AN EYE FOR DETAIL

17TH-CENTURY DUTCH AND
FLEMISH PAINTINGS FROM THE
COLLECTION OF
HENRY H. WELDON

AN EYE FOR DETAIL

17TH-CENTURY DUTCH AND FLEMISH
PAINTINGS FROM THE COLLECTION OF
HENRY H. WELDON

Nancy T. Minty and Joaneath Spicer

*with contributions by Sir Oliver Millar and Anke
van Wagenberg-Ter Hoeven*

THE WALTERS ART GALLERY
BALTIMORE

1,000 copies of this catalogue were published in conjunction with the exhibition *An Eye for Detail: 17th-Century Dutch and Flemish Paintings from the Collection of Henry H. Weldon* (June 20-September 5,1999), organized by the Walters Art Gallery, Baltimore

The entries by Nancy Minty, with the exception of no. 11, and that by Sir Oliver Millar are included here with the permission of the New Orleans Museum of Art, publisher of *In the Eye of the Beholder: Northern Baroque Paintings from the Collection of Henry H. Weldon*, New Orleans 1997.

ISBN 0-911886-50-8

Library of Congress Catalog Card Number 99-61728

Designed by Jeanne Arnold
Printing by Pressroom Printer, Hong Kong
on behalf of Sotheby's, Inc.
Majority of photography by Gavin Ashworth

FRONT COVER:
Adriaen van Ostade (Haarlem 1610-Haarlem 1685), *A Man with Pince-Nez, Reading Notices* (no. 35).

BACK COVER:
Adriaen Coorte (active in Middelburg? c. 1683-1707), *Wild Strawberries on a Ledge* (no. 13).

FRONTISPIECE:
Anthony van Dyck (Antwerp 1599-Blackfriars 1641), *Study of Boy's Head and Hands* (no. 16, detail).

SECOND FRONTISPIECE:
Peter Paul Rubens (Siegen 1577-Antwerp 1640) and Jan Brueghel the Younger (Antwerp 1601-Antwerp 1678), *Landscape with Pan and Syrinx* (no. 42, detail).

CONTENTS

PREFACE

It is a pleasure for me to have the opportunity to say a word or two about what seems to me to be an almost perfect fit: the Weldon collection of Dutch and Flemish paintings being lent for exhibition to the Walters Art Gallery. Not only is this an alliance of a favorite institution with a collection of a close friend, it is fully appropriate to consider the analogous collecting interests of Henry Weldon and those of Henry Walters.

The Weldons, both Henry and Jimmy, came from families who were collectors. Henry Weldon, who was born in the Netherlands, saw the destruction of his first collection of Georgian glass, silver, and twentieth-century art in Liverpool in 1940 when the family was relocating from London to New York. Subsequent important collections were formed by the Weldons which included Chinese tomb figures from the Han and T'ang Dynasties and Zhou bronzes. More recently the Weldons have formed the finest and most comprehensive collection of eighteenth-century English pottery in private hands.

The sharing of common collecting interests with those pursued by Henry Walters cannot be overlooked. That both Henrys vigorously pursued, fine seventeenth-century Dutch and Flemish painting, and Chinese and English ceramics, albeit in distinct manifestations, make it particularly fitting for The Walters to be exhibiting these works. The end result for the viewer is that one plus one is several times larger than two.

Collected over a period of four decades, these cabinet paintings in and of themselves are very beautiful and include supreme, well known masters such as Rubens, van Dyck, Post, and Ruisdael, as well as wonderful, lesser known artists such as Coorte and Steenwijk. For those who come to view the exhibition, the opportunity presents itself to renew their experience of, or to experience for the first time, the universal appeal of Dutch and Flemish painting.

The Weldons manifestly enjoy their own collection and are, in turn, providing us the same opportunity by sharing it. It is my great pleasure to welcome these fine paintings to the Walters Art Gallery. I am sure that the Weldons join me in thanking the Gallery, the director Gary Vikan, Adena Testa, Chairman of the Board of Trustees, and curator Joaneath Spicer for making this exhibition possible.

Francis D. Murnaghan, Jr.
Chairman Emeritis, Walters Art Gallery
Board of Trustees

ACKNOWLEDGEMENTS

First we must thank Henry and Jimmy Weldon, not only for their great generosity in parting with their beloved paintings over the summer, but also for their friendship and support of The Walters. However, exhibitions involve much more than friendship and love of art; and the cooperation of John Bullard and the staff of the New Orleans Museum of Art, where a somewhat different selection of paintings from the Weldon collection was exhibited in 1997, is gratefully acknowledged. Nancy Krieg, paintings conservator in New York, cleaned and treated many of the paintings, while Gavin Ashworth provided the photography for the New Orleans catalogue.

The 1997 catalogue benefitted significantly from the advice of Egbert Haverkamp-Begemann, the John Langeloth Loeb Professor Emeritus in the History of Art at the Institute of Fine Arts, New York University, while Jan Leja assisted with iconographic questions and Donald Spanel provided editing assistance. The present catalogue has benefited from the advice of Michael Abromaitis, Maia Gahtan, Walter Liedtke, Anne-Marie Logan, Fred Meijer, and M. Shreve Simpson, and the encouragement of Peter and Judy Van Dyke. The staff of the following institutions were very generous with their help: Frick Art Reference Library, New York; New York Public Library; Stephen Chan Library, Institute of Fine Arts, New York University; Rijksbureau voor Kunsthistorische Documentatie, The Hague; the Witt Library, London; and the library of the Walters Art Gallery, Baltimore.

Mounting exhibitions at The Walters involves virtually the entire staff in some capacity, but I would like to signal the particular contributions of Johanna Biehler, Anne Bornscheuer, Terrie Chavis, Karen French, Todd Jackson, John Klink, Marietta Nolley, Michelle Nesbit, John Shields, M. Shreve Simpson, Susan Wallace, and Lynn Wolf. The support of Francis Murnaghan, chairman emeritus of The Walters' board of trustees, and Walters director Gary Vikan was critical to the initiation of the project.

The production of the catalogue has been efficiently and sensitively carried out by Sotheby's with the assistance of George Wachter, Richard Buckley, and Maura Dorment.

We are especially grateful to Nancy Minty, the primary author of the 1997 catalogue and a doctoral candidate at the Institute of Fine Art in New York, who studied Dutch and Flemish art at the University of Toronto with a certain Professor Spicer (whose PhD was also supervised by Prof. Begemann, then at Yale). She worked closely with the Weldons to select the "highlights" that would be extensively researched and then carried through on that research, in conjunction with which Sir Oliver Millar agreed to write an entry on Van Dyck. It is our pleasure to thank him again. Our great desire to exhibit the Weldons' collection in the summer of 1999 was not matched by the time available to prepare a revised catalogue, and the willingness of Anke van Wagenberg-Ter Hoeven to join the project on short notice was invaluable.

Joaneath Spicer
The James A. Murnaghan Curator
of Renaissance and Baroque Art
Walters Art Gallery

Entries by
Nancy T. Minty   NTM
Sir Oliver Millar   OM
Joaneath Spicer   JS
Anke van Wagenberg-Ter Hoeven   AvW-TH

AN EYE FOR DETAIL

Fig. 1 Jacob Marrel, *Flowers Resting on a Ledge* (no. 29, detail)

Introduced by Adriaen van Ostade's *Man with Pince-Nez, Reading Notices* (cover and no. 35) that invites us to follow the man's infectiously inquisitive gaze, this exhibition is about the enjoyment of detail. The particular fascination of being slowly drawn into the detailed world of a little painting that seems to exist just for us is a pleasure that is increasingly rare for museum visitors. The selection and installation of paintings in most museums are shaped by the twin desires to make art accessible to as many people as possible and at the same time to keep that art secure. In the case of paintings, this may prompt curators to favor medium to large-sized works intended to be seen from a certain distance.

There are, however, some schools and periods of old master painting, most notably Dutch and to a lesser extent Flemish painting of the sixteenth to eighteenth centuries, in which many of the greatest masters conceived their works for viewing at close quarters, often in private,

domestic spaces intended for contemplative thought known as "cabinets.." The wonderfully rewarding experience of looking carefully at such Dutch and Flemish cabinet paintings—as those which the Weldons have lovingly chosen for their New York apartment[1]—is one for which our more accustomed way of responding to larger paintings does not prepare us. While we are quite aware that actually looking at Michelangelo's frescoes on the ceiling of the Sistine Chapel would be different from looking at reproductions of the frescoes in a book or on a screen, we might assume that in the case of paintings that may be the same size, or nearly so, as the reproductions in this catalogue, there is not much to be gained from having the painting itself before our eyes.

What is to be gained is an unexpectedly intimate and personal experience, due in large part to the engaging power of detail. We are especially engaged by detail that is intended to create an illusion of reality, when the painted, framed image is physically part of our own space.

One of the great attractions of a still life painted in life-like detail and composed to accommodate the viewer's gaze lies in the almost magical way that such a painting seems to be an extension of the viewer's space, especially when it is possible to commune with it privately. In addition, the still life may represent objects such as fragile blossoms that in real life we delight in touching. In Jacob Marrel's remarkable *Flowers Resting on a Ledge* (no. 29), one of the Weldons most recent acquisitions, we see a glass vase with a bouquet of flowers tipped over on a stone ledge, the spilled water dripping over the edge (fig. 1). The closeness of the flowers to the picture plane combines with the delicate modeling and precise detail to lend the separate blossoms a striking physical presence. This physicality is most pronounced in the case of the luscious flame tulips, not too surprising given that Marrel had been a dealer in tulip bulbs. This appeal not only to the sense of sight and smell but also to the sense of touch is accentuated by the presence of the little lizard, at home in so many of Marrel's flower pieces. As the creature stretches toward a tiny moth flitting above his head, his claws spread to keep his balance. The light catches the claws, increasing our sense of the fragility of the delicate lilies-of-the-valley nearby, much as a black beauty mark was at one time applied in order to highlight a woman's pale, flawless complexion.

Among the paintings in which similar strategies were used to beguile us, the two little gems by Adriaen Coorte stand out. In *Wild Strawberries on a Ledge* (no. 13 and back cover), a handful of freshly picked wild strawberries lies near the rim of a stone ledge, one flowering sprig jauntily inserted into the midst of

Fig. 2 Hendrick van Steenwijk, *Prison Interior with Sleeping Guards and the Deliverance of St. Peter* (no. 51, detail)

the fruit. A soft bath of light from the left catches the tiny bumps on the strawberries, creating bursts of beaded light like miniature fireworks. The entrancing physicality of these strawberries is matched in the artist's *Chestnuts on a Ledge* (no. 14). The same focus on just a few fragile objects is found as well in Willem van Aelst's *Peaches, a Plum and Grapes on a Ledge* (no. 1) and Balthasar van der Ast's *Roses, Lizard, Butterfly, and Grasshopper on a Ledge* (no. 3). At the end of the century Rachel Ruysch continued to explore these sensibilities in the amazingly sensuous, soft petals of her *Nosegay of Roses, Marigolds and Larkspur, with Insects and Bumblebee* (no. 45). Here the languor of the full-blown white rose is set off by the contrast with the tiny thorns of the adjacent stem, their brilliantly lit spikes profiled against the shadowed side of the stone ledge. The effect prompts a comparison with Marrel's little lizard. In Otto Marseus van Schrieck's magical *Still Life with Thistle and Frog Before a Woodland Waterfall* (no. 49) it is instead a frog, snails, a delightful, dangling spider, and other insects, together with the prickly, furled leaves of the thistle that are caught as if by torch light on a nocturnal walk. This unassuming patch of forest undergrowth takes on aesthetic significance by virtue of our gaze, guided by the artist.

Many of the Weldons' landscapes engage us through their serenity, such as Jan Both's fine *Italianate Landscape with Mountain Path and Ford* (no. 6), the tips of the foliage dusted by early morning light. We are likewise soothed by the fine color modulations in Jan Brueghel's exquisite *Woodland Road* (no. 9). Others offer a vicarious experience of exciting natural phenomena. These include the simple thrill of seeing a rainbow begin to arch across the sky, as in David Teniers' *River Landscape with Rainbow* (no. 52), or lightning in a storm, as in Simon de Vlieger's *Lightning over Rough Seas with Sailboats* (no. 59). They spur the senses by calling on the viewer's own past experiences.

The effect of Saverij's *Alpine Landscape with Torrent and Hunter* (no. 48a) is also enhanced by prompting our own memories of thrilling waterfalls. Though nowadays we may take the picturesque character of mountain waterfalls for granted, Saverij seems to have been the first European artist to have depicted them.[2] Obviously travelers through the Alps had seen waterfalls, but artists such as Pieter Bruegel the Elder who passed through the Alps in the 1550s didn't think they were worthy of depiction; apparently they were too threatening. The French essayist Montaigne traveled through the Alps in 1581 and wrote of alpine waterfalls in the same vein that he wrote of robbers. However, when he reached Italy and visited the tourist sites around Rome, he felt safe enough to wax lyrical about the cascades at Tivoli.

Probably in 1606, Saverij, then working at the court of the Holy Roman Emperor Rudolf II in Prague, was sent into the Alps to search for wonders of nature to enhance the emperor's famous collection of natural and man-made wonders. Instead of objects, the artist brought back drawings of immense, strangely shaped boulders, a rainbow, and the phenomenon that fascinated him the most, the thundering alpine waterfalls. These drawings became the point of departure for paintings. Saverij was not traveling through the Alps to reach Italy by the quickest route; he went into the mountains looking for wondrous new aesthetic experiences. In his drawings Saverij shows himself standing or sitting close to the falls and looking at them pensively; however, in his paintings the travelers depicted give the falls a wide berth.

A marvelously sophisticated use of perspectival detail underlies the *frisson* we are encouraged to feel in entering Hendrick van Steenwijk's *Prison Interior with Sleeping Guards and the Deliverance of St. Peter* (no. 51 and detail fig. 2). By including the vaulted ceilings in the same recessional system and closing off all exits either by granite walls or deepest darkness, Steenwijk creates a haunting sense of enclosure. The light of torches and the smoldering embers of fires lit by the guards cast an eerie glow in the foreground and middleground, while in the deepest recesses of the dark corridor we can just make out the tiny figures of St. Peter and his angelic deliverer caught in the dim light of a wall torch. It is remarkable the way that this last, barely perceptible detail can unify our experience of the painting, resolving the perspectival recession that is broken by the deep shadows.

An entrancing detail may also consist of a single brushstroke, as in Anthony van Dyck's sublimely subtle *Study of a Boy's Head and Hands* (no. 16). Here, as in the artist's other brilliant studies in the Weldon collection, *Young Woman Resting her Head on her Hand* (no. 15) and his *Portrait of Martin Ryckaert* (no. 17), we are very much aware of the artist's hand deftly manipulating the brush. The longer the eye dwells on the flick of white at the back of the boy's neck, the less its evocation of the boy's shirt seems important and the more the visual excitement of the stroke as a stroke predominates. This is in contrast to many of the paintings discussed above, in which the entrancing realism of detail is achieved by making the individual brush strokes disappear. Given how satisfying it is to let the eye follow every brush stroke in *Boy's Head*, it is a bit of a jolt to realize that the artist didn't intend for us to do that. As in the case of the other two studies by van Dyck in the collection, the *Boy's Head* was not meant for the delectation of an art lover. Van Dyck apparently made this oil sketch on paper in preparation for a portrait of the child to be included in his painting *Suffer the Little Children to Come Unto Me*, now in the National Gallery of Canada, Ottawa (no. 16, fig. 1). In a marriage of portrait and religious painting that is rare in van Dyck's *oeuvre*, a family presents their son—this boy—to be blessed by Christ. As has been proposed, the painting was very likely commissioned to celebrate the boy's first communion. The parents would have seen in the study a likeness of their son, not a swirl of brushstrokes to be enjoyed for their virtuosity. We who do not know the boy are free to enjoy the subtlety of the strokes as they create form.

When a study such as this is subsequently "collected" and enjoyed as a prized possession, as the provenance of the *Boy's Head* makes clear it was already in the seventeenth century, then it takes on a new function that is distinct from its initial one. Framed and enjoyed as an object that is deemed complete as an aesthetic experience in itself, *Boy's Head* prompts us to look yet again at the paintings by Marrel, Coorte, Steenwijk, Ruisdael, Rubens, and so many others that were created in the first place as prized, aesthetic objects that invite the gaze. Not only will this dialogue add a new dimension to our enjoyment of these paintings, it just might give us something in common with the Weldons—an eye for detail.
JS

1 For the Weldons as collectors, please see Haverkamp-Begemann's "Introduction" to the 1997 version of this catalogue.
2 For Saverij's "discovery" of the alpine waterfall see Spicer 1997.

CATALOGUE

1 Willem van Aelst

(Delft 1625/1626-Amsterdam c. 1683)

Peaches, a Plum, and Grapes on a Ledge

1646
oil on copper
16.75 x 21.75 cm.
Inscribed, bottom center: *W.V. Aelst. Ao. 1646.*

PROVENANCE:
Possibly Pallavicini Collection, Budapest; Acquired at auction, New York.

EXHIBITIONS:
Providence 1964, no. 1; New York 1966, no. 1; Zurich 1990, no. 13 (ill.); New Orleans 1997, no. 1(ill.).

Willem van Aelst is best known as a painter of flower and fruit still lifes, but his *oeuvre* also includes paintings of fish, birds, hunters' paraphernalia as well as breakfast pieces and sumptuous banquet still lifes. He seems to have received his training in Delft from his uncle Evert van Aelst (1602-1657),[1] also a still-life painter, and became a member of the painters' guild in 1643. In 1645 he left for France, traveling and working there until 1649, by which time he was in Italy. In Rome and Florence van Aelst worked as a court painter to Ferdinand II de' Medici, Grand Duke of Tuscany. According to the biography of van Aelst published in 1718 by Arnold Houbraken, during these years the artist was friends with the Dutch still-life painter, Otto Marseus van Schrieck (1619/1620-1678) (no. 49), with whom he carried out many pranks.[2]

In the late 1650s van Aelst returned to the Netherlands and enjoyed considerable financial success: according to Houbraken he owned a house on the fashionable Prinsengracht in Amsterdam.[3] Here the flower painter Rachel Ruysch (see no. 45) became his most famous pupil. Both Ruysch (1664-1750) and Jan van Huysum (1682-1749) carried on van Aelst's pictorial style into the eighteenth century.[4]

Peaches, a Plum, and Grapes, dated 1646, was painted during van Aelst's stay in France when the artist was only about twenty years old. Other small decorative fruit pieces from these years include a similar composition dated 1645 (Sotheby's, London, July 23, 1924) and another fruit still life dated 1646 is in the Perman collection, Stockholm.[5] The extremely soft lighting from the left and slightly fuzzy modeling of the surfaces, especially of the peaches, lends this elegant arrangement of luscious summer fruit the sensuous appeal for which van Aelst is so appreciated. The way that the artist already at this early date makes use of this small format to distill the sensuousness of such delicate surfaces would culminate in such later works as his 1674 *Peaches, Grapes, and a Mouse*, German private collection, the cover image for the catalogue of the 1983 Amsterdam exhibition on Dutch and Flemish fruit still lifes, *A Fruitful Past.*   AvW-TH

1 For Evert van Aelst and the circle of still-life painters in Delft, see most recently Kersten and Lokin 1996, pp. 30-33.
    2 Mitchell 1973, p. 34.
    3 Houbraken 1718, vol. I, p. 358.
    4 Houbraken 1718, vol. I, p. 229.
    5 Taylor 1995, pp. 175-177. For biographical information see also Bergström 1956, pp. 220-224; Mitchell 1973, pp. 33-35; Warner 1975, pp. 12-15.

2   Balthasar van der Ast
(Middelburg 1593/94 - Delft 1657)

Bouquet on a Ledge with Landscape Vista

1624
oil on copper
13.3 x 10.2 cm.
Inscribed, bottom, left of center: *.vand[er]ast. A /*
bottom right: *1624*

PROVENANCE:
Private collection

EXHIBITIONS:
Amsterdam 1984, no. 13 (ill.); David Koetser Gallery, Zurich, 1985, no. 50; New Orleans 1997, no. 2 (ill.); Washington 1999, no. 4 (ill. 34).

Van der Ast pays tribute to his brother-in-law and probable teacher, Ambrosius Bosschaert the Elder (1573-1621), in this delicate still life on copper which juxtaposes the minute wonders of a varied bouquet, shells, and insects, to a distant, misty riverview. A glass, decorated with thorn prunts and overflowing with a multitude of flowers, stands on a ledge, as if on a window, centered before a landscape of a river and its rocky, turreted banks. At the base of the glass, a fly, shell, snail, and grasshopper cast fine shadows on the ledge. The glory of nature is writ small and large with the tiny microcosm of each specimen set against the seemingly endless landscape.[1]

Along with his apparent mentor, Ambrosius Bosschaert the Elder, the leader of the Bosschaert dynasty of still-life painters, and Roelandt Saverij (1576-1639), van der Ast developed the flower genre from the Flemish still-life tradition of Jan Brueghel the Elder (1568-1625). Flemish characteristics which pervade the present painting are the degree of detail and the correspondingly fine technique, as well as the convention of the expansive "world landscape," borrowed from South Netherlandish landscape painting.[2] During Bosschaert's residency in Breda (1619-21), he devised this composition of bouquet against riverscape,[3] perhaps in response to precedents popularized in prints.[4] His brother-in-law, van der Ast, was painting in his elder's manner when the genre emerged.[5]

The Weldon painting, probably the only one of this type in van der Ast's *oeuvre*, resembles and deliberately emulates the work of Bosschaert as in, for example, the elder artist's *Bouquet of Flowers on a Ledge*, 1619, Carter Collection, Los Angeles, and the *Vase with Flowers*, c. 1618-19, Mauritshuis, The Hague.[6] While the Los Angeles painting presents a similar outlook, the bouquet in the Mauritshuis composition is framed in a niche, in turn set before a riverscape. Both paintings demonstrate Bosschaert's influence on the composition of the present work: Bergström observed that van der Ast has even borrowed flowers from the Mauritshuis painting, notably the crowning yellow iris and the striped tulip.[7] Van der Ast's technique also derives from his model. He employed a succession of glazes achieving a range of color saturation, and modeling forms and shadows. However, he departs from his elder in the subtlety and relative softness of his colors and outlines, in part through the selective application of slightly cloudy glazes.[8]

Van der Ast's culling of floral samples from his master's works is entirely in keeping with the contemporary practices of flower painting. The individually naturalistic specimens were characteristically arranged in fantasy bouquets which featured flowers that blossomed at different times and included exotic, rare and expensive samples. Artists would necessarily have relied on their own studies, botanical prints, and the work of their colleagues in order to compose lavish, varied arrangements where each important flower is shown to full advantage.[9]

The collecting and cultivation of flowers reached fetishistic proportions in Holland during the first half of the seventeenth century culminating in the tulip boom (when a single bulb fetched the astronomical price of 4000 guilders) and subsequent bust of 1637.[10] Bol has characterized the gardens of adamant flower collectors and botanists as "the open-air counterparts of the cabinets filled with foreign shells,"[11] another exotic collectible that was prized by amateurs.

(actual size)

Just as flowers became a fashion, so too did paintings depicting them. During the first three decades of the seventeenth century the genre grew to represent twenty percent of the still-life market.[12] Flower paintings were not only plentiful, but sometimes expensive: Bosschaert was reputedly paid the princely sum of 1000 guilders for a single floral still life and archival evidence indicates that he lived very well.[13] Van der Ast also maintained a comfortable lifestyle and his considerable output, of which approximately two-hundred paintings are extant, suggests that the demand for his work was high.[14]

Apart from alluding to the prestigious pursuits of flower collectors, this genre of painting has been invested with religious and moral significance. Flowers, among nature's most beautiful creations, were viewed as symbols of God's glory. In the words of the contemporary poet Petrus Hondius, "Each flower that he sees offers him God's wondrous work".[15]

Floral still lifes have also been overlaid with *vanitas* meaning, particularly those featuring withering leaves and blooms as well as preying insects. An inscription from a print of a bouquet, dated 1604, contains the following message which elucidates the theme of earthly transience: "The flower, mirror of life, blossoms and passes away like a sigh of the wind."[16] The present painting, which exemplifies the artist's painstaking recreation of nature's beauty, seems to represent an homage to the Creator rather than a reference to worldly vanity.[17]

Van der Ast's lovely *Roses, Lizard, Butterfly, and Grasshopper on a Ledge* (no. 3), also in the present collection, illustrates the artist's departure from his master's example with a looser technique at a later

moment in his career, probably 1630-40. Bergström has demonstrated how van der Ast used Bosschaert's flower basket paintings as a point of departure for his own "ledge" works which simply feature flowers lying on a surface, as if he had excerpted the stray fallen blooms of the basket paintings, making them into autonomous compositions.[18] This motif became a sub-specialization of the artist in a number of charming paintings which doubtless influenced the ledge compositions of Adriaen Coorte (active c. 1686-1707), a Middelburg successor to the Bosschaert dynasty, in characteristic works like his strawberry and chestnut still lifes, both in the present collection (nos. 13,14).[19] NTM

1 An interpretation of Ambrosius Bosschaert's *Vase with Flowers*, c. 1618-19, Mauritshuis, The Hague, which similarly features a detailed bouquet against a distant landscape, offered in Münster/Baden-Baden 1979-80, pp. 17-22, suggests a simultaneously microscopic and macrocosmic view of nature.

2 For a discussion of this Flemish landscape convention, see the entries on Jan Brueghel the Elder's *Woodland Road with Wagons and Travelers* and Adriaen van de Venne's *Winter Pleasures* in this catalogue, nos. 9, 56.

3 Los Angeles/Boston/New York 1981-82, p. 15.

4 Segal in Osaka/Tokyo/Sydney 1990, p. 49, where the author cites and illustrates the print *Flower Piece with Birds*, 1599, by Hendrick Hondius (1573-1650) after Elias Verhulst. See also San Francisco/Baltimore/London 1997-98.

5 In Amsterdam 1984, p. 45, Bergström states that it is only in van der Ast's "very early years" that his work closely resembles Bosschaert's.

6 Bergström made the above observation and comparisons in a letter to D. Koetser, Zurich, 1982. The Carter painting is on copper, 28 x 23 cm., illustrated and catalogued by Spicer in San Francisco/Baltimore/London 1997-98, no. 75 and the Mauritshuis painting, panel, 64 x 46 cm., reproduced and catalogued in Broos 1987, no. 13.

7 See note 6 above.

8 These and other aspects of the two artists' techniques are discussed in Taylor 1995, pp. 148-49.

9 This is a much-discussed aspect of Dutch flower painting, which Bol 1960, p. 20, likened to the

contemporary practice of group portraiture: ..."individual portraits placed beside and above each other, each being given its full pound of clear recognizability." See also Brenninkmeyer-de-Rooij 1990 (revised and translated into English in Brenninkmeyer-de-Rooij 1996, p. 70) and Taylor 1995, p. 119 with regard to the flower paintings of Jan Brueghel the Elder.

10 As recorded in Taylor 1995, p. 10. On the tulipomania, see also Osaka/Tokyo/Sydney 1990, pp. 43-45.

11 Bol 1960, p. 16.

12 Taylor 1995, p. 125.

13 This information is based on Bok's biography from Amsterdam 1993-94, pp. 302-3.

14 For a brief biography of the artist which estimates his probable means, see Meijer in ibid., p. 299. The artist's *oeuvre* is estimated by Bergström in Amsterdam 1984, p. 61, note 1, where he indicates that of the total number, approximately fifty paintings are dated. On p. 45, the author indicates that Bol 1960 had catalogued 126 paintings.

15 From Hondius' poem entitled *Hof-weten*, published in Leiden, 1621, as cited and translated in Taylor 1995, p. 30, where the author discusses the religious significance of the genre of flower painting, and places the phenomenon within the context of medieval tradition.

16 As cited and translated in Brenninkmeyer-de Rooij 1996, p. 13. The print in question is by Jan Theodor de Bry (1561-1623) after Jacob Kempener (reproduced in Broos 1987, p. 83).

17 Brenninkmeyer-de Rooij 1990, pp. 236-38, favors an analogous interpretation for the flower paintings of Jan Brueghel the Elder. The *vanitas* aspect of certain flower paintings was overemphasized until she corrected this misperception with regard to Brueghel's work. Taylor 1995, pp. 47, similarly suggests that Bosschaert's *Vase with Flowers*, Mauritshuis, The Hague (see note 6 above) is less a *vanitas* than it is a celebration of creation.

18 Bergström 1983. The ledge compositions probably also relate to contemporary developments in Savery's *oeuvre*, as for example his *Rose with Mouse and Grasshopper*, c. 1622, (illustrated and catalogued in Müllenmeister 1988, no. 286) which, in turn, bears a strong resemblance to Jan Brueghel the Elder's small copper paintings of the same subject, *A Mouse and a Rose*, before 1618, Bibilioteca Ambrosiana, Milan, and *A Mouse, a Rose, and Insects*, Piet and Nellie de Boer Foundation, Amsterdam.

19 For other ledge paintings by van der Ast, see Bol 1960, nos. 43-55.

3   Balthasar van der Ast

(Middelburg 1593/94 - Delft 1657)

Roses, Lizard, Butterfly, and Grasshopper on a Ledge

c. 1630-40
oil on panel
16.75 x 18 cm.
Inscribed, bottom center and right, along stone ledge:
.B van der. / .ast.

PROVENANCE:
Private collection.

EXHIBITIONS:
New Orleans 1997, no. 3 (ill.).

Please refer to entry no. 2 for a brief discussion of this
painting.

4 Gerrit Berckheyde
(Haarlem 1638 - Haarlem 1698)

The Binnenhof in The Hague

c. 1690
oil on canvas
51.5 x 61 cm.
Inscribed, lower left: *Gerrit Berkheÿde*

PROVENANCE:
Possibly John, 2nd Lord Northwick, Northwick Park;
George, 3rd Lord Northwick, Northwick Park; by
descent to Edward George Spencer-Churchill (Sale,
Christie's, London, Spencer-Churchill Collection,
October 29, 1965, no. 78, ill.); Alan Jacobs Gallery,
London (by 1975); Private collection.

EXHIBITIONS:
London 1975-76, p. 36 (ill.); Birmingham 1995, no.
1(ill.); New Orleans 1997, no. 4 (ill.).

LITERATURE:
Northwick Park 1864 (reprinted 1908), no. 330 (as
Street in Holland: The Bumanky [sic] at the Hague);
Borenius 1921, no. 174; Weltkunst 46 (October 15,
1979) p. 2493 (ill.); Gaskell 1989, p. 301 and note 11;
Dumas 1991, p. 670, fig. 5, pp. 671, 673, note 21;
Lawrence 1991, p. 75, note 29c. To be included in
Lawrence's forthcoming catalogue raisonné of
Berckheyde's work.

Berckheyde's town view presents a scene of civic order and prosperity centered on the twin-towered Ridderzaal/Knight's Hall of the inner square of the court complex in The Hague. Fashionably attired figures with plumed hats, embroidered overcoats, and colorful capes stroll and gather before the imposing façade of the Knight's Hall which is portrayed both monumentally and precisely. The space is animated by the crowd whose cordiality is underscored by its elegant gestures and occasional polite greetings, as in the bowing pair of gentlemen in the middle ground. The geometric play of light and dark on the square, and the long shadows cast by the figures further enrich the scene, while the sunshine enhances the general atmosphere of well-being.

In her book on Berckheyde, Lawrence has aptly described such views as portraits of buildings, and she has emphasized their significance as images of civic pride and political and social order.[1] Indeed, by juxtaposing the prosperous and orderly citizens of The Hague with the court complex of the Binnenhof/Inner Court including the Knight's Hall, the seventeenth-century seat of the States General, and a partial view of the Stadholder's quarters to the far left, the artist has married the concepts of good government and social order.

Berckheyde painted views of the court center of The Hague late in his career, beginning in the mid-1680s. Lawrence has attributed his shift of focus from earlier depictions of Haarlem and Amsterdam to The Hague to the restoration to power of the House of Orange under Willem III in 1672. The site of the former castle and ancestral residence of the dynasty in The Hague was the Binnenhof and surrounding buildings. More specifically, Lawrence relates the proliferation of images of the court in The Hague in Berckheyde's late *oeuvre* to Willem's increase in stature because of his appointment to the throne of England in 1689 through his marriage to the daughter of the English King Charles II.[2]

There are five additional extant variations of this view by the artist in which he repeats the architectural setting while changing the staffage. Dumas has posited that all of the paintings may originate from an exact study of the site.[3] Although they vary in size and support, two of the versions are also painted on canvas and are of virtually the same dimensions as the Weldon painting.[4] Although none of the six examples is dated by the artist, the present work and the Thyssen-Bornemisza painting, which it closely resembles, have both been placed around the year 1690.[5]

The depiction of the view in the Weldon painting is consistent with formal characteristics that Lawrence has generally identified with Berckheyde's portraits of buildings. The vantage point is high, the scale of the central structure slightly exaggerated, and the site manipulated in order to highlight the main subject. The elements of light, shadow, and staffage are also employed as foils to enhance the importance of the building.[6]

Berckheyde's rendering faithfully replicates details of the site and the Ridderzaal; however, its brushwork is characteristically and relatively broad in comparison to the architectural paintings of his contemporary Jan van der Heyden (1637-1712). In spite of Berckheyde's technical generalization of architectural minutiae, he is careful to include all of the important elements of the landmark such as, for example, the two bones which hang on the wall of the antechamber to the Ridderzaal. In seventeenth-century Holland, whale jawbones adorned courthouses as public symbols of the law.[7] Hence, their inclusion in a depiction of a building that was the seat of government and contained the Rolzaal,[8] or trial chamber, is significant.

Berckheyde successfully recreates the architectural complexity and historical importance of the Knight's Hall in his painting. Furthermore, in his portrayal of the courtiers he evokes the vitality of the square which one contemporary poet described as the hub of the city: "The world, everyone comes here seeking new tidings...."[9] NTM

1 Lawrence 1991, pp. 7-11.

2 Ibid., p. 67. Dumas 1991, pp. 667-73 offers a comprehensive history of the Binnenhof/Ridderzaal site in which he discusses and illustrates the present painting, as well as other depictions by Berckheyde, see note 3 below.

3 Dumas 1991, p. 671, discusses the versions, and on p. 673, note 21, he lists all six paintings of the Binnenhof (including the Weldon painting). Lawrence 1991, pp. 74-5, and note 29 also lists all six versions. The five additional paintings are: 1. *The Binnenhof*, The Hague, c. 1690, canvas, 53 x 62.8 cm., Fondación Colección Thyssen-Bornemisza, Madrid (illustrated and catalogued in Gaskell 1989, no. 65) 2. *The Courtyard of the Binnenhof*, The Hague, canvas, 53.5 x 61.5 cm., formerly L. and G. Guterman, New York (Sale, Sotheby's, New York, January 14, 1988, no. 3, ill.) 3. *The Binnenhof with the Ridderzaal*, c. 1690, panel, 32.5 x 46 cm., formerly Kunsthandel D. Katz, Dieren (illustrated and discussed in Dumas 1991, pp. 671, 673, fig. 6) 4. Untitled, canvas, 54 x 70 cm., N. Bacon, Norfolk. 5. Untitled, canvas, 121.5 x 150cm., W. R. Hearst, San Simeon (Sale, Dorotheum, Vienna, 15-18 July, 1971, no. 6, ill.).

4 Nos. 1 and 2 in note 3 above.

5 Dumas 1991, p. 670, published the Weldon painting with the date of c. 1690, as did Lawrence 1991, p. 75. The Thyssen-Bornemisza painting was published with an estimated date of c. 1690, based on the artist's choice of "pale tones and transparent shadows," the smooth surface of the paint, and the style of the costumes, in Amsterdam/Toronto 1977, no. 105, and this date and description were subsequently maintained by Gaskell 1989, no. 65, and Lawrence 1991, p. 75.

6 Lawrence 1991, pp. 10-12.

7 Dumas 1991, p. 667.

8 Lawrence 1991, p. 74.

9 Van der Does 1668, p. 131, as cited in Dumas 1991, p. 668, excerpted and translated by the present author.

(detail)

11

5 Abraham Bloemaert

(Gorinchem 1566 - Utrecht 1651)

Farmyard with Dovecote

c. 1630-35
oil on panel
38.25 x 29.75 cm.
Inscribed, bottom, left of center: *A Blomart fe.*

PROVENANCE:
Possibly K. Wetzlar, Amsterdam (c. 1960); Sale, Kunsthauses am Museum, Cologne, October 26, 1963; Private collection.

EXHIBITIONS:
London 1964, no. 34 (ill.); Providence 1964, no. 1A (ill.); New York 1966, no. 2; New Orleans 1997, no. 5 (ill.).

LITERATURE:
Weltkunst, October 15, 1963, p. 31 (ill.); Roethlisberger/Bok 1993, vol. 1, no. 512, and pp. 308 (under no. 478), 353 (under no. 572), vol. 2, fig. 696; Spicer in San Francisco/Baltimore/London, 1997-1998, under no. 18; Seelig 1997, p. 303, no. B179; San Francisco/Baltimore/London 1997-98, pp. 184, 415 (note 14).

This bucolic scene offers a rare view of Abraham Bloemaert as a painter of pure landscape with no apparent narrative. A farmyard is defined by the central motif of a dovecote and low thatched buildings to the right. A woman and a boy labor over pots on the brightly lit ground in front, which contrasts with the dark shadow cast across the bottom of the yard where two goats and a sheep lay and graze. From the darkness of the cottage doorway a figure appears to look outside. While the human element animates the landscape in this painting, it is the picturesque potential of the dilapidated farm buildings in dramatic light which seems to have captured the artist's imagination.

The element of landscape in Bloemaert's *oeuvre* functions most frequently as a setting for elaborate religious and mythological narratives. Although independent landscape compositions by the artist occur in his drawings, and in prints thereafter by his son Frederick (c. 1614/17-1690), they are infrequently the subject of paintings. Bloemaert's early conception of landscape grew out of his Mannerist paintings of the late 1590s to early 1600s in which he employed a luminous palette, strong contrasts of light and color, meticulous brushwork and complicated, often contorted forms.[1] Throughout his career he continued to depict landscapes in narrative paintings where he frequently subsumed the subject and gave prominence to the rural setting, as in his *Landscape with Tobias and the Angel*, 1630, in which the biblical protagonists are scarcely visible on the horizon behind a farmyard filled with peasants and livestock.[2] His growing interest in farm settings and bucolic genre elements, manifested in many drawings which appear to be from life,[3] was coupled with a stylistic

shift, probably resulting from the influence of the more indigenous landscape painting of Esaias van de Velde (1587-1630), Pieter de Molijn (1595-1661), and Jan van Goyen (1596-1656).[4] Around the year 1630, a mellower, quieter approach emerges in Bloemaert's landscapes.[5]

The Weldon painting represents Bloemaert's mature landscape style with vestiges of Mannerism still visible. The slightly acid green and yellow of the yard, the red of the woman's dress and the overall glow, recall his more luminous tones, and the swelling shapes and lines are reminiscent of his early sinuous figures and contours. In particular the pose of the woman — somewhat twisted, with her tiny head and her back turned — reflects Bloemaert's early attenuated figure style. Nonetheless, local brilliance is muted and movement minimized, imparting a softness which seems to be dictated by the sloping lines and subtle tones of the shambling structures.

Roethlisberger has dated the Weldon panel to the early 1630s, citing its stylistic resemblance to the small peasant paintings of the same period.[6] He has also identified a drawing, which he attributes to Bloemaert and dates to the 1630s, of a similar dovecote, proposing it as a model for the structure in the Weldon painting.[7] He has further likened the Weldon panel to an earlier work, a canvas of the same format, albeit larger, the *Farm Landscape with Tobias and the Angel*, in which a dovecote also dominates.[8] However, his comparison rests on the compositional resemblance of the two paintings rather than the handling, which he describes as "exceptionally minute" in the Tobias painting, dated to the second decade of the seventeenth century.

A survey of Bloemaert's painted and graphic *oeuvre* yields additional precedents for the composition of the Weldon painting. The motif of the dovecote recurs in several other paintings and a number of works on paper.[9] The earliest painting in which it appears is the *Farm Landscape with the Rest on the Flight*, c. 1605-10, where it acts as a repoussoir and a shelter to the holy family and is set in Bloemaert's typically horizontal landscape.[10] The artist continued to use the farmyard setting and the dovecote in several larger horizontal paintings until at least 1635 when it appears in his *Farm Landscape with the Expulsion of Hagar and Ishmael*, a painting that is roughly contemporary with the Weldon panel.[11]

Despite several paintings by the artist featuring dovecotes, it is in his son Frederick's prints, most probably modeled on the father's drawings, that the closest parallels with the Weldon panel may be found. Frederick's print entitled *Farmyard with Dovecote*, which Roethlisberger associates with a lost drawing by Abraham of around 1620, presents a pure landscape devoid of biblical narrative with a dovecote at center, rundown farm sheds, and a pair of workers wattling a fence.[12] Likewise, his print entitled *Landscape with Dovecote*, which also probably reflects an original composition by his father, offers a simple landscape view with similar structures and two figures.[13] Furthermore, Frederick's genre prints, also presumably based on Abraham's drawings, provide a motif which closely echoes the woman and boy in the Weldon painting. In *The Young Thief*, a sleeping woman, seen from behind, crouches diagonally, while a boy in front reaches across to rob her. Although the narrative of the print is entirely different, its forms are almost

identical to those of the Weldon painting.[14] In subject matter, intimacy, and simplicity these prints more closely approximate the Weldon panel than the elaborate biblical paintings in which Bloemaert applies similar motifs and techniques, albeit to achieve an expansive effect.[15]

Bruyn has suggested a moralizing interpretation of lust for the elements of the dovecote and the goat in Bloemaert's Utrecht *Tobias* landscape, as well as a general theme of decay suggested by the tumble-down farm buildings.[16] Roethlisberger rejects his claim and repeatedly denies similar readings of the same motifs in other paintings by the artist. With regard to the Weldon panel, he posits and then dismisses a possible association of the domesticity of the woman and virtues of the dove.[17] It seems unlikely that in an *oeuvre* filled with representations of biblical stories, the artist would have chosen this simple non-narrative painting as a specifically moralizing vehicle. NTM

1 Haak 1984, p. 314, succinctly chronicles Bloemaert's development as a landscapist. He cites the artist's *John the Baptist Preaching*, Rijksmuseum, Amsterdam, as an example of Bloemaert's mannerist style. For a more detailed discussion of the artist's landscapes, see Müller 1927.

2 Gemäldegalerie, Berlin.

3 Van Mander 1604, fol. 298, refers to a group of farm landscape drawings by Bloemaert:

Furthermore, with art lovers there are very subtle landscapes by him with some well-observed and burlesque peasant houses, peasants' implements, trees and pieces of ground — things which are to be seen in great variety round about Utrecht and which are drawn by him; for he does a great deal after life... As translated in Miedema 1994, vol. 1, p. 298 recto.

4 Stechow 1966, pp. 25-26.

5 Haak 1984, p. 314.

6 Roethlisberger/Bok 1993, vol. 1, no. 512. The peasant paintings, which number about half a dozen, are dated to the first half of the 1630s. For a painting that approximates the Weldon panel in scale, style, technique, and rustic subject matter, see Roethlisberger/Bok 1993, no. 507, *A Peasant Woman Feeding a Child*, c. 1634, private collection.

7 Ibid., p. 353, under no. 572, which is an entry

on the print, *Landscape with Dovecote*, that Frederick Bloemaert made after the drawing that Roethlisberger attributes to his father. The drawing is entitled *Landscape with Barnstable*, Art Institute of Chicago, inventory no. 1922.1888. According to the museum records, its attribution to Abraham Bloemaert has been questioned by some scholars.

8 Ibid., no. 478, Centraal Museum, Utrecht, 65.3 x 54.5 cm. The author suggests that the Utrecht painting may have been cut from a horizontal format, and he notes that the Weldon painting is the only landscape that features an upright format. See note 15 below regarding the size of the present painting.

9 Ibid., vol. 1, p.144, where the author cites, but does not list a total of eight paintings, four prints, and "several" drawings.

10 Ibid., vol. 1, no. 101. There is a drawing of *Abraham Casting out Hagar and Ishmael*, Schlossmuseum, Weimar, which also features a dovecote and which has recently been dated to c. 1603-4 by Bolten in Amsterdam 1993-94, cat. 222. In Roethlisberger/Bok 1993, vol. 1, no. D26, it is dated to the first half of the 1630s.

11 Ibid., no. 511, private collection, Switzerland. There is also a painting of the same subject at the J. Paul Getty Museum, Malibu, where a dovecote is shown. While Roethlisberger/Bok 1993, vol. 1, no. 547, dates it to 1638, Bolten in Amsterdam 1993-94, no. 222, note 3, gives the date as 16[2]8 and he states that it is "possibly a studio work."

Other notable paintings which combine elements of the dovecote and the farmyard are the much more complex *Landscape with the Parable of the Tares*, 1624, Walters Art Gallery, Baltimore, discussed along with the related prints by Spicer in San Franciso/Baltimore/London 1997-98, no. 18 (Roethlisberger/Bok 1993, vol. 1, no. 391) and the *Farmyard with Tobias and the Angel*, 1629, Hamburger Kunsthalle; ibid., no. 482.

12 Ibid., no. 465. From "The Large Landscape Series" of engravings, executed after 1635.

13 For a citation of the print and the discussion of a related drawing, see note 6 above.

14 On the print, see Roethlisberger/Bok 1993, vol. 1, no. 368, where the author estimates the date of Abraham's model for it to the decade of the 1620s, and he groups the print with three others, entitling the series "Four Genre Scenes." Roethlisberger relates the imagery in this group to that of the "Leisure" series.

15 Given that virtually all of the extant dovecote paintings are much larger and in a horizontal format, one might expect the Weldon panel to be a fragment of an originally bigger painting. However, the presence of beveling on all four margins on the back of the panel suggests that the painting has never been cut.

16 Amsterdam/Boston/Philadelphia 1987-88, p. 86.

17 Roethlisberger/Bok 1993, vol. 1, no. 478, where he cites and refutes Bruyn, and no. 512, where he discusses meaning in the Weldon painting.

6   Jan Both

(Utrecht ? c. 1615 - Utrecht 1652)

Italianate Landscape with Mountain Path and Ford

c. 1645-50
oil on canvas
70.8 x 88 cm.
Inscribed, lower right, on rock: *JBoth* [with first two initials in monogram ligature]

PROVENANCE:
Major J. C. T. Mills, Norfolk (by 1964); Sale, Christie's, London, December 13, 1985, no. 70 (ill.); Private collection.

EXHIBITIONS:
Norwich 1964, no. 5; Birmingham 1995, no. 2 (ill.); New Orleans 1997, no. 6 (ill.).

Jan Both's sunny mountain prospect epitomizes the classical vision of Italianate painting developed by the artists of the second generation of the Dutch southern landscape school, among whom he was a leader. A mountain path cuts a ledge skirting a rocky precipice with trees on either side; these, in turn, frame a view of a tower on a farther hill. To the left, a vista of water and mountains merges with the distant horizon. Gold and pink clouds drift across a blue sky, suffused with the soft light of a sun concealed by the mountains at right. Humble travelers wind along the path, interrupted by a ford which several of the wayfarers cross in the immediate foreground. Most prominent is a man bearing a woman on his back as he emerges from the water, casting a long shadow on the path before him.

Jan Both lived in Rome from the late 1630s until 1641 when he returned to, and settled in, his native Utrecht. Many of his paintings developed from the landscape motifs that he studied in Italy and the styles and conventions of the artists he worked with there. The influence of Herman van Swanevelt (c. 1610-1655), who had absorbed the innovations of the pioneer of Italianate landscapes, Cornelis van Poelenburgh (nos. 37-39), is most strongly manifested in the composition of the present painting. Swanevelt's particular configuration of a low foreground bracketed by high cliffs and trees and leading to faraway hills, developed from the 1630s to early 1640s, is echoed in the Weldon painting and is common in Both's *oeuvre*.[1]

The motif of the ford with crossing figures recurs in at least three other paintings by the artist, dated to the years 1645-50.[2] Among them, the *Landscape with Ford*, Nationalmuseum, Stockholm, is a variant of the present painting. With the exception of details like the distant tower in the Weldon composition, absent in the Stockholm painting, the works are virtually identical. Burke has dated the Stockholm version to c. 1645-50. The

practice of replicating and varying compositions is characteristic of Both's working method, and may be seen in the Munich and Detroit ford paintings, c. 1645 and c. 1650, respectively; here the artist modeled the second, larger painting on the first.[3] The dates for all four ford paintings are based on a hypothetical chronology of stylistic development for the artist since only a couple of paintings from Both's extant *oeuvre* are inscribed with dates.[4]

The ultimate source for the rustic staffage in the Weldon painting, repeated in the Stockholm version, is the genre imagery of the Dutch artist Pieter van Laer (1599-after 1642). He was both a friend of Jan's brother Andries (c. 1612- c. 1642), also a painter, and a member of the Schildersbent, the fraternity of Dutch artists in Rome with whom the Boths associated. The figures are robust and identifiable as the peasant types of van Laer, rather than the classical or historical staffage of other Italianate painters.[5] Despite Andries's figure painting, which is more closely associated with van Laer, and his contribution of the staffage in some of Jan's landscapes, his death around 1642 precludes his possible collaboration on the present painting which probably dates from the end of that decade.[6] It is likely that the staffage was painted by Jan in the manner of Andries.

By the end of the seventeenth century, Both's Italianate scenes were among the highest-priced landscape paintings in the Netherlands.[7] Subsequently they were avidly collected by the English. Both's success was not only posthumous: during his own lifetime he worked alongside Lorrain (c. 1604/5-1682), Poussin (1594-1665), and others for the Spanish court on a landscape cycle for the Buen Retiro Palace in Madrid, and his landscapes were acquired by the Utrecht collector of landscapes and patron of Poelenburgh, Baron van Wyttenhorst.[8] The artist's significance may also be measured by his considerable influence on his successors and followers in the Italianate landscape genre. The paintings by Jan Hackaert and Willem de Heusch in the present collection (nos. 22, 23) are a testament to Both's legacy. NTM

1   For a similar painting by Swanevelt, dated 1643, see his *Landscape with Tall Rocks*, Rijksmuseum, Amsterdam, illustrated and discussed by Chong in Amsterdam/Boston/Philadelphia 1987-88, no. 102, where the author traces the development of Swanevelt's conception of the view. Examples of other paintings in Both's *oeuvre* which employ a similar composition are the *Landscape with a Draftsman*, c. 1645, Collection of Mr. and Mrs. E.W. Carter, Los Angeles, *and A Rocky Italian Landscape with Herdsmen and Muleteers*, c. 1645, National Gallery, London. There is a drawing at the British Museum, London, *A Winding Road by a River*, inventory no. Gg. 2-269, which was attributed to Jan Both in Hind 1926, vol. 3, p. 49, no. 5, and which exactly represents the site of the Weldon painting. However, this drawing is apparently not accepted by Burke 1976, who omits it from his catalogue of drawings. For Both's Utrecht paintings see most recently Spicer in San Francisco/Baltimore/London 1997-98, pp. 41-42 and nos. 70-72.

2   Burke 1976, includes the three paintings in his catalogue raisonné, omitting the present work. They appear as no. 19, *Landscape with a Ford*, c. 1650, Detroit Institute of Arts; no. 78, *Landscape with a Ford*, c. 1645, Bayerische Staatsgemäldesammlungen, Munich; and no. 108, *Landscape with a Ford*, c. 1645-50, Nationalmuseum, Stockholm.

3   As stated by Burke 1976, no. 19.

4   The paintings are Both's *Landscape with Mercury and Argus*, Bayerische Staatsgemäldesammlungen, Munich, whose date is read as 1650 in Burke 1976, no. 79, and the *Southern Landscape*, 1649, private collection; Burke 1976, no. 117. The date on the second painting was first published in Montreal 1990, no. 17. There is also one dated drawing attributed to Both, Museum of Fine Arts, Budapest; Burke 1976, no. D-10. The information about the drawing and the Munich painting is taken from Los Angeles/Boston/New York 1981-82, no. 5, note 11.

5   Sutton in Amsterdam/Boston/Philadelphia 1987-88, p. 42. On van Laer, see, Janeck 1968 and Durantini 1972. The central motif of the man carrying the woman does, however, ultimately derive from Italian Renaissance and, in turn, classical models. See, for example, the figures of Aeneas and his father, Anchises, fleeing Troy in Raphael's *Fire in the Borgo*, Stanza dell'Incendio, The Vatican.

6   On Andries, see Haverkamp-Begemann 1976. On Jan and Andries, see Waddingham 1964. The artistic relationship of the brothers is also discussed in Burke 1976, pp. 133-37, where the author traces the confusion regarding the attribution of staffage in Jan's paintings, to Andries, to a statement from von Sandrart 1675-79. The present painting is recorded in Norwich 1964, no. 5, as having once been given to both artists.

7   Chong in Amsterdam/Boston/Philadelphia 1987-88, pp. 115-16, and table 3, p. 117.

8   For references on van Wyttenhorst's collection, see the entry on Poelenburgh's *Italianate Landscape with Sleeping Venus and Spying Satyrs* (no. 37).

(detail)

7a, b **Bartholomeus Breenbergh**
(Deventer 1598 – Amsterdam 1657)

Pastoral Landscapes with Ruins

c. 1629/1630
oil on silvered copper
13.3 x 26.7 cm.

PROVENANCE:
Private collection, Ireland; Richard L. Feigen & Co.,
New York; Gebr. Douwes Fine Art; Private collection,
the Netherlands.

EXHIBITIONS:
Chicago 1984; London 1991.

LITERATURE:
Roethlisberger 1981, p. 9, nos. 109a, 109b, ill.;
Roethlisberger 1991, no. 5, ill.

Bartholomeus Breenbergh was born in Deventer and is thought to have received his initial training as a painter in Amsterdam, where he is signaled in 1619; however, by the end of the same year he was in Rome. The impact of his encounter with the remains of Roman architecture, the soft penetrating Italian light, and the art of the contemporaries he encountered there, chiefly the Fleming Paul Bril (1554-1626), Cornelis van Poelenburch (1594/5-1667) who had arrived from Utrecht in 1617, and possibly the Italian Filippo Napoletano (1587-1638), would shape him as an artist.[1] By the end of 1630 the artist seems to have been back in the Netherlands and settled in Amsterdam.

Other than the many drawings of ruins that Breenbergh made in Rome, he also produced a small number of paintings there. In his monograph on the artist, Roethlisberger dates the Weldon *Pastoral Landscapes* to c. 1630 and places them among a group of small works on copper or panel with pastoral subjects and blond coloring which he considers to have been produced "perhaps partly in Rome and partly upon his return in Amsterdam."[2] Though Breenbergh made drawings of famous as well as little-studied ruins while in Rome, his paintings are often imaginary variations of these.[3] The ruins are isolated out from any surrounding architecture and the figures of shepherds, gypsies, or other passersby are small, giving life to these peaceful, sun-drenched scenes from the Italian Campagna without rivaling the monumental ruins for our attention.

Though Roethlisberger found it difficult to establish whether these *Pastoral Landscapes* were painted in Italy or Amsterdam, they very likely predate the artist's *Voyage of Eliazar and Rebecca*, dated 1630, private collection, Montreal.[13] From this point on, the ruin is now less a subject in its own right than a setting for a narrative subject taken from the Bible or from Greco-Roman mythology, reflecting the great popularity in these years of history painting in Amsterdam. In addition, Breenbergh used copper—the support for *Pastoral Landscapes*—primarily during the Roman years, and it is also to this period that other examples of paired landscapes can be assigned. JS

1 For Breenbergh's Italianate landscapes, see Roethlisberger 1991, Utrecht 1965, Salerno 1977, Boston 1987.

2 Roethlisberger 1991, under no. 5.

3 Roethlisberger (1981, under no. 109; 1991, under no. 5) has identified the ruin in our 7a as the same one as that represented in a painting attributed to Filippo Napoletano, *An Ancient Tower and a House in the Campagna*, private collection, Rome (Salerno 1977, no. 38.2, ill. p. 205).

7a

7b

8   Jan Brueghel the Elder
(Brussels 1568 - Antwerp 1625)

Fantastic Forest Scene

c. 1600
oil on panel
18.2 cm. (diameter)

PROVENANCE:
Kunsthandel P. de Boer, Amsterdam (by 1934); Geus van den Heuvel,
Nieuwersluis (by 1955); Private Collection.

EXHIBITIONS:
Amsterdam 1934, no. 59; Stedelijk Museum, Schiedam, 1952-53, no. 14;
Dordrecht 1955, no. 26; Laren 1958, no. 75; Arnhem 1960-61, no. 8 (ill.); Laren
1963, no. 47; Amsterdam 1963A, no. 8 (ill.); Cologne/Utrecht 1985-86, no. 76
(ill.); New Orleans 1997, no. 10 (ill.).

LITERATURE:
Puyvelde 1934, p. 21, plate II, fig. B; Ertz 1979, no. 69.

Please refer to entry no. 9 for a brief discussion of this painting.

(actual size)

9   Jan Brueghel the Elder
(Brussels 1568 - Antwerp 1625)

Woodland Road with Wagons and Travelers

c. 1609
oil on copper
9.2 x 15 cm.
Inscribed, lower left *BRVEGHE[L]*

PROVENANCE:
Possibly J. Allnutt Collection (Sale, Christie's, London, June 18-20, 1863, no. 338, described as "J. Brueghel, *A landscape with post-wagons and figures on a road*," or no. 395, described as "J. Brueghel, *A landscape with figures and post-wagons*"); Grace Shearer, thence by descent; Christie's, London, April 10, 1987, no. 20 (with provenance given as "Major Allnutt; Miss Grace Shearer, thence by inheritance").

EXHIBITION:
New Orleans 1997, no. 1 (ill.).

Close scrutiny of this diminutive, refined and jewel-like landscape by Jan Brueghel the Elder effectively reveals how the artist earned the moniker "*de Velours*" or "Velvet" for his detailed, yet subtle craftsmanship. On a copper surface, slightly smaller than a postcard, the painter has rendered the illusion of a view along a road into the woods and beyond to a distant village, down a hill to the left. The scene is animated by tiny, brightly clothed figures, wayfarers, travelers on horseback, and wagons. The wooded setting framing the scene offers an abundance of rich and varicolored foliage. The proliferation of detail and its finesse lend credence to the claim of Brueghel's first biographer, Karel van Mander, who maintained that one of the painter's early teachers was the miniaturist Mayeken Bessemer, his maternal grandmother.[1]

Brueghel's extensive landscape *oeuvre* has been divided into types by Ertz, who groups this painting with four similar works under the larger heading of Waldstraßen or woodland roads,[2] a category that is an extension of the forest landscape which was first developed by Brueghel just prior to 1600. The artist's earlier roundel also in the present collection, the *Fantastic Forest Scene* (no. 8), dated c. 1600, provides an example of the woodland landscape, a genre which he conceived, at least in part, from the drawings of forest interiors of his father, Pieter Bruegel the Elder (c. 1525/30-1569).[3] Jan's pure forest scenes, like those of his fellow Flemish landscapist Gillis van Coninxloo (1544-1607), tend to be characterized by fantasy, as in the Weldon roundel in which the trees are mannered, even decorative, and the craggy cliff and fortress are pure fabrication. However, the invented landscape does reveal a close study of nature in the details, such as the tiny birds, reeds, roots, and irises in the foreground.

The woodland road type, the earliest example of which is dated 1605, features a lower horizon, a more indigenous topography, and by and large a more earthbound prospect, imparting a generally realistic impression.[4] Nonetheless, these paintings incorporate conservative, imaginary elements of the Flemish landscape tradition. Most notable in the present painting is the telescopic view of the faraway village, illuminated between two stands of trees at left, which is reminiscent of the panoramic world landscapes of Joachim Patinir (c. 1475-1524), Pieter Bruegel the Elder and others. The tripartite color scheme of brown for the foreground, green for the middleground and blue for the distance and horizon is also consistent with Brueghel's landscape heritage. The general disposition of the main road and the groupings of the trees, which appear in other paintings by the artist, seem to correspond to a drawing by him in the Kupferstichkabinett, Berlin.[5]

Ertz has dated the present painting c. 1609, largely on a comparison with four analogous woodland road scenes that span the period from 1607 to 1611.[6] More recently, Sutton has identified eight paintings that relate to a similar work and are dated 1608.[7] The subject matter and the technique of the Weldon painting certainly situate it securely in this period. NTM

1 Van Mander 1604, p. 234. Van Mander reports that Brueghel's other early teacher was the Antwerp artist Pieter Goetkindt. These claims remain inconclusive as no paintings attributed to Bessemer or Goetkindt are extant.

2 Weldon curatorial file, letter and report from K. Ertz, July 13, 1992, who has inspected the painting. Ertz cited the following paintings as a context for the present work: 1. *Woodland Road with Travelers*, c. 1607, private collection, Belgium; Ertz 1979, no. 156, 2. *Woodland Road*, c. 1607, Munich, Alte Pinakothek; Ertz 1979, no. 158, 3. *Woodland Road with Travelers*, 1611, formerly David Koetser, Zurich; Ertz 1979, no. 232, 4. *Woodland Road with Travelers*, c. 1611, Apsley House, London; Ertz 1979, no. 241.

3 Sutton, "Introduction," in Amsterdam/Boston/Philadelphia 1987-88, p. 17. On Pieter Bruegel the Elder's forest landscapes, see, Arndt 1972.

4 The painting which Ertz identifies as the first dated *Waldstraße* is *Road in a Wood*, 1605, Munich, Alte Pinakothek; Ertz 1979, no. 112.

5 This observation was made by Sutton in his catalogue entry for Brueghel's *A Road with a Ford in a Wood*, 1608, private collection, in Boston/Toledo 1994, no. 82.

6 See note 2 above for a list of the paintings. When Ertz examined the Weldon painting, he reported an inscribed date of 160(9?). However, this date is no longer visible.

7 See note 5 above.

(detail)

10a, b, c   Pieter Brueghel the Younger
(Brussels 1564 – Antwerp 1638)

Threesome, Two Monks and Two Men, Two Couples

oil on panel
11 x 24 cm. (each)

PROVENANCE:
Private collection, Netherlands; Confiscated, German Occupation Authorities, 1940; Sale H.W. Lange, January 27, 1943, no. 14 (ill.); Allied Central Collecting Point, Baden-Baden, 1945, nos. 1320 A-C; Stichting Nederlandsch Kunstbezit, 1946, inv. no. 2326; Private collection, Germany; Sale, March 14, 1963, Lempertz, Cologne, no. 59; Kunsthandel P. de Boer, Amsterdam 1963; Private collection.

EXHIBITIONS:
Amsterdam 1963, no. 12 (ill.); London 1963, nos. 37-39; Providence 1964, nos. 2-4; New York 1966, nos. 3-5; New Orleans 1997, nos. 7-9.

LITERATURE:
Marlier 1969, pp. 421-422, c-e, figs. 268-270; New Orleans 1997, nos. 7-9 (ill.).

Pieter Brueghel the Younger belonged to the prominent Flemish Brueghel family of artists.[1] He was the oldest son of Pieter Brueghel the Elder (ca. 1520-1569) and brother of Jan Brueghel the Elder (1568-1625) represented in the Weldon collection by two fine landscapes (nos. 9 and 10).

Pieter Brueghel the Elder had explored the representation of peasant life as a vehicle for moralizing about human nature or for commenting on the larger world of human affairs. Pieter the Younger's many reinterpretations of some of his father's most important paintings made their imagery accessible to a wider public. Nevertheless, in his own compositions it is clear that he was less concerned with these more intellectual approaches. Unlike his brother Jan, Pieter Brueghel the Younger never travelled to Italy and did not depict mythological and allegorical themes. When he began to develop his own subjects, they often reflect a more tolerant—and sometimes ironic—view of the harsh conditions of peasant life. He is a chronicler. Especially in his earlier works, dated from 1593 onwards, Pieter Brueghel the Younger favored the "traditional" Brueghel subject matter, inspired by his father: peasant weddings (for example the *Peasant Wedding Dance*, dated 1609 in The Walters), *Four Seasons*, peasants scenes, and religious themes.[2]

However, from 1616 on his *oeuvre* undergoes a change and he begins to distance himself a little from his father. This is expressed in a change in signature ("P. Breughel", as opposed to his father's "Bruegel") as well as in compositions that no longer depend on his father's. The subjects of his paintings are now slightly different, tending towards descriptions of village life, like *St. Michael's Inn, Drunk Lead Home by his Wife, Return from the Fair*, the *Swan Inn, St. George's Fair*, and *Dance Around the May Tree*.[3]

In his monograph on Pieter Brueghel the Younger, Georges Marlier suggests that the Weldon panels of *Threesome*; *Two Monks and Two Men*; *Two Couples* (which Marlier titles respectively *The Meeting*; *Two Monks Arriving at an Inn*; *Two Peasant Couples in a Field*) were part of a series of five paintings and were intended for a cabinet.[4] Such small, oblong panels were often made to decorate the drawers of ebony wood cabinets that held precious objects and were popular with wealthy collectors in Flanders. The other two panels in the series as described by Marlier depict *Drunkard Escorted by Relatives* and *Peasant Dance*. At the time of Marlier's publication (1969), the latter two were in a private collection in Amsterdam.[5]

Peasants in an Open Wagon in the Bonnefantenmuseum, Maastricht (fig. 1) [6] was almost surely the sixth panel of this series, as was suggested already by Jacqueline Folie in her editing of Marlier's text after his death[7]. It is closely related in subject and composition and identical in dimensions. All panels have trees anchoring the foreground and the characteristic sixteenth-century three-color scheme to create depth with warm brown tones in the foreground, greens in the middle-ground and cooler blues in the background, with some bright red accents throughout the paintings.

In a small number of paintings Pieter Brueghel the Younger depicted the events leading up to a peasant wedding or dance. According to Klaus Ertz, the impulse for this did not derive from his father but rather from Martin van Cleve (1527-1581), who painted several series of popular traditions that accompany weddings.[8] One of these series, sold at auction in Brussels, in 1930, consists of five paintings, showing the *Train of the Bride, Train of the Bridegroom, Handing of the Gifts, Meal in the Open*, and *Blessing of the Wedding Bed*.[9] A second series by van

10a

10b

10c

Cleve appeared at auction in Cologne, in 1986, depicting the same subjects, though this series was enlarged with a painting of marital life after the wedding, *Dismissal of the Lovers*.[10] While Marten van Cleve may be considered the *inventor* of the pictorial series surrounding a popular wedding, Pieter Brueghel the Younger, created his own interpretation.

The subject matter of Pieter Brueghel the Younger's companion panels under discussion suggests that the series as a whole probably represented motifs associated with a wedding. We might speculate that the six panels—representing the events before (traveling, meetings), during (dance), and after (drunk) a wedding feast—were initially completed by a representation of the feast itself. The recognition that the Weldon panels were part of a larger series, gives us a greater appreciation for the importance of the whole in achieving what would have been an impressive ensemble. AvW-TH

1   For Pieter Brueghel the Younger in general see most recently Essen 1997-98.

2   Idem, pp. 10-11, see also pp. 16-20.

3   *St. Michael's Inn* in Private collection (Essen 1997-98, cat. 141); *Drunk Lead Home by his Wife* in Montreal, Museum of Fine Arts (Essen 1997-98, cat. 126); *Return from the Fair* (Essen 1997-98, p. 19, fig. 5) and Private collection (Essen 1997-98, cat. 145); the *Swan Inn* for instance in Stockholm, Hallwylska Museet (Essen 1997-98, p. 19, fig. 6); *St. George's Fair* in Antwerp, Koninklijk Museum voor Schone Kunsten (Essen 1997-98, cat. 143); and *Dance Around the May Tree* in Innsbruck, Tiroler Landesmuseum (Essen 1997-98, cat. 144).

4   Marlier 1969, p. 422.

5   Marlier 1969, p. 420-422, figs. 267, 271.

6   Panel, 11.3 x 24 cm., Essen 1997-98, cat. 134. Marlier 1969, p. 4 22, fig. 272. The panel is on loan from the Rijksdienst Beeldende Kunst, no. 1410. Rijksdienst Beeldende Kunst, 1992, p. 58, no. 350.

7   Marlier 1969, p. 422, note 1, signed J.F.

8   Ertz in Essen 1997-98, p. 394.

9   Marlier 1969, p. 342, fig. 207-210). Only the Handing of the Gifts (Marlier fig. 209) reappeared, in the De Pauwschen Collection at 10 Sotheby's, London, 9 April, 1986, no. 30, as Marten van Cleve, panel, 42.2 x 76.4 cm.

10 Essen 1997-98, p. 396, fig. 3.

Fig. 1 Pieter Brueghel the Younger, *Peasants in an Open Wagon*, after 1616, oil on panel, Rijksdienst Beeldende Kunst, The Hague, on loan to Bonnefantenmuseum, Maastricht

11 Abraham Calraet, attributed to
(Dordrecht 1642-Dordrecht 1722)

A Portrait of a Horse in a Landscape

oil on panel
48.2 x 59.3 cm.
Inscribed, lower left: *A. Cuyp* [indistinctly]

PROVENANCE:
Sale, J. West, London, March 21, 1835 (for £34:13s);
W. Russell, Amsterdam; Leonard Koetser Gallery,
London (by 1972); Galerie J. Kraus, Paris (by 1978).

EXHIBITIONS:
London 1972, no. 34 (ill.); Dordrecht 1978, cat. 26
(ill.); Paris 1978, no. 6 (ill.); Birmingham 1995, no. 5
(ill.); New Orleans 1997, no. 12 (ill.).

LITERATURE:
Smith 1829-42, Supplement, 1842, no. 43; Hofstede
de Groot 1907-28, vol. 2, 1909, no. 574; *Burlington
Magazine* (June 1978) xxv (ill.); Chong 1992, no.
Calr 15.[1]

A dark brown horse stands before an expansive landscape, against a lightly clouded sky - perfectly still, and displayed to advantage, as in a portrait. His ample, well-groomed form is defined by highlights, most notably in the curved lines at his flank, along his belly and the muscles of his chest. His physiology is further particularized in details like the veins on his chest, the white blaze on this face and his single white stocking.

In van Mander's poem on the art of painting, published in 1604, he devoted over half of his section on animals to horses,[2] introducing and distinguishing them with the following lines: "The most noble, the most highly prized kind of all livestock, namely the obliging, spirited horses. Noble (I say), for many fine traits have been observed in horses: they remain as faithful as hounds to their master, and love him alone."[3] The sturdy, brown horse of the Weldon panel does indeed appear noble, as defined by Van Mander, if not in the aristocratic sense.

In the course of the seventeenth century, the portrayal of horses became a subgenre of animal painting in the Netherlands, and a small portion of the representations display the characteristics of portraiture. Following on the examples of the earlier equine portraits by Jacob de Gheyn the Younger (1565-1629) and Roelant Saverij (1576-1639), Paulus Potter (1625-1654) seems to have conceived some of his horse paintings as portrayals of prized, identifiable mounts, as for example *The Gray Horse* of 1653.[4] Much like the artist of the Weldon portrait, Potter brought a greater degree of realism to his depictions than is found in the idealized specimens conceived by his predecessors. Nonetheless, Potter's equine subjects still appear to be prized stallions. By

comparison, the brown horse of the Weldon panel, though well-maintained, is a relatively humble beast. His sturdy build is less that of a favorite war horse or hunter, than a working animal and he even bears the blemishes of a chestnut on his left foreleg and the nail holes from his shoes in his hooves.

Long thought to be the work of the Dordrecht artist Aelbert Cuyp (1620-1691), the Weldon painting has recently been reattributed to his colleague and townsman Abraham Calraet in the catalogue raisonné of Cuyp's work.[5] The landscape certainly displays qualities characteristic of Cuyp's paintings, yet the portrait type of a single horse, unfettered and unaccompanied by a human being never occurs in Cuyp's *oeuvre* while it is a recurrent theme in the work of Calraet. Furthermore, Cuyp's horses are often shown in the broader aristocratic context of a hunt or a noble patron's portrait, as accessories to the human sitters rather than the subjects in and of themselves.[6] Finally, the type of horse depicted here - with furry fetlocks and sturdy pasterns, a massive neck, a heavy body and a forward lean - seems to be characteristic of Calraet's style, rather than the slimmer, more elegant horses of Cuyp.[7]

An excellent example of Calraet's horse type, as probably portrait, and an apt comparison to the present panel is the *Brown and White Skewbald Horse with a Saddle Beside It,* from the National Gallery, London, where it was attributed to Cuyp up until 1921.[8] Although the horse is seen from a different angle, and he is spotted, he is of the same type as that shown in the Weldon panel. He also bears a similar relationship to the landscape behind and a diagonal tree trunk in the lower left corner. A second painting attributed to

Calraet which features two horses and a more extensive landscape is the *Horses in a Marsh Landscape* [9] (fig. 1). The foremost dark brown horse in this painting is virtually identical to the Weldon horse.

In Bredius's annotations to the inventory of Calraet's mother's estate, he was the first to suggest that a number of small horse portraits, *Pferdeporträts*, then given to Cuyp should be reattributed to the workshop of Abraham Calraet and his younger brother Barent (1649-1737), also a painter. The inventory lists many horse paintings and, as indicated by Bredius, in three instances, names are given which probably denote the owners, thereby suggesting that they were in fact commissioned portraits. [10] In addition, the same document includes items specified as copies of Cuyp's horse paintings.

Abraham's brother Barent Calraet was recorded as Cuyp's pupil by the eighteenth- century biographer Houbraken. Given the nature of Abraham's emerging *oeuvre*, it is probable that he also had contact with Cuyp. [11] Abraham's work was initially identified by Bredius when he separated a number of still-life paintings, monogrammed A.C., from the *oeuvre* of Cuyp and correctly restored them to Calraet. [12] In 1926, following on Bredius's discovery, Hofstede de Groot, who had listed over 800 paintings in his 1909 catalogue of Cuyp's *oeuvre*, began the process of identifying Calraet's hand in a number of horse paintings that he had previously attributed to Cuyp. [13] Since then, a growing group of horse paintings, of relatively small format and on panel, formerly recognized as being in Cuyp's first manner,

has become associated with the *oeuvre* of Calraet. While the present painting was published under the name of Aelbert Cuyp in the catalogue to the 1978 Dordrecht exhibition on the Cuyp family, the substance of the entry suggests that Calraet was probably responsible for many such representations. [14] In Chong's catalogue, he attributes 170 paintings to Cuyp and 86 to Calraet, and he characterizes the attributional issue as a "major problem." [15] NTM

1 In all citations and exhibitions, except for Chong 1992, the painting is attributed to Aelbert Cuyp. On the issue of attribution, see text below and especially notes 5 and 7.

2 As discussed in Dordrecht/Leeuwarden 1988-89, p. 268.

3 Van Mander 1604, folio 39, as translated in Miedema 1973, vol. I, pp. 220-21, and cited in The Hague 1994-95, p. 102.

4 Kunsthalle, Hamburg. A portrait of a captured Spanish charger that was presented to Prince Maurits was executed by de Gheyn the Younger, *Spanish War-Horse*, in 1603, Rijksmuseum, Amsterdam, can be compared to Saverij's 1605 *Stallion and Groom,* private collection, the Netherlands, which belonged to the emperor Rudolf II, Kaufmann 1988, no. 19.7. The evolution of the horse portrait in the Netherlands is outlined with the above examples and others, and discussed by E. Buijsen in The Hague 1994-95, under cat. 16 and on p. 28.

5 Chong 1992, cat. Calr 15. Smith 1842 and Hofstede de Groot 1909 probably never saw the painting as both cite sales records rather than listing its owner. Hofstede de Groot, in fact, seems to have simply transcribed and slightly altered Smith's entry. While the catalogue entry in Dordrecht 1978 gives the traditional attribution to Cuyp, the substance of the text raises the possibility that Calraet may have been the author. See text and note 14 below.

6 For an example of Cuyp's aristocratic portraiture which includes horses, see *Michiel and Cornelis Pompe van Meerdervoort with their Tutor,* Metropolitan Museum of Art, New York, Chong 1992, no. 143. Cuyp comes closest to the horse portrait in his *A Man Behind his Horse*, Collection W. van der Vorm, Museum Boymans-van Beuningen, Rotterdam, Chong 1992, no. 145, where the dismounted rider is virtually obscured by the animal and a groom holds the reins. Occasionally Cuyp also depicted less exalted horses, as in drawings like the *Study of a Horse*, Fitzwilliam Museum, Cambridge.

7 While Chong 1992, Calr 15, likens the horse to his number B15, a painting which falls under his section of works "that cannot be firmly attributed to Cuyp," he states that the Weldon horse "resembles even more closely horses by Calraet," without making specific comparisons. (A comparison of Calraet's *A Boy Holding a Gray Horse*, National Gallery, London, illustrated and discussed in Brown/ MacLaren 1992, no. 2548, and Cuyp's *An Officer with his Horse*, H. M. Queen Elizabeth II, Buckingham Palace, London, Chong 1992, no. 144, effectively illustrates the differences between Calraet's shaggier, heavier horse type and Cuyp's smoother, more groomed horses.)

8 Brown/MacLaren 1990, no. 1683 (ill.). The support is panel and the dimensions are 34.2 x 44.4 cm.

9 Catalogued and illustrated in Norwich 1964, cat. 9, where support and dimensions are given as panel, 15 x 20 1/8 in. (Approximately 38 x 51 cm.) The painting was then in a private collection, U.K. It is not catalogued in Chong 1992 whose study includes sections on paintings which "cannot be firmly attributed to A. Cuyp," the *oeuvre* of Calraet, and "doubtful attributions to... Calraet," in addition to the main catalogue of paintings securely attributed to Cuyp.

10 Bredius 1915-22, vol. I, 1915, p. 313, no. 93 and note 1, p. 314, nos. 111-12 and note 1.

11 Houbraken 1718-21, vol. III, 1721, p. 292.

12 Bredius 1917.

13 C. Hofstede de Groot in Thieme-Becker 1907-50, vol. 19, 1926, pp. 482-4. De Groot's earlier catalogue of Cuyp's *oeuvre*, 1909, was based on that of Smith in vol. IV and IX (Supplement), in Smith 1829-42, which included 313 paintings. This information is provided in Chong 1992, pp. 63-66.

14 Dordrecht 1978, cat. 26: "Daarbij moeten wij ons wel realiseren, dat deze voorstellingen waarschijhlijk zeer gevraagd zijn geweest en door epigonen als A. Calraet veel zijn nagevolgd in de stijl van Cuyp." Moreover, we should realize that these representations were probably much in demand, and many were imitated in the style of Cuyp by followers like Calraet.

15 Chong 1992, p.66.

Fig. 1 *Horses in a Marsh Landscape*, oil on panel, Private Collection, U.K.

12 Pieter Codde

(Amsterdam 1599 - Amsterdam 1678)

A Musical Company

c. 1624-29
oil on panel
39.8 x 58 cm.
Inscribed, bottom right, on book page: *P Codde f /162[?]* [initials
P C as inverted Cp monogram]

PROVENANCE:
D. Gaskell, Lupset Hall, Wakefield; G. Milnes-
Gaskell; H. Schickman Gallery, New York (by 1968);
Private Collection, Connecticut (by 1972); Private
collection.

EXHIBITIONS:
New York 1968, no. 2 (ill.); Birmingham 1995, no. 3
(ill.); New Orleans 1997, no. 13 (ill.).

LITERATURE:
Playter 1972, pp. 65, 67 and pl. 64; Liedtke 1988, pp.
96, 99, and fig. 5-12.

The elegant simplicity of Pieter Codde's early high-life interiors is exemplified by this musical company. A finely-dressed group of players and singers perform in concert, seated informally at a rectangular table. A woman whose lips are parted in song faces out from the group as if she were inviting the viewer to join in. To her right, a flutist whose glance also engages the viewer plays his instrument beside a singer who is absorbed in her music book. At the far end of the table a lutenist accompanies the voices. A couple of vocalists focused on their broadsheet sit across from the flutist; the man is seen in profile, while the woman's back is fully turned. The musical subject and the subtle coloration and brushwork in the painting perfectly match its theme of harmony.

Pieter Codde's *oeuvre* is largely composed of interiors depicting well-to-do revelers whose groupings and architectural settings became increasingly complex beginning around 1630.[1] The genre was developed by Codde and his Amsterdam contemporaries Willem Duyster (1588/9-1635) and Simon Kick (1603-1652), who were probably influenced by the earlier Haarlem scenes of Willem Buytewech (1591/92-1624) and his follower Dirck Hals (1591-1656).[2]

While the final digit of the artist's date on the Weldon painting is unclear, the decade of its execution is established by the presence of the "2," and Playter has placed it late in the 1620s, relatively early in the artist's career.[3] The painting has characteristics evident in several works which date from the mid-1620s through the 1630s. The emphasis on the figure making contact with the viewer is reflected in both a number of the artist's contemporary group scenes and his genre paintings of individuals. Playter has stated that this motif in the Weldon panel marks its first appearance in Codde's company paintings.[4] His later use of a woman in a similar, albeit reversed, pose who likewise seems to beckon to the viewer may be seen, for example, in his *Merry Company* of 1631, private collection, Montreal.[5] The motif of the figure looking out is also the subject of interiors which focus on individuals, as in *The Seated Woman Holding a Mirror*, 1625, National Gallery, London, and the *Young Scholar in his Study*, c. 1630-33, Musée des Beaux-Arts, Lille.[6] The opposite and complimentary motif of the figure facing away, shown here as the female singer holding the music, is also found in Codde's contemporaneous company and single-figure paintings as, for example, in the *Woman Seen from Behind Seated at a Virginal*, private collection.[7]

The small number of figures in the Weldon panel and the room they occupy are features of other early company paintings. The closest parallels are found in two versions of the *Musical Company*, which Playter likened to the Weldon painting and dated slightly later.[8] The compositions of both paintings feature a compact group of five fashionably dressed musicians seated and standing around a table in a small, simple space.

The sober tonalist palette of the Weldon panel situates it in the artist's *oeuvre* and in the larger context of the contemporary technical innovations in Dutch painting. The artist employed a subdued color range, featuring the fashionable black silks and brocades of the day, combined with subtle accents, as in the green underskirts of the two foreground women and the cape of the man

33

seen in profile. Virtually all of the muted colors in the painting are united in the pattern of the oriental carpet at the center of the composition. Sutton has associated the restricted palette of Codde's paintings with the period beginning in the late 1620s, and has likened it to similar developments in the techniques of landscape and still-life painting.[9] The understated coloration is enriched by the textures crafted by the artist's fine brushwork such as the brocade pattern in the black dress of the woman whose back is turned, the trim at the hem of her skirt, and her delicate lace collar. Codde's finesse as a painter of costume is echoed and elaborated in roughly contemporary portraits, such as the *Portrait of a Married Couple*, 1634, The Hague.

The theme of the musical concert in the Weldon painting surely alludes to harmony. Music figured prominently in the culture of the Dutch Republic in the seventeenth century and it was frequently represented in conjunction with the theme of love.[10] Emblematic illustrations and inscriptions explicitly link these subjects. An example is Crispin de Passe's print for the emblem *Amor Docet Musicam/Love Teaches Music* in which a lute-wielding Cupid points toward a musical trio.[11]

A number of features of the Weldon painting make it clear that Codde's concert may be interpreted as an inducement to love. At the left foreground tenderness is expressed by the man who gently places his hand on his partner's chair back and appears to look as much at her as at the music in her hands. The allusions to the lute, symbol of love, in the presence of the lutenist whose obscured instrument is also represented by the prominent black case on the floor in the foreground (the lute was used to accompany a singer, underscoring the theme of the harmony and companionship, and it was also the preferred instrument of the lover's serenade as depicted in contemporary paintings).[12] Finally, Codde makes his point with the woman in the foreground, his most prominent figure. She appears to invite the viewer to partake in the pleasures, and in her hand she holds a single pink rose, a token of love.[13] NTM

1 In addition to paintings of musical companies, sometimes including dancers, as well as depictions of feasters, card players, and other festive groups, the artist specialized in the subject of guard rooms, populated by equally elegant figures. Early in his career, Codde also painted a number of single-figure interiors. To a lesser degree, Codde was a portraitist. On his *oeuvre*, see Playter 1972 and Torresan 1975.

2 Liedtke in New York 1992-93, p. 101, citing Sutton in Philadelphia/Berlin/London 1984, pp. xxxii-xxxiii, where he summarizes these developments in genre painting.

3 Playter 1972, p. 65. She states that the alleged date of 1624 is too early stylistically. Her criteria for dating the painting to the late 1620s are the nature of the composition, the tonalism, the placement of figures in the room, and the use of empty space around them.

4 Ibid., p. 67.

5 Catalogued and reproduced in Philadelphia/Berlin/London 1984, no. 29.

6 The London painting, probably his earliest dated work, is illustrated and catalogued in Brown/MacLaren 1992, no. 2584. The Lille panel was recently catalogued by Liedtke in New York 1992-93, no. 13, where he dated it to 1630-33, while Sutton in Philadelphia/Berlin/London 1984, no. 27, had placed it around 1628-30.

7 Reproduced and catalogued in Boston 1992, no. 27. For an example of the use of this motif in a group composition, see the two versions of the *Musical Company*, National Museum, Warsaw, and the Staatliches Museum, Schwerin, illustrated and catalogued in Warsaw 1969, no. 228, and Schwerin 1982, no. 70, respectively.

8 Playter 1972, p. 66. For references to the paintings see note 7 above.

9 Philadelphia/Berlin/London 1984, p. xxxiii. On tonalist landscape techniques, see the entries on Salomon van Ruysdael's *Riverview with Boats and Liesvelt Castle Tower* and Jan van Goyen's *Outlook on the Dunes* in this catalogue, nos. 46, 20. For a tonalist still life, see Jan Fris's *Still Life with Pipe and Jug*, also in the Weldon collection, no. 18.

10 For an overview of this subject, see The Hague/Antwerp 1994. For a succinct account of the love symbolism of music in Jan Vermeer's *The Concert*, c. 1665-66, present location unknown, see Wheelock 1995A, pp. 116-117.

11 The emblem is from Gabriel Rollenhangen's *Nucleus Emblematum*, Cologne, 1611, and it is illustrated and interpreted in Haarlem/Worcester 1993, p. 126.

12 As discussed in ibid. For an account of the symbolism of the instrument in Dutch art, see de Jongh in Haarlem 1986, pp. 285-88.

13 On the love symbolism of the rose in Dutch painting, see Segal in Osaka/Tokyo/Sydney 1990, p. 36.

(actual size)

13 **Adriaen Coorte**
(active in Middelburg? c. 1683-1707)

Wild Strawberries on a Ledge

1704
oil on paper, laid down on panel
13.5 x 16.5 cm.
Inscribed, lower left, on stone ledge: *A Coorte/ 1704*

PROVENANCE:
S. Gratama, Antwerp; Bequest to Gemeentemuseum, The Hague, 1932; Sold 1960, to H. Terry-Engell Gallery, London; E. Hodgkins Esq., U. K. (Sale, Sotheby's, London, April 12, 1978, no. 12, ill.); Alfred Brod Gallery, London; Private collection, Switzerland.

EXHIBITIONS:
Zurich 1956, no. 58; Dordrecht 1958, no. 13 (ill.); London 1960, no. 11 (ill.); Osaka/Tokyo/Sydney 1990, no. 58 (ill.); New Orleans 1997, no. 14 (ill.).

LITERATURE:
Mededeelingen van den Dienst voor Kunsten en Wetenschappen der Gemeente's-Gravenhage (1933) III, part V, p. 74; Knuttel 1935, p. 48 ; Van Gelder 1950, p. 69; Swillens 1957, p. 77; Bol 1952-53, no. 43; Bernt 1962, vol. 4, fig. 56; Bol 1977, no. 62 (ill.), and pp. 8, 9, 15, 57; Osaka/Tokyo/Sydney 1990, no. 58 (ill.).

Adriaen Coorte has distilled his subject of wild strawberries to its very essence in this intimate still life of 1704. A pile of tiny round strawberries, known in Holland as maandbloeyers, is tidily heaped at the corner of a stone ledge.[1] A single white blossom springs from the berries. The vibrant red of the fruits, varied in spots with green and yellow and meticulously highlighted with fine white fibers, glows against the dark surroundings. The brilliant illumination of the berries is contrasted to the shadows cast on the ledge. The heightened illusionism of the painting, most evident in the description of the fruit, is maintained in the rendering of the ledge where the divide and seemingly random chips are carefully crafted.

The enigmatic still-life painter Adriaen Coorte, most probably from Middelburg, is better known to us through his distinctive paintings, of which this is a classic example, than from contemporary sources. In fact, his posthumous reputation was relatively obscure until Bol "rediscovered" his work and presented it in an exhibition in Dordrecht in 1958. Coorte is placed in Middelburg because many of his paintings appear in eighteenth-century inventories from that city, and there is one record of him in its artist's guild for the period 1695-99.[2] Furthermore, his work seems to have evolved from the style and formulation of still-life painting practiced by the Bosschaert dynasty originating in Middelburg. The ledge composition, an innovation of Balthasar van der Ast (c. 1593/4-1657), seen in his *Roses, Lizard, Butterfly, and Grasshopper on a Ledge* in the present collection, (no. 3) a formulation which probably evolved from the works of Ambrosius Bosschaert the Elder (1568-1625), the leader of the dynasty, is adapted, simplified, and often exploited by Coorte.[3]

Strawberries were certainly a favorite subject of the artist. Of the approximately one hundred recorded paintings by Coorte, nearly one-fifth feature the fruit.[4] While the painter depicted the berries in more complex compositions which include receptacles and other fruits such as, for example, his *Bowl of Strawberries* and *Bunch of Asparagus*, 1703, location unknown,[5] there are a handful of ledge compositions dating from 1700 onwards which closely resemble the Weldon painting. A gradual simplification and reduction in the size of works, as seen in the strawberry paintings, is consistent with the general evolution of Coorte's *oeuvre*, which in later years tended toward small, modest compositions.[6] Two ledge paintings, one dated 1700 and the other 1705, are essentially variations on the pile of strawberries with a blossom accent, seen in the present work, albeit both show the composition in reverse.[7]

Coorte sometimes conceived his ledge paintings as pairs in which he would juxtapose a bright subject, like the present one, to a monochrome fruit, often nuts, reversing the composition of each pendant so that the stone corners and fruits would mirror and face each other.[8] While the Weldon *Wild Strawberries* and Coorte's *Chestnuts on a Ledge*, 1705 (no. 14), also in the present collection, are not technically a pair since the mirror effect is not achieved, their complimentary light and dark palettes closely approximate the effect of the artist's known pendants. NTM

1 In Amsterdam 1984, p. 90, Bergström identified the whitish variety of strawberry - fragaria vesca - and provided the Dutch term which translates literally as "month(ly) bloomers." Bol 1977, p. 18, indicates that although of the wild variety, these berries were cultivated.

2 The most comprehensive study on Coorte remains Bol 1977, who discusses the few known facts of the artist's biography on pp. 5 ff. His catalogue of Coorte's *oeuvre* includes about one hundred paintings, many of which are known only through catalogue and inventory descriptions. They consist mostly of fruit still lifes (including nuts and asparagus), and, to a lesser degree, shell, flower and *vanitas* compositions. The dated paintings span the years 1683 to 1707.

3 Ibid., p. 22, Bol briefly discusses the importance of van der Ast and Bosschaert, stating that the likeness to Coorte is "one of motif only." Bol , pp. 22-4, considers that the Middelburg painter Johannes Godaert (1617-1668) and the Dordrecht artist Isaac van Duynen (1628-c. 1677/81) were "preludes" to Coorte.

4 On Coorte's *oeuvre*, see note 2.

5 Sotheby's, New York, May 16, 1996, no. 120 (ill.), formerly L. and G. Guterman Collection, New York.

6 Bol 1966, p. 15, discusses the tendency toward simplification. In spite of this general trend, the artist continued to depict berries in receptacles while he was painting his ledge paintings, as, for example, his *Wild Strawberries in a Wan Li Bowl*, Mr. and Mrs. E. W. Carter Collection, Los Angeles, catalogued and illustrated in Los Angeles/Boston/New York 1981-82, no. 36, where the Antwerp painter Jakob van Hulsdonck's (1582-1647) similar compositions are plausibly suggested as precedents.

7 Respectively, Bol 1977, no. 47 (ill.), 13.5 x 15.5 cm., location unknown, and no. 24 (ill.), 13.5 x 15.5 cm., location unknown.

8 On this aspect of Coorte's *oeuvre*, see Bergström in Amsterdam 1984, p. 87, where the author states that the artist painted many such pairs. The pendants sometimes even bear the dates of successive years. Probable pairs catalogued in Bol 1977 are nos. 51, 52, *Two Peaches*, 1702, and *Five Chestnuts*, 1703, and nos. 96, 97, *Cherries and Chestnuts*.

(actual size)

14 **Adriaen Coorte**
(active in Middelburg? c. 1683-1707)

Chestnuts on a Ledge

1705
oil on paper, laid down on panel
13.7 x 16.2 cm.
Inscribed, lower left, on stone ledge: *A Coorte/ 1705*

PROVENANCE:
Private collection, The Netherlands.

EXHIBITIONS:
Zurich 1989-90, no. 8 (ill.); Birmingham 1995, no. 4 (ill.); New Orleans 1997,
no. 15 (ill.).

Please refer to entry no. 13 for a brief discussion of this painting.

15 Anthony van Dyck

(Antwerp 1599 - Blackfriars 1641)

Young Woman Resting Her Head on Her Hand
(probably *The Penitent Magdalene*)

c. 1616-181
oil on paper, laid down on panel
49 x 37.5 cm.

PROVENANCE:
Sir Francis Cook, Doughty House, Richmond (by 1869); thence by descent; Sale, Christie's, London, December 2, 1983, no.121 (ill.); Private collection.

EXHIBITIONS:
Manchester, City Art Gallery, temporary loan; Washington 1990-91, no. 89 (ill.); New Orleans 1997, no. 16 (ill.).

LITERATURE:
Bode 1909, p. 37; Schaeffer 1909, no. 22 (ill.); Kronig 1914, no. 248 (ill.); Glück 1931, pp. 72, 527 (ill.); van den Wijngaert 1943, p. 30, fig. 5; Larsen 1980, no. 42 (ill.); Ottawa 1980, p. 147; Larsen 1988, vol. II, no. 227 (ill.), and under no. 28; Washington 1990-91, no. 89 (ill.), and pp. 327, 347.

This study of a young woman, probably depicted as a penitent Magdalene, reveals the youthful van Dyck as a brilliant technician and a sensitive conveyer of fleeting emotion — in this instance abandon and distraction. The sitter, whose likeness is framed by an abundance of auburn hair, rests her cheek on her right hand and tilts her head, looking heavenward. The vulnerable expanse of a pale throat and neck emerges from a thickly painted white chemise and tapers to a delicately featured, rosy face. The woman's lips are slightly parted, and her blue eyes look outwards, gazing beyond the confines of the picture and seemingly transcending the viewer's realm.

Van Dyck probably painted this study head at a pivotal period in his career, around 1616-18, when he was both the preferred studio assistant of Rubens (1577-1640) and emerging as an artistic personality in his own right. A letter of 1620, written to the distinguished collector Thomas Howard, Earl of Arundel, who was trying to lure the young painter from Antwerp to England, succinctly sums up his position: "Van Dyck is still with Rubens, and his own work is coming to be appreciated as much as his master's."[2] The present painting represents a workshop practice of Rubens' prior to 1620, the creation of study heads, sometimes painted from life, known to contemporaries as *tronie*,[3] which were employed as models for larger compositions. Many such works are described in Antwerp inventories, and a group of them appears in Rubens's own estate as "A good number of faces, from life, on canvas and panel, both by Mons. Rubens and Mons. van Dyck."[4]

While van Dyck may have borrowed the practice of making study heads from Rubens, the "robust" technique shown in the present painting is entirely his own,

and it demonstrates his independence from his master even at an early age.[5] Rubens' contemporary paintings are characterized by cooler tonalities and a relative smoothness whereas van Dyck was employing a loaded brush, often dry, and a ruddier palette to achieve a vigorous, even a rough effect.[6] In the present painting, van Dyck's bold touch is especially evident in the slashing strokes of the white collar and the long squiggling brush mark that defines the exposed wrist and forearm. Likewise, the lush hair is described by lively, broad strokes and a whole range of colors.

Van Dyck's emphasis on the Magdalene's hair, her religious attribute, is apt. In accounts of the saint's life, it both denotes her earthly beauty as a sinner and symbolizes her redemption when she dries Christ's feet with it after she has bathed them in her tears. Van Dyck's choice of the subject of a Magdalene is consistent with his contemporary *oeuvre* which includes several depictions of the saint as well as of other repentants like St. Jerome, in Counter-Reformation imagery validating the sacrament of penance.[7] Much like his illustrious teacher, van Dyck was a devout Catholic: his family included many clerics and he joined a Jesuit confraternity in 1628.[8] The subject of the repentant saint occupied Rubens while van Dyck was in his employ in his *Ecstasy of the Magdalene*, c. 1619-20, Musée des Beaux-Arts, Lille.[9] A comparison of the characterization of the overwrought Magdalene of the Rubens painting and the quiet despair of the Weldon saint underscores van Dyck's artistic autonomy. Not only did his technique differ, but he also distinguished himself in his sophisticated and refined interpretations of human emotion.

Van Dyck's *oeuvre* includes large-scale representations of the saint such as the *Magdalene in Penitence*, Rijksmuseum, Amsterdam.[10] However, the most relevant points of reference for the present painting are other study heads of young women, some of which are also interpreted as depictions of the Magdalene.[11] The *Study of a Woman's Head*, Gemäldegalerie, Vienna, offers the closest comparison. It appears to show the same model looking to the left and the technique is equally broad.[12] True to contemporary studio practice, this head was used for the figure of the woman to the right in a larger painting, *Moses and the Brazen Serpent*, c. 1620-21, Museo del Prado, Madrid.[13] A *Magdalene Repentant*, Solomon Collection, Los Angeles, offers a profile view of the saint who looks downward and contemplates a skull.[14] Finally, there is a *Study Head of a Young Woman*, Metropolitan Museum of Art, New York, in which the artist has depicted an auburn-haired model looking to the side and downward and where he has employed the same medium and support but with a thinner touch. While this study has been grouped with the Vienna and Los Angeles paintings, Held maintains that it dates from a later period, c. 1630.[15]

Although the Weldon painting does not appear to have been the model for a larger composition of the *Magdalene*, it has been identified as the study used for the figure of the maenad in van Dyck's *Drunken Silenus*, c. 1620, Gemäldegalerie, Dresden (fig. 1).[16] Ironically, for this bacchanalian subject the penitent saint has been transformed into the object of desire of the lustful peasants, as well as the support for the faltering Silenus. NTM

1   As stated by Held in his entry on the painting in Washington 1990-91, no. 89.
2   The letter was written by Francesco Vercellini, Venetian secretary to the Earl of Arundel, July 17, 1620, from Antwerp where he was sojourning with the countess of Arundel. As cited in Barnes's essay in Washington 1990-91, p. 24.
3   The term translates as "face."
4   As cited from Denucé 1934, p. 70, in French in Held 1980, vol. 1, p. 597. Held 1990, vol. 1, pp. 597-99, offers a summary on this practice in Rubens's studio and to a lesser degree on van Dyck's use of *tronie*, which is the source for the brief discussion above.
5   The term robust is taken from Held's description of the present painting in his entry for a related study, *Head of a Young Woman*, Metropolitan Museum of Art, New York, in Washington 1990-91, no. 95.
6   On these differing techniques, see Barnes' comparison of the *Drunken Silenus* paintings of Rubens, 1617/8-1626, Alte Pinakothek, Munich, and van Dyck, c. 1620, Gemäldegalerie, Dresden, in Washington 1990-91, pp. 106-108, from which the present description is taken.
7   This religious sacrament had been denied by Protestantism. Schaeffer 1909 and Bode 1909, were the first authors to publish the *Young Woman* as a *Magdalene*. Held in Washington 1990-91, no. 89, accepts and elaborates on this interpretation. His discussion of the significance of depictions of the *Magdalene* to Counter-Reformation imagery is the source for the text above. For a description of the political, religious and artistic climate that revived Catholic imagery in the southern Netherlands, see Freedberg's essay in Boston/Toledo 1993-94, pp. 131-45.
8   Ibid., p. 45.
9   Illustrated and catalogued by Liedtke in New York 1992-93, no. 3.
10   Illustrated and catalogued in Larsen 1988, no. 457.
11   Bode 1909, p. 307, was the first author to discuss the Magdalene paintings as a group. Glück 1931, pp. 72, 527 compares the Weldon and Vienna heads. Liedtke 1984, vol. 1, pp. 77-79, discusses the *Study Head of a Young Woman*, Metropolitan Museum of Art , in the context of the Vienna head and the *Magdalene Repentant*, Collection of Mr. and Mrs. Bernard C. Solomon, Los Angeles. Larsen 1988, vol. 2, no. 28, relates the Vienna and Weldon heads, as well as the Los Angeles Magdalene. Held in Washington 1990-91, nos. 89, 95 discusses the Vienna, Weldon, Los Angeles, and New York (Metropolitan Museum of Art) paintings.
12   It employs the same medium and support as the Weldon painting, but is larger, 56.5 x 41.6 cm.
13   The painting is catalogued and illustrated in Washington 1990-91, no. 117, where the Vienna head is discussed as a model.
14   Illustrated and catalogued in Princeton 1979, no. 8. In Washington 1990-91, p. 347, Held likens the technique and probable date (c. 1616-18) for this painting to those of the Weldon and Vienna paintings.
15   56.5 x 41.6 cm., illustrated and catalogued in Liedtke 1984, vol. 1 pp. 77-79, where he discusses it in conjunction with the Vienna and Los Angeles paintings and dates it c. 1618. In Washington 1990-91, no. 95, Held discusses the thinner, smoother technique of the Metropolitan Museum painting and favors a date of c. 1630. Nonetheless, the range of technique seen in the Böhler *Apostle* series, dated to c. 1620-21 by Barnes in Washington 1990-91, nos. 19, 20, suggests that the artist easily varied his manner within a given period.
16   Glück 1931, p. 67. The *Silenus* painting is illustrated and catalogued in Washington 1990-91, no. 12.

Fig. 1 Anthony van Dyck, *Drunken Silenus*, c. 1620, oil on canvas, Gemäldegalerie, Dresden

16 Anthony van Dyck

(Antwerp 1599 - Blackfriars 1641)

Study of Boy's Head and Hands

c. 1620-21
oil on paper, laid down on canvas
43 x 28.9 cm.

PROVENANCE:
William, 4th Duke of Hamilton (1658-1712), Inventory, August 12, 1695, no. 15, London;1 Inventory, October 13, 1704, no. 273, Kinneil Castle, Scotland;2 Inventory, June 7, 1759, no. 72, Hamilton Palace, Scotland;3 By descent to William Alexander Louis Stephen, 12th Duke of Hamilton, Hamilton Palace, Scotland (Sale, Christie's, London, The Hamilton Palace Collection, July 8, 1882, no. 1033, to E. Warneck, for £ 47 5s.); E. Warneck , Paris (Sale, Georges Petit, Paris, Collection Warneck, May 27, 1926, no. 37 (ill.), to F. Hess, Esq.); F. Hess, Berlin (Sale, Cassirer-Fisher, Lucerne, Die Sammlung Hess, September 1, 1931, no. 13, ill.); Private collection, U.K.

EXHIBITION:
New Orleans, 1997, no. 17 (ill.).

LITERATURE:
Bode 1906, p. 264; Bode 1919, pp. 347-8; Burchard 1978, pp. 29-30, and fig. B; Compin 1978, p. 384; Princeton 1979, p. 92; Ottawa 1980, p. 155; Laskin/Pantazzi 1987, p. 100; Larsen 1988, vol. II p.108; Genoa 1997, pp. 74-75 (ill.).

Van Dyck, throughout his career, made studies in oil of heads which were to be incorporated into his compositions, but such studies occur less frequently in his later years than during his early days in Antwerp. From his London years only one such study survives: the enchanting sketch of the heads of the two youngest children of Charles I, heads which could be incorporated almost *verbatim* into the large group which he painted in 1637 of the King's five eldest children.[4] There are in the Ashmolean Museum in Oxford two lightly handled head-studies for two of the sitters in the large painting of the Magistrates of the City of Brussels grouped round the figure of Justice: painted by van Dyck when he was in Brussels in 1634-35 and destroyed in the bombardment of the city in 1695.

These studies were for heads in compositions containing a number of figures. It is by no means certain that van Dyck made head-studies before painting single commissioned portraits. It has, however, been suggested recently that a number of paintings of heads which are closely connected with portraits painted by van Dyck while he was in Genoa are in fact preliminary *ad vivum* sketches;[5] but this has not yet been generally accepted.

From van Dyck's years in Antwerp a large number of oil studies of heads have survived. They are frequently to be associated with his larger and more formal paintings of Apostles: subjects for which he made preliminary studies of picturesque handsome male heads. In this van Dyck was following Rubens' practice and a number of the heads recorded in this way by van Dyck can be actually recognized in pictures painted in Rubens' studio in the second decade of the century. Such studies proliferate and many more from time to time have been attributed without justification to van Dyck.

The studies which can be attributed to him are, like those *Apostles* which are certainly by him, among the most brilliantly and spontaneously painted works from that immensely exciting period in the painter's career.

In that period van Dyck also produced a number of studies of heads in oil on paper, subsequently mounted, perhaps not in his time, on panel. The use of oil on paper produces a distinctly dramatic, dragged texture, less lustrous and smooth than the natural effect of oil on wood, but allowing sometimes for more of the original drawing of the study to remain visible and displaying a great deal of sensitivity and spontaneity in the actual touch with which the paint is applied. These studies were obviously made from the model in the studio and were then worked into the composition with which van Dyck was occupied. The most famous of these studies is of the drawn features and long golden hair of a young woman, painted in heavily worked, rather sticky paint.[6] The head is then dramatically inserted on the right of the large *Moses and the Brazen Serpent* in the Prado.[7] A comparable study of a young woman, conceivably intended for a painting of the Magdalene, is in the Weldon collection (no. 15). A particularly significant work in this context is the study of a man's head in Berlin.[8] The study was used by van Dyck, for example, in painting his *Saint Peter* in the set of *Apostles* and the head appears again as one of the *Disciples in the Descent of the Holy Spirit* in Potsdam.[9] The model's identity is known – his name was Abraham Grapheus – and Jordaens also made use of his features. Indeed, the addition to the panel on all sides of the sketch in Berlin may have been made by Jordaens.[10]

Fig. 1 Anthony van Dyck, *Suffer the Little Children to Come Unto Me*, c. 1620-21, National Gallery of Canada, Ottawa

This by no means exhausts the list that could be compiled of the studies on paper, a list to which the *Study of a Boy's Head and Hands,* with its distinguished provenance, makes a delightful addition. The study is of precisely the kind which van Dyck would have felt it necessary to make if a family group – with a number of different sitters – had to be incorporated in a composition, particularly perhaps, in so unusual a composition as *Suffer Little Children To Come Unto Me* (fig. 1).[11] The study is exceptionally well preserved. The features and the hands are swiftly drawn in rather sticky, and in places, heavily impasted paint. Very little medium is used outside these areas – the parts of the image van Dyck needed accurately to record. Indeed, apart from the highly characteristic swift strokes of white which indicate the collar, the forms of the chest and the arms are barely indicated. The position of both head and hands are very slightly altered in the final painting. The hands are lowered and point downwards. A certain tension, and a certain nervous subtlety in the head, may have been

smoothed out on the canvas. The biblical portrait is a strange picture, with a marked change in mood and quality between its two halves. It is all the more interesting that the partly shadowed head on the left of the composition is probably derived from another oil sketch by van Dyck: a study of two heads in the Musée des Beaux-Arts, Lyon.[12] This is almost certainly on paper mounted on canvas. The two heads are tightly, economically, crammed onto the single sheet. Both heads were used at some stage by van Dyck in building up his series of *Apostles*; and the sketch, as delicately drawn as this new study of a very different head, is an excellent example of an aspect of van Dyck's practice in his formative years.
OM

1 *A list of the right honourable the earle of Arans pictures at London*, August the 12, 1695, no. 15, "A Boyes Head with two Hands by Vandyke," *Hamilton Inventories*, Beckford MSS, Bodleian Library, Oxford. Up to, but not including, the Hamilton Palace Sale, 1882, the provenance information derives from the documentation provided by the proprietor of the painting at the time of its sale to the Weldons. Subsequent provenance information was confirmed in sales catalogues available in New York libraries.

2 *Hamilton Inventories*, Beckford MSS. No. 12, no. 273, Bodleian Library, Oxford, as "A Boys head with 2 hands by Vandike."

3 *Hamilton Inventories*, Beckford MSS. No. 13, no. 72, Bodleian Library, Oxford, as "A Boy praying by Vandyke."

4 The sketch, *Princess Elizabeth and Princess Anne*, Scottish National Portrait Gallery, Edinburgh, is illustrated and catalogued in Washington 1990-91, no. 101. The formal portrait, *The Five Eldest Children of Charles I*, is in the collection of H. M. Queen Elizabeth II.

5 Barnes puts forth this theory in the catalogue of the exhibition Genoa 1997, pp. 74-75.

6 *Study of a Woman's Head*, Gemäldegalerie der Akademie der bildenden Künste, Vienna.

7 Catalogued and illustrated in Washington 1990-91, no. 15.

8 Gemäldegalerie, Berlin (illustrated in Bock 1986, p. 43).

9 Staatliche Schlösser und Gärten.

10 Jaffé in Ottawa 1968-69, no. 25.

11 National Gallery of Canada, Ottawa. The best account of the picture is by Barnes in Washington 1990-91, no. 18. It is surely time finally to reject the untenable view, put forward by a number of scholars, that the family is that of Rubens and Isabella Brant: untenable on the obvious grounds of likeness and of the ages, and numbers, of their children.

12 *Two Study Heads* (illustrated in Glück 1931, p. 36).

17   **Anthony van Dyck**
(Antwerp 1599 - Blackfriars 1641)

Portrait of Martin Ryckaert

after 1627
oil on panel
24 x 19 cm.

PROVENANCE:
Tesse Collection, Berlin; Baron Albert von
Oppenheim, Berlin (Sale, Berlin, Lepke, October 27,
1914, no. 11, ill.); E. Sittenfeld, Berlin; Consul
Becker, Darmstadt; L. and M. Kaplan, New York (by
1950); Leonard Koetser Gallery, London (by 1962);
Private collection.

EXHIBITIONS:
Cologne, 1876, no. 50; New Orleans 1997, no. 18
(ill.).

LITERATURE:
Chronique des Arts et de la Curiosité (1905) p. 126;
Glück 1931, p. 332; Bode 1914, no. 11;
Valentiner/Wescher 1950, no. 9 (ill.); Spicer 1994, p.
362.

Van Dyck's grisaille portrait of his
elder and colleague the Antwerp landscape
painter Martin Ryckaert (1587-1631) presents the sitter as a venerable and distinguished gentleman. Seated and frontally
posed, Ryckaert is richly attired in a fur-
lined cap and cape, a sumptuous tunic
and sash, and a white shirt. His thought-
ful countenance bears directly on the
viewer, with highlighted eyes staring from
the shadow of his brow. A single, beautifully articulated hand loosely grips the
armrest of the chair in a gesture suggesting strength and authority.

Van Dyck probably executed this oil
sketch after his monumental *Portrait of
Martin Ryckaert*, c. 1627-31, Museo del
Prado, Madrid (fig. 1), as a model for the
engraving made by Jacob Neefs (1610-
after 1660) (fig. 2) in preparation for the
print series of illustrious men and women
which became known, in posthumous editions, as the *Iconography*.[1] Although the
artist worked on the portrait series from
the mid-1620s until the late 1630s, his
precise goal with regard to the final prod-
uct remains unclear.[2] The initial publica-
tion(s) of eighty prints, not necessarily as
a series, occurred between 1635 and 1641
at the Antwerp press of Martin van den
Enden. The prints consisted of representations of artists and collectors, princes
and militiamen, and statesmen and
philosophers. The serial publication as
the *Icones...Centum*, enlarged to one hundred prints, was issued in Antwerp in 1645
by Gillis Hendricx. As collections, the
numerous series which appeared after the
artist's death, including that of Hendricx,
were probably the inventions of various
publishers. Nonetheless, as a concept the
Iconography occupied much of van Dyck's
life and its genesis rests on his artistic
labor and vision.

An understanding of the steps
involved in the artistic production of the
prints is only gradually emerging. While
nineteenth-century scholars tended to dis-
miss the grisaille sketches as workshop
production, in 1915 Hind assigned them
an important role in the genesis of the
prints, and attributed many to the artist's
hand: "One of the strongest arguments for
van Dyck's authorship is that they are no
whit less brilliant, and sometimes more
brilliant, than the undisputed chalk
sketches."[3] His conclusions were drawn
chiefly from the largest group, about forty
grisailles in the collection of the Duke of
Buccleuch.[4] Hind proposed the following
sequence for the production of the prints:
1. Van Dyck's original drawing; 2. an oil
grisaille, incorporating detail as a guide
for the printmaker; 3. the print. Hind also
acknowledged the importance of the large,
formal portraits executed by van Dyck, as
in the present case, for approximately thirty subjects, although he did not propose
them as immediate models for the printmaker.[5] Recently, his hypothesis has been
generally accepted and elaborated.[6] The
acceptance of many of the grisailles,
including the *Martin Ryckaert*,[7] as the
work of van Dyck is indicated not only by
their technical brilliance but also by documentary evidence. The 1682 inventory of
the master's pupil Peter Lely includes the
description of "Thirty Seven pictures in
Grisaille done by vandike after the Life, of
the most eminent Men in his time, from
which the Plates were Graven."[8]

The Weldon sketch is marked by the
painterly excellence that is associated with
the best grisailles from the series. A
tremendous amount of detail is provided
for the engraver in a fluid, lively technique. While the forms are fully modeled,
the paint surface remains thin. The use of
highlights effectively completes and animates the figure such as, for example, in
the eyes, along the nose and in the left side
of the face.[9] Furthermore, the technique
is analogous to that used in van Dyck's
grisailles of larger compositions in preparation for the printmaker such as, for
example, his *St. Augustine in Ecstasy*, c.
1630, Yale University Art Gallery, a monochrome reduction of the painting in
Antwerp.[10]

An examination of the formal portrait, the Weldon grisaille and the print by
Jacob Neefs, which characteristically
reverses the composition, reveals a number of changes.[11] Moreover, it clarifies the
fact that the grisaille rather than the large
portrait was the engraver's model. While
the format of the painting shows the sitter
almost in full, the grisaille and the print
reduce the composition to a waist-length
view. This is consistent with virtually all
of the portraits in the *Iconography* which
omit the legs of the sitter. Further, in the
large portrait the painter's right sleeve is
conspicuously empty, a reflection of the
fact that he had only one arm. In both the
grisaille and the print the drapery over the
sitter's missing limb cloaks his form and
minimizes this feature. Nonetheless, the
inscription on the print proclaims him as
"unimanus."[12] The grisaille and the print
differ in one respect: the print extends the
composition further on the sitter's cloaked
side to include the second finial and armrest of the chair as in the formal portrait.
It is possible that this difference is a result
of a reduction in the size of the Weldon
panel along the right margin at some time
after it was engraved.[13]

In comparing the grisaille with the
Prado portrait, it is notable how well the
artist gave "color" to his monochrome
likeness by using highlights as, for example, in the way he emulated the richness of
the drapery in the tunic which appears as
red velvet in the large painting.

Regardless of the variations in the
successive presentations of the sitter,
Martin Ryckaert is consistently portrayed
as a figure of tremendous authority and
substance. This characterization is in
keeping with the grand tenor of the
Iconography project in which artists are
presented with the same dignity as the
princes, statesmen and other illustrious
sitters.[14] Given van Dyck's own lifestyle, it
is hardly surprising that he would have
chosen a noble persona for the figure of
the artist. He cultivated the image and
lifestyle of an aristocrat, probably at first
in emulation of Rubens's princely example. Bellori recorded that when the young
artist was in Italy he lived and dressed lav-
ishly, adopting the manners "more of an
aristocrat than of a common man."[15] The
artist's status soon equaled his courtly
demeanor. By 1630 van Dyck had been
named painter to Her Majesty Infanta
Isabella and in 1632, just after his move to
England, the artist was knighted and
declared "Principalle Paynter" to King
Charles I.[16]

Ryckaert's pose recalls the young painter's monumental portraits of the statesmen and high clergy of the Italian nobility executed during his southern sojourn from 1621-27. The seated pose is an adaptation of Italian portrait conventions employed by Titian (1488/90-1576) and his predecessors in likenesses of popes and high church officials. Van Dyck's use of this imposing format, by which he emulated his beloved Titian, is particularly effective in his *Portrait of a Genoese Senator*, 1621-23, Gemäldegalerie, Berlin, the pendant to the unknown senator's wife. Like Ryckaert, the senator grips his chair arm and unflinchingly addresses the viewer with his gaze.[17] In the *Iconography* the dignified and significant seated pose is assigned to only four other individuals, the majority of whom were indeed illustrious men: Jean Malderus, Bishop of Antwerp; Nicolaes Rockox, Burgomaster of Antwerp and celebrated patron; Jean-Charles della Faille, Jesuit and mathematician of the same city; and one of the two brothers De Wael, in the double portrait of the artists.[18]

The grisailles, drawings and prints for the *Iconography* are notoriously difficult to date. None of the work executed by van Dyck, preparatory studies drawn or painted, nor prints, is dated. The sitters depicted in a group of drawings attributed to van Dyck, which number around forty, are for the most part artists whom he knew during the period 1627-37.[19] Likewise, the late twenties and early thirties are generally assigned to van Dyck's own group of eighteen portrait etchings which were eventually incorporated into the *Iconography*. It appears that this period was marked by the artist's intensive participation in the project. This is consistent with the chronology of the Ryckaert portrait and grisaille. Given that the grisaille probably postdates the Prado portrait, which is ascribed to the period of van Dyck's return to Antwerp from Italy (c. 1627), and must predate Ryckaert's death in 1631,[20] it could have been painted anytime after about 1627.[21] NTM

1 The Prado painting is on panel, 148 x 113 cm., catalogued and illustrated in Balis/Díaz Padrón/van de Velde/Vlieghe 1989, no. 70. There are four copies of the painting listed in Larsen 1988, vol. 1, nos. 131/1-4. The Neefs print is catalogued in Maucquoy-Hendrickx 1991, no. 113.

2 On the project see Spicer 1994 and Maucquoy-Hendrickx 1991. See also van den Wijngaert 1943, Puyvelde 1959, chapter XI, Vey 1962,
pp. 48-50, and Paris 1981. Succinct summaries are also provided by Brown in New York/Fort Worth 1991, pp. 190-93 and by Haverkamp-Begemann/Dickey in Yokohama 1990, pp. 28-30.

3 Hind 1915, p. 36.

4 This group is intact. Recent scholarship has attributed some of these sketches to van Dyck and others to assistants. See, for example, Held in Washington 1990-91, p. 340.

5 Hind 1915, p. 22.

6 See especially Spicer 1994, which includes illustrations of works which document the various stages. Her contribution to the scholarship on the genesis of the series is fundamental. In note 103, p. 355, Spicer offers a brief account of the scholarship on the grisailles. There are a number of dissenting scholars as, for example, Vey 1962. The grisailles pose a complex art-historical problem which will be readdressed by Vey in a study being prepared for the forthcoming quartercentenary celebrations of 1999 marking van Dyck's birth. S. J. Barnes kindly informed me of this study.

7 Glück 1931, p. 332, published the Weldon sketch, Oppenheim Collection, Berlin, 1918, in conjunction with the Prado portrait, as the grisaille vorlage/model, for the Neefs engraving. Held, who knows the grisaille from a reproduction, proposed that it was from the "best group" of oil sketches (as stated in a letter to the owner, March 21, 1994).

8 As cited by Haverkamp-Begemann/Dickey in Yokohama 1990, p. 30, note 9, where the Lely sketches are identified as those now in the collection of the Duke of Buccleuch.

9 For descriptions of technique, see Hind 1915, p. 36, who is emphatic about the use of highlights, and Puyvelde 1959, p. 229.

10 The Yale painting is illustrated and catalogued in Washington 1990-91, no. 94. The larger painting, Kunsthistorische Musea, City of Antwerp, is also reproduced and illustrated there, no. 46. See Held in the same catalogue, p. 328, where he discusses the attribution and technique of this separate category of grisailles and likens the practice to Rubens, while distinguishing the style of van Dyck.

11 To date no drawings have been identified for this sequence.

12 The inscription was the addition of the publisher and does not necessarily reflect van Dyck's intention.

13 A simple examination, without technical means, of the reverse of the cradled panel is inconclusive with regard to this question. The suggested reduction would have occurred before 1950 as the painting is reproduced in its present state in Valentiner/Wescher 1950. The dimensions of the panel, 24 x 19 cm., are smaller than those of the copper plate for the print, 27 x 20 cm. at the Musée du Louvre (as recorded in Maucquoy-Hendrickx 1991, no. 113). Generally the grisailles reflect the dimensions of the plate size. The Buccleuch grisailles measure approximately 23 x 18 cm.

14 On the conventions of portraits of artists and the Italian precedents for the *Iconography*, see Raupp 1984, especially pp. 137-53 on van Dyck. See also Barnes 1989, on the development of the Uomini Illustri tradition in Italy.

15 Bellori 1672, p. 255, as cited and translated by Barnes in Washington 1990-91, p. 24, in her description of van Dyck's lifestyle.

16 These appointments are recorded in the chronology for the artist in Washington 1990-91, p. 76.

17 The Berlin pair is reproduced and catalogued in Washington 1990-91, nos. 26, 27. Although the pose of the senator resembles that of Ryckaert, he is not presented completely frontally, rather at an angle, in keeping with the conventions of pendant portraits where the sitters face one another.

18 The prints listed above are, respectively,
Maucquoy-Hendrickx's nos. 133, 165, 158 and 136 Perry Chapman, 1990, pp. 93-94, discusses the pose in the print of Ryckaert as a possible influence on Rembrandt.

19 Paris 1981, p. 5.

20 In Balis/Díaz Padrón/van de Velde/Vlieghe 1989, no. 70, Balis dates the painting to 1627/28-1631, based on stylistic evidence, the dates of van Dyck's residency in Antwerp, and Ryckaert's death. Larsen 1988, vol. 1, no. 609, gives a date of c. 1630.

21 In her comprehensive study of the *Iconography* project, Spicer 1994, pp. 329, 343, has proposed that the grisaille production took place from 1634-5. However, as she states, p. 344, the analysis of the grisailles is not her main purpose.

Fig. 1 Anthony van Dyck, *Portrait of Martin Rychaert*, c. 1627-31, Museo del Prado, Madrid

Fig. 2 Jacob Neefs (1610- after 1660), after Anthony van Dyck, *Portrait of Martin Rychaert*, for the *Iconography*, engraving from the "Chalcographie du Louvre", The Metropolitan Museum of Art, Harris Brisbane Dick Fund, 1930

18 Jan Fris
(Amsterdam 1627 - Delft 1672)

Still Life with Pipe and Jug

c. 1650
oil on panel
37.8 x 29.2 cm.

PROVENANCE:
J. Danster Nijman, Amsterdam; Macalester Loup, The Hague; Henry Philip Hope, London (died 1839); thence by descent, Henry Thomas Hope, London (died 1862); Adèle Bichat (widow of H.T.H.); Henry Francis Hope Pelham-Clinton-Hope (by 1884); Asher Wertheimer (dealer), London, 1889; Private collection, U.K., 1898; Private collection, U.K.

EXHIBITIONS:
Providence 1964, no. 8 (ill.); New York 1966, no. 11; Birmingham 1995, no. 6 (ill.); New Orleans 1997, no. 19 (ill.).

LITERATURE:
Paris 1983, p. 52.

Jan Fris' simple monochrome tobacco piece, a type of still life known to contemporaries as *toebackje*, is a classic example of the genre which was developed in the Dutch Republic in the 1620s, and became increasingly popular in the succeeding decades. A gray, earthenware jug dominates the composition, which consists of smoking accessories in front on the table corner and a deck of cards behind. The smoking paraphernalia include a clay brazier containing glowing coals, a white Gouda pipe with an open tobacco packet laid on top and cylindrical lighters. The white of the pipe and the tobacco wrapper, as well as judiciously placed highlights, stands out among predominantly gray and brown tones.

The Haarlem still-life painters Pieter Claesz (c. 1597-1660) and William Claesz. Heda (1594-1680) evolved the *toebackje* from the genre of the monochrome banquet piece in the early 1620s.[2] As the type developed, the compositon was simplified to a few objects, the palette became more restricted and the brushwork freer. By mid-century there were a number of artists, many based in Amsterdam like Fris, who painted tobacco pieces which adopted a vertical format and a composition dominated by like objects such as the earthenware jug, the brazier, the Gouda pipe, and the lighters. The practitioners of this genre whose work is closest to Fris' are Jan Jansz van de Velde (c. 1619-c 1663 or later), Jan Jansz Trek (c. 1606-c. 1652), both of Amsterdam, and the younger Leiden artist Edwaert Collier (c. 1640-after 1706).[3]

There is a variation on the present painting from Fris's *oeuvre*, signed and dated 1650, Fondation Custodia, Paris.[4]

The Paris panel which is only slightly larger features the same objects with the exception of the cards. Given the strong resemblance of these two paintings, it is likely that the Weldon panel dates from the same time. Nihom-Nijstad has identified the jug in the Paris painting as a *wapenkruik*, a pitcher featuring the seal of a coat of arms, albeit with an unintelligible mark. She has further noted that similar jugs in paintings by Fris dated 1660 and 1666 bear the arms of the city of Amsterdam,[5] a crest featuring a vertical line of three Xs with rampant lions on either side. The pitcher in the Weldon painting appears to bear this coat of arms, appropriate to the work of an Amsterdam painter.[6]

The tobacco still life has been interpreted as a symbol of the ephemerality and idleness of earthly existence. Indeed, in one of the earliest *vanitas* paintings that includes smoking accessories, Willem Claesz. Heda's *Vanitas Still Life*, 1621, Bredius Museum, The Hague, the juxtaposition of a human skull, a glowing brazier, pipes, and tobacco delivers an unequivocal message. If the present painting partakes of this tradition, its meaning is probably less emphatic, much like that of a contemporary riddle: "Tobacco, so well-loved by so many/Into a clay pipe is packed/Its smoke like its aroma are vanity/And so the enigma is explained."[7] Smoking certainly had negative connotations for Fris' contemporaries, and this habit combined with the gambling and drinking implicit in the cards and the pitcher of this painting completes the trinity of vices.[8] On the other hand, the composition may simply allude to the modest pleasures of these activities. NTM

1 This provenance is taken from the information provided by the owner of the painting when it entered the Weldon collection. At present it is difficult to confirm the early Dutch collectors Nijman and Macalester Loup, as well as the ownership of the Hope family. The Hope Collection, which originated with the Dutch branch of the family, eventually went to London where it was highly prized and said to rival that of the Prince Regent. On the collection, see The Hague/San Francisco 1990-91, pp. 420-22.

2 On Claesz, Heda, and the genre of the monochrome banketje, see Vroom 1980.

3 On these artists, see ibid., where example(s) of paintings by each show close parallels with the composition and format of the present work.

4 The painting entitled *Tobacco Still Life*, panel, 41 x 32.5 cm., is reproduced (in reverse, for an unreversed image, see Vroom 1980, vol. 1, p. 163, fig. 217) and catalogued by Nihom-Nijstad in Paris 1983, no. 30, where she likens it to the Weldon panel.

5 Ibid., p. 52, notes 5 and 6, where the paintings are listed from former sales, with neither current location given.

6 The Amsterdam coat of arms is also shown on *wapenkruiken* in paintings by Fris's colleagues, as, for example, Jan Jansz van de Velde's *Tobacco Still Life*, 1656, National Museum, Budapest, illustrated and catalogued in Vroom 1980, no. 696.

7 From J. van der Veen's *Raadstelen/Enigmas*, 1653, as cited in Broos 1987, p. 22 (present author's translation).

8 For a brief discussion of the meaning of these activities in contemporary genre painting, see the entry on Adriaen van Ostade's *Peasants Playing Cards*, (no. 35).

19   Jan van Goyen
(Leiden 1596 - The Hague 1656)

Summer Landscape

1620
oil on panel
22.5 cm diameter.
Inscribed, bottom center: *I V GOIEN/1620*

PROVENANCE:
Sale, F. Muller & Cie, Amsterdam, coll. de K...., April 25, 1911, no. 39 (sold to Douwes for fl. 320); Kunsthandel gebr. Douwes, Amsterdam; Sale, F. Muller & Cie, Amsterdam, P. Smidt van Gelder collection, December 13, 1921, (sold for fl 450); D. Komter, Amsterdam (by 1924); D.A. Hoogendijk, Amsterdam (by 1926); Dr. H Schäffer, Berlin; J.M.C. Hoog, Haarlem; by descent to T. Hoog, Haarlem (by 1960); Kunsthandel P. de Boer, Amsterdam (by 1966); Private collection.

EXHIBITIONS:
Amsterdam 1924, no. 47; Berlin 1932, no. 42; Haarlem 1936, no. 12 (ill.); Leiden/Arnhem 1960, no. 1; Amsterdam 1966-67, no. 16 (ill.); London 1967 ; New Brunswick 1983, no. 62, (ill.); Birmingham 1995, no. 7 (ill.); New Orleans 1997, no. 20 (ill.).

LITERATURE:
Hofstede de Groot 1907-28, vol. 8, 1927, no. 496; van de Waal 1931, p. 6 (ill.); Dobrzycka 1966, no. 1 (ill.); Beck 1973, vol. 1, no. 99 (ill.); Amsterdam/Boston/Philadelphia 1987-88, p. 319.

In van Goyen's earliest dated painting, the *Summer Landscape* of 1620, the artist reveals more of his training with the landscape pioneer Esaias van de Velde (1587-1630) than he foretells of his own innovative future in the tonalist and realist movement in Dutch painting, as exemplified by his *Outlook on the Dunes*, 1651, also in the present collection (no. 20).[1] Compositional elements borrowed from van Goyen's teacher and other predecessors structure the summer roundel: the device of the rustic dovecote frames the composition at left, and the tall tree anchors the gently sloping fields which lead to a distant village and forest at the foot of faraway hills. The staffage also bespeaks the influence of van de Velde: the scene is filled with the quiet comings and goings of the countryside, a rider at center, a ferryboat beyond and pedestrians throughout. In the foreground, a brightly attired couple and a seated man pause to chat near the base of the tree.

During van Goyen's early years as a painter in his native Leiden, he executed over fifteen pairs of roundels depicting the seasons of summer and winter.[2] This statistic is both a testament to the enduring popularity of the Flemish form of season- or month-roundels in the northern Netherlands,[3] and an indication of van de Velde's influence on his student. The older Haarlem artist painted a number of roundel pendants beginning in 1615, just prior to van Goyen's tutelage under him.[4] The Weldon panel is reminiscent of van de Velde compositionally and technically, particularly in the meticulous brushwork and bright palette seen in the foreground figures.

While the winter pendant to this panel is currently unknown, later winter roundels by van Goyen offer an idea of the lost composition. In *Winter* of 1625, Rijksmuseum, Amsterdam, the artist portrays a skating scene with a large tree and castle to the left, an arrangement which is strikingly similar to Hendrik Averkamp's *Winter Scene with Skaters near a Canal*, before 1610, National Gallery, London.[5] Adriaen van de Venne's *Winter Pleasures*, in the present collection (no. 56), of c. 1615, painted at the same time as van de Velde's early roundels, is also analogous to van Goyen's *Amsterdam Winter*, with the exception of its pronounced bird's-eye perspective, a more conservative element of the Middleburg artist's style.

Although van Goyen comfortably masters traditional forms and techniques in this painting, he also hints at further developments in his work. The large tree suggests the expressionistic oaks that dominate later paintings like the *Landscape with Two Oaks*, 1641, Rijksmuseum, Amsterdam, and the free brushwork of the clouds promises the incipience of his atmospheric skies.[6] NTM

1 Fox-Hofrichter characterized the painting in terms of van Goyen's debt to van de Velde in the entry in New Brunswick 1983, no. 62. For a discussion of van Goyen's innovations as a landscape painter, see the entry for no. 21.

2 Madrid 1994, p. 114. The Leiden period spans the years 1620-32. Although most of the season roundels are from those years, there are some that date as late as 1650.

3 On conventions of the Flemish landscape and seasonal roundel traditions, see the discussions of Jan Brueghel the Elder's two landscapes in the Weldon collection (nos. 8, 9), and van de Venne's *Winter Pleasures* (no. 56).

4 Van Goyen studied with van de Velde around 1617.

5 See de Bruyn Kops's entry on the van Goyen roundel, where Averkamp's role is also discussed, in Amsterdam/Boston/Philadelphia 1987-88, no. 32.

6 Van de Waal 1931, p. 6, offers a brief stylistic analysis of the painting in which he praises the technique in the sky.

20 Jan van Goyen
(Leiden 1596 - The Hague 1656)

Outlook on the Dunes

1651
oil on paper, laid down on panel
23.5 x 36 cm
Inscribed, bottom left: *VG.1651* [with initials in monogram ligature]

PROVENANCE:
Sale, Phillips, London, October 11, 1954, no. 221 (for £540); Duits, London; Private collection.

EXHIBITIONS:
London 1955, no. 6 (ill.); Providence 1964, no. 9 (ill.); New York 1966, no. 13; New York, Metropolitan Museum of Art, temporary loan, 1972; Birmingham 1995, no. 8 (ill.); New Orleans 1997, no. 23 (ill.).

LITERATURE:
Burlington Magazine 97 (November 1955) p. v (ill.); *Apollo* 62 (November 1955), p. 130; Beck 1960, no. 8, fig. 2, pp. 177-78; Beck 1973, no. 250 (ill.).

Van Goyen demonstrates his command of draughtsmanship and his mastery of atmospheric rendering in this dunescape of 1651. The immediate topography is defined at either side by the subtly swelling dunes which give way to an expansive panorama and distant spires. The immense cloud-filled sky lowers the horizon which is studded with figures. The group of rider and three pedestrians to the left of the spire offers a sampling of the artist's technique which is rapid, yet convincing: by means of highlights and quick dark outlines van Goyen defines the roughed-in forms of the horse who stands solidly, leaning into the distance, his master, and the crouched and standing figures before them, each assuming a different position.

In this painting, the artist has reconciled style and subject, rendering his indigenous landscape in a manner that appears realistic. In spite of the use of continued artistic conventions such as the repoussoir of the collapsing fence at the left, this view is certainly more faithful to the topography surrounding Haarlem, where the artist then lived, than the hilly fantasy of his early *Summer Landscape* (no. 19) is to his native Leiden. Indeed, the type of the dunescape appears to have provided Haarlem artists with their first opportunity to experiment with a monochrome palette, a development in Dutch landscape painting characterized as tonalism. Led by their slightly older colleague Pieter de Molijn (1595-1661), van Goyen and Salomon van Ruysdael (c. 1600/03-1670) (no. 46) became the most celebrated practitioners of the technique which exploits media, supports, and brushwork to lend a muted, suffused look to the landscape.[1]

The present painting was executed in 1651, along with approximately thirty works in which the artist employed oil on a paper support. They are of roughly similar dimensions. As noted by Beck, these studies are entirely monochrome, brown in brown, and were created as independent works of art. They incorporate techniques which are seen in the artist's contemporaneous panel paintings and in his drawings.[2] From the group of oils on paper, the artist's *Hillock in the Dunes*, 1651, private collection, Germany, most closely resembles the Weldon painting in its outlook with figures and the expansive, flat view.[3] With regard to the staffage of the present painting and the general configuration of the landscape, there is a dune drawing in Rotterdam, also dated 1651, which features a similar mounted figure shown to the left of a spire and gazing at the sea.[4] The motif of the valley-like dune and the outlooking rider also occurs in a drawing from one of van Goyen's sketchbooks, dated to the early 1650s.[5] This virtual contour sketch records the artist's immediate response to the scene, and it is likely that this and other plein-air drawings were the models for van Goyen's paintings on paper. In the Weldon painting and the related works, the small, solid grouping of horse and rider looking out and leaning into the view, effectively communicates both the allure and the vastness of the landscape. NTM

1 For the development of tonalism, first seen in paintings in the late 1620s, see Sutton in Amsterdam/Boston/Philadelphia 1987-88, pp. 35 ff., and on tonalism and the Haarlem school of landscape, see London 1986. For a further discussion of tonalism in the present catalogue, see cat. 47.

2 Beck 1960, p. 177. Most of the oil on paper paintings are signed and dated 1651 or 1652, and feature dune or riverscapes. For the majority, the dimensions are about 25 x 38 cm. In Beck's catalogue raisonné, 1973, they appear as nos. 245-271e, and G82, 2119, 543, 1032A, 1053, 1113. In the same year that the artist began these free renderings of landscape, he also executed his most detailed and technically traditional painting, the *View of the Hague*, 1651, commissioned for the Town Hall, now in the Gemeentemuseum, The Hague.

3 Ibid., no. 249.

4 *A Covered Wagon*, 1651, Boijmans Van Beuningen Museum, Rotterdam; Beck 1973, no. 201.

5 Folios 90-91, from the Bredius-Kronig sketchbook, J. Kronig Collection, Monaco; Buijsen 1993.

21 Pieter de Grebber
(Haarlem c. 1600 - Haarlem c. 1652/3)

Portrait of a Woman

c. 1625-30
oil on panel
39.1 x 34 cm

PROVENANCE:
J. Unger Canstatt (Sale, Berlin, March 21, 1917, no. 12); Dr. A. Welcker, Amsterdam; Private collection.

EXHIBITIONS:
London 1958, no. 18; Providence 1964, no. 10 (ill.); Allentown 1965, no. 32 (ill.); New York 1966, no. 15; New York, Metropolitan Museum of Art, temporary loan, 1972; Birmingham 1995, no. 9 (ill.); New Orleans 1997, no. 22 (ill.).

LITERATURE:
Burlington Magazine 100 (June 1958) pp. 216, 221, fig. 38; *Daily Telegraph and Morning Post*, April 10, 1958, p. 12 (ill.).

This bust-length likeness of a young woman represents de Grebber's skill at portraiture, a genre which differs markedly from his widely recognized, classical history paintings. A round-faced sitter with a broad forehead and delicate features looks up, seemingly to the bright light source from the left which illuminates her face and is reflected in her expressive brown eyes. Her loosely bound hair and sober attire denote modesty. She wears a dark wrap which covers her shoulders and torso, except for the pink border of her dress and the emerging white blouse. Ornamentation is minimal: a fine pattern on the pink fabric and a small tie at her neck. The palette is nearly monochrome, with the accents of red in the lips and flesh tones as subtle as the decoration of the clothing. The drama of the image is achieved principally through the artist's manipulation of light and the mystery of its hidden source.

Pieter de Grebber's extant *oeuvre* numbers about seventy paintings, mostly religious histories with about twenty portraits.[1] His success as a painter is indicated by the numerous civic and royal commissions he received, his financial prosperity, and the inclusion of his name in contemporary treatises and guidebooks.[2] While his official commissions are documented and recognized,[3] his identity as a portraitist is relatively vague since much of his work in the genre has been attributed to other artists. One of the names which occurs most frequently in association with de Grebber's portraits is that of the Leiden artist Jan Lievens (1607-1674). The presence of a label fragment on the back of the Weldon panel indicates that it also was once attributed to Lievens. Early in Lievens's career, around 1625-30 when he was in Leiden with Rembrandt (1606-1669), the two artists developed a type of portraiture which outwardly resembles the present work in format, coloration and, most of all, in the pronounced chiaroscuro.[4] De Grebber directly emulated the style of Rembrandt and Lievens in at least one early religious painting dated 1632,[5] and it is likely he was also influenced by them in his portraiture. The intimate nature of his portraits was certainly more suited to their early somber and solemn manner than his large commissions for which he employed his hallmark classical style.

There are a number of depictions of women by de Grebber, both portraits and religious paintings, which offer points of reference for the present work. The closest painting, also a *Portrait of a Woman*, is known only through reproduction.[6] While the pose of the woman is slightly different (she is seen in fuller profile and her eyes are level), her physiognomy is virtually identical. Both feature a round face, large forehead, hooded eyes, fine nose, small bee-stung lips, and sloping chin. It appears that the same sitter is portrayed in these paintings. Nonetheless, a survey of de Grebber's work reveals that he favored a certain aesthetic and this facial type does recur.[7] There is also a *Portrait of a Young Woman Singing*, Nationalmuseum, Stockholm, which closely resembles the Weldon painting with regard to the lighting, placement, and attire of a similar figure, albeit a different sitter.

The heavenward gaze of the Weldon woman, her demure demeanor and the general resemblance she bears to de Grebber's devotional images, suggest that she may also have been imbued with religious significance. This hypothesis is substantiated by particulars of the artist's life: he was an ardent Catholic and he devoted most of his *oeuvre* to Christian imagery.[8]

In de Grebber's painting entitled *Consolation*, 1628, Szépmüvészeti Museum, Budapest, the biblical narrative of the widow and the unjust judge, a parable of faith, is the subject (Luke 18:1-8). The dominant figure of the widow is shown in profile, looking left with a dark veil over her head.[9] A painting in Hannover which is attributed to de Grebber and features only the veiled head of a woman looking upwards with a bright light in her eye has been related to the Budapest widow.[10] While both of these paintings may show a sitter different from the Weldon woman, they exhibit common characteristics, namely a pious spirit, the same lighting and format, and a comparable technique.

De Grebber's representations of the penitent Mary Magdalene also bear a resemblance to the Weldon painting. The Magdalene is depicted frontally with head turned to the left and gazing heavenward in a drawing by the artist which was a model for his etching of the subject.[11] In a second print by de Grebber, based on a painting, the Magdalene is depicted in profile, eyes cast upward.[12] These representations approximate aspects of the Weldon composition, notably lighting effects, the physical type of the model, and the devotional spirit.

The religious content of the painting is not restricted to the surface image. An earlier composition depicting the story of the expulsion of Adam and Eve is preserved beneath the portrait and fully revealed in an x-ray (fig. 1). A careful examination of the painting with the naked eye shows circular strokes in the background to the right of the woman's head and white highlights at the front of her shawl which could be mistaken for a pattern in the fabric. These features respectively represent the figures of Adam and Eve and the avenging angel in the composition below, which is oriented along the vertical axis of the present portrait. As a representation of Adam and Eve, the painting had a horizontal format with the angel appearing at upper left and the sinners at lower right. The x-ray of the painting(s) shows the first composition with the exception of the figure of Adam, ahead of Eve, who is difficult to discern and whose presence is barely indicated by his foreleg overlapping Eve's left ankle. De Grebber's rendering of the subject appears to be consistent with the tra-

ditional iconography.[13] Moreover, discernible aspects of the first painting correspond with extant works by the artist. The angel, particularly in the features of his physiognomy and massive wings, may be likened to the angel in de Grebber's *Annunciation*, 1633, Pakzad Collection, Hannover,[14] and Eve's body type resembles the semi-nude principal figure in the later painting of *Bathesheba at her Toilet*, 1644.[15] NTM

1 On the painter and his *oeuvre*, see Dirkse 1978 and Hazeleger 1979.

2 For a concise yet comprehensive biography of the artist, see van Thiel-Stroman in Haarlem/Worcester 1993, pp. 220-221.

3 See, for example, his *Conferment of the Sword on the Haarlem Coat of Arms*, 1630, Town Hall, Haarlem.

4 For an example of this type of portraiture, see Lievens's *Portrait of Rembrandt*, c. 1628, Collection Daan Cevat, Geurnsey. On the work and relationship of Rembrandt and Lievens during these years, see Leiden 1991.

5 See de Grebber's *Raising of Lazarus*, 1632, Galleria Sabauda, Turin, reproduced in Haak 1984, p. 255, where the author stresses the general influence of Rembrandt's chiaroscuro on de Grebber during the early 1630s. The painting of the same subject by Rembrandt, c. 1630, is at the Los Angeles County Musuem of Art, and that of Lievens, 1631, is at the Art Gallery and Museum, Brighton.

6 Canvas, 40.5 x 33 cm. Formerly Baszanger Collection, Geneva, reproduced and catalogued in Réau 1950, no. 41.

7 Two paintings which feature a similar woman are *Bathsheba at her Toilet*, 1644, Rijksdienst Kastelenbeheer, reproduced in Amsterdam/Jerusalem 1991, p. 246, and the group portrait, *Family in a Landscape*, Museu Nacional de Art Antiga, Lisbon, reproduced in Haak 1984, p. 256.

8 De Grebber executed numerous commissions for "hidden" churches in the Netherlands where the official religion was Protestantism, as well as Catholic churches in Flanders. He also painted many portraits of Catholic priests. From 1634 until his death, he lived, unmarried, in a lay order community in Haarlem. This information is taken from the biography of the artist in Haarlem/Worcester 1993, pp. 220-21.

9 Reproduced in Bernt 1979, vol. 1, p. 479.

10 *Study of a Woman*, panel, 50 x 39 cm., Niedersächsischen Landesgalerie, Hannover, catalogued by von der Osten in Hannover 1954, no. 112, where it is suggested as a study for the Budapest painting. The figure faces right in this painting.

11 The drawing, *Saint Mary Magdalene*, is in Berlin. It is catalogued and reproduced in Bock/Rosenberg 1931, p. 146,

no. 2473. The print, which reverses and slightly alters the composition is reproduced in Hollstein 1949- , vol. 8, p. 174, no. 11.

12 The print is illustrated in ibid., no. 10. The painting, present location unknown, on which it may have been based is reproduced in a photograph (no number) in the artist's file at the Frick Art Reference Library.

13 For a roughly contemporary representation of the narrative which features the same elements in a comparable format, see Cornelis van Poelenburgh's *Expulsion from Paradise*, after 1625, Rijksmuseum, Amsterdam.

14 The painting is catalogued and illustrated in Washington/Detroit/Amsterdam 1980-81, no. 47.

15 For a full citation of this painting, see note 7 above.

Fig. 1 Pieter de Grebber, *Portrait of a Woman*. X-ray is turned sideways here to make the underlying *Expulsion From Paradise* easier to see.

22 Jan Hackaert
(Amsterdam c. 1629 - Amsterdam 1685 or after)

Landscape with Travelers Attacked by Bandits

oil on panel
25.5 x 36 cm.
Inscribed, bottom left: *J.H.*

PROVENANCE:
C. Cope collection (Sale, Christie's, London, June 8, 1872, no. 31, to Johnson, for £ 44); Sale, Christie's, London, G. Field Collection, June 10, 1893, no. 22; Private collection.

EXHIBITIONS:
London, Royal Academy, 1888; Vienna 1979-80, no. 17 (ill.); New Orleans 1997, no. 23 (ill.).

LITERATURE:
Hofstede de Groot 1907-28, vol. 9, 1926, no. 164a.

23 Willem de Heusch

(Utrecht 1625 - Utrecht 1692)

Italianate Landscape with Shepherds

oil on panel
31 x 38 cm.
Inscribed, lower right, on rock: *WDHeusch: f* [initials in monogram ligature]

PROVENANCE:
Possibly Duke of Sutherland, Stafford House, U.K.; Private collection.

EXHIBITIONS:
Providence 1964, no. 11(ill.); New York 1966, no. 17; New Orleans 1997, no. 24
(ill.).

23A Meindert Hobbema

(Amsterdam 1638 - Amsterdam 1709)

Cottage at the Edge of a Wood

oil on panel
27.2 x 33 cm.
Inscribed twice at the lower left and lower right: *M. Hobbema*
(signature illustrated in Broulhiet 1938, p. 374, pl. 582)

PROVENANCE:
Baroness Vincent Maximilian van Tuyll, Utrecht, 1836; W. Gruyter, Amsterdam,
1882; Collection Edward Warneck, 1911; Sale Edward Warneck, Paris, May 1926
(label on verso); European noble family; Purchased 1999.

EXHIBITION:
Paris 1911, no. 71 (ill.).

LITERATURE:
Hofstede de Groot 1912, vol. IV, no. 60a; Broulhiet 1938, p. 398, no. 172, ill. p. 188.
Paris, 1911; Stechow 1959, p.16.

24   Jan van Kessel the Elder
(Antwerp 1626 - Antwerp 1679)

Fish Still Life in Harbor Landscape
(Possibly *The Element of Water*)

1660
oil on panel
27 x 37.2 cm.
Inscribed, bottom right: *J. V. Kessel f 1660*

PROVENANCE:
Schoenman Galleries, New York; W. P. Chrysler, Jr.; Private collection, Mass.;
Sale, May 8, 1957, New York, Parke Bernet Galleries, no. 1757.

EXHIBITIONS:
Providence 1964, no. 12 (ill.); New York 1965, no. 60 (ill.); Red Bank 1965,
no. 80; New York 1966, no. 18; New Orleans 1997, no. 25 (ill.).

25   Theodoor Mertens (also Maertens)
(active in Antwerp ? c. 1666)

Still Life with Fruit and Oysters on a Table

1666
oil on panel
24.4 x 35 cm.
Inscribed, top right: *Tho . mertens . fecit 1666 .*

PROVENANCE:
Private collection.

EXHIBITIONS:
Zurich 1989-90, no. 24 (ill.); New Orleans 1997, no. 27 (ill.).

LITERATURE:
de Maere/Wabbes 1994, no. 773 (ill.).

26 Nicolaes Maes
(Dordrecht 1634 - Amsterdam 1693)

Portrait of a Woman, Age Forty-one

1671
oil on panel
43.3 x 30.5 cm.
Inscribed, bottom right: *AET 41/N. MAES/1671*

PROVENANCE:
Private collection.

EXHIBITIONS:
Birmingham 1995, no. 10 (ill.); New Orleans 1997, no. 28 (ill.).

Nicolaes Maes' vivid representation of an unidentified forty-one-year-old woman[1] is a fine example of the genre of society portraiture which the painter mastered in his maturity. The figure is set in a painted oval, depicted frontally to the waist, with a slight turn to the left. The gaze of her highlighted brown eyes is direct and her expression, while not dour, is difficult to gauge. Although she is rendered with fine features and a stylishly pale complexion with high color in her cheeks,[2] the painter has allowed minor irregularities, such as the slightly unmatched angle of her upper eyelids, to show thereby lending "character" and individuality to a conventional genre. In keeping with current fashion the sitter is elegantly dressed in black with a translucent white shawl collar and white sleeves and with the luminous accents of pendant pearl and gold earrings and a pearl clasp at her neck.

From the mid-1650s until his death, the Dordrecht artist Nicolaes Maes devoted himself increasingly to portraiture, abandoning his first specialization of genre painting, presumably in order to earn a living. While he is highly acclaimed for his genre subjects today, of which approximately forty examples survive, he was far more prolific as a portraitist, and he achieved financial and artistic success in this manner.[3] His skills were sought by some of the leading families of the day including, for example, the Sixes of Amsterdam and the Trip family of Dordrecht.[4]

Maes' change in subject matter was accompanied by a shift in technique. In his society portraits he increasingly favored looser brushwork and settings and styles which reflected the courtly aspects of Flemish portraiture, namely the innovations of Anthony van Dyck (1599-1641).

Maes' early biographer, Houbraken, attributed this transition to an alleged trip to the southern Netherlands in the 1670s, and also associated it with the artist's move to Amsterdam which occurred in 1673.[5] Houbraken described the second manner in a way which, to some extent, befits the present portrait : "[Maes] soon gave up [Rembrandt's] way of painting when he started painting portraits and he discovered that young ladies took more pleasure in white than in brown."[6] There is, however, no documentation to support Houbraken's claim about the journey to Flanders and, as Robinson has recently noted, the transition in Maes' style actually began in 1661. Moreover, as Robinson and others have shown, Flemish conventions of portraiture had influenced Dutch painters since the 1640s and Maes would have been exposed to them at home.[7]

Painted in 1671, the Weldon panel certainly postdates the onset of the artist's second manner. Nonetheless, in its relatively conservative composition, a simple bust against a plain ground, its sober colors, and small size, it combines earlier conventions of Dordrecht portraiture, as practiced by the Cuyp family, with technical elements of the late work.[8] Given the date of the painting which precedes the artist's move to Amsterdam by two years, it most probably depicts a Dordrecht sitter. Hence it is not surprising that it would incorporate the local tradition.

The modest format and refined rendering were perhaps also dictated by the sitter. A consideration of the painting alongside other portraits by Maes of women who appear to be at the same station in life reveals a similar manner and format. It should be noted that many of these paintings of women and possibly the Weldon panel were originally part of a double commission which would have

included a likeness of the husband who would have been shown facing right, to the left of his wife.[9] *A Portrait of a Woman*, 1667, Kunstmuseum, Basel, where the sitter's age is inscribed as fifty-three, while larger and painted on canvas, employs the same general format (with the exception of the oval inset), composition, and technique.[10] Likewise a *Portrait of a Woman*, also dated 1667, Musée des Beaux-Arts, Arras, shows comparable tendencies.[11] Finally, the *Portrait of Sara Ingelbrechts*, 1675, Kunsthistorisches Museum, Vienna, features the oval inset format, a comparable rendering of the sitter, and a similar technique, albeit somewhat flashier, especially in the drapery.[12]

Except for the fact that Ingelbrechts is bare-headed, her attire is virtually identical to that of the sitter in the Weldon painting. The presence of similar garments in other works by the artist, as well as many other contemporary portraits attests to their currency. The Weldon woman wears a peaked cap, headwear which was fashionable from the 1640s on and was not necessarily reserved for widows.[13] Pendant earrings, as seen in the Weldon painting and which had been worn in the 1630s, became increasingly popular as the large ruff, or millstone collars went out of style.[14] The change in collar styles also brought about the lowering of necklines which culminated in French-style *décolletage*.[15] While the dress of the Weldon woman certainly does not feature a plunging neckline, the combination of a diaphanous kerchief and a lower cut does reflect a modest version of French fashion. NTM

1 The sitter's age is characteristically indicated in the inscription.

2 On this cosmetic effect, a fashion imported to the Netherlands from France, see du Mortier in Washington/London/Haarlem 1989-90, p. 52.

3 The estimate for the number of genre paintings, dating from 1654-58, is taken from Robinson 1992, p. 100. Hofstede de Groot 1907-28, vol. 6, 1915, records over 400 portraits, a good number of which would probably be discounted from the artist's *oeuvre* today. Studies on the artist, such as Valentiner 1924, have tended to focus on his genre output. Robinson 1992 offers an overview of his portraiture for the years 1655-61, while Robinson 1997 provides a survey of the artist's *oeuvre* from 1653-1661, as well as a study of his life. The numerous late portraits remain to be studied in depth, although many of them are illustrated and catalogued in Sumowski 1983, vols. 3, 5, 6.

4 See, for example, the pendant portraits of *Jacob Trip* and *Margaretha de Geer*, Szépmüvészeti Múzeum, Budapest, and the various Six portraits listed in Hofstede de Groot 1907-28, vol. 6, 1915, nos. 256a-261.

5 Houbraken 1718-21, vol. 2, 1719, as cited by Robinson 1992, pp. 112-13.

6 Houbraken 1718-21, vol. 2, 1719, pp. 274-5 (present author's translation).

7 Robinson 1992, pp. 113-14, where the author names Jan Mytens (c. 1614-1670) and Adriaen Hanneman (1601-1671), both of The Hague, as early exponents of the "van Dyckian style." While Slive 1959, p. 33, accepts that Maes probably went to Flanders around 1665-67, earlier than Houbraken claimed, he alludes to the presence of van Dyckian tendencies in the aristocratic portraiture of The Hague as early as 1640.

8 Robinson 1992, p. 104, stresses the impact of the Dordrecht tradition, originating in the late 1640s and early 1650s, on Maes's initial work as a portraitist, rather than the alleged influence of Rembrandt's portraiture of the early 1650s.

9 On the conventions of marriage portraiture in Holland, see Smith 1982.

10 73.6 x 60.1 cm., illustrated and catalogued in Sumowski 1983, vol. 3, no. 1403.

11 Canvas, 90.3 x 72.2 cm., illustrated in Gaskell 1989, p. 175.

12 Illustrated in Vienna 1991, pl. 539, no. 9005.

13 Du Mortier in Washington/London/ Haarlem 1989-90, p. 51. The presence of this type of hat in genre paintings depicting young mothers and in portraits of couples demonstrates that it was not reserved for widows.

14 Ibid., p. 52. For examples of paintings in the present collection which feature women in millstone collars, see Adriaen van de Venne's *Winter Pleasures* and Pieter Codde's *Musical Company*, cats. 56 and 13.

15 Ibid., p. 52.

27   Jacob Marrel (Jacobus Marellus)

(Frankenthal c. 1613/14 - Frankfurt am Main 1681)

Bouquet in a Niche with Cherries and Insects

c. 1635
oil on copper
18.2 x 13.3 cm.
Inscribed, lower right, at corner of niche: *J. Marrel*

PROVENANCE:
Private collection.

EXHIBITIONS:
Zurich 1985, no. 45; New Orleans 1997, no. 29 (ill.).

Please refer to entry no. 27 for a brief discussion
of this painting.

Jacob Marrel renders nature's blooms with a miniaturist's precision, arranging them with poetic lyricism in this still life which probably dates from his early years in Utrecht. A splendid striped tulip crowns an abundant bouquet which is barely contained in a small glass, known as a *roemer*.[1] At least fifteen varieties of flowers are represented, from the tiniest and most delicate forget-me-nots on the ledge and the lily of the valley at the base of the bouquet, to the full pink, white and yellow roses at center, and the lush tulip and irises at the top. Minutely described insects populate the niche and explore the flowers. Among them are a caterpillar inching its way up the base of the arch, a tiny fly lighting on the white rose, a dragonfly approaching the columbine at left, and a grasshopper and butterfly at upper right. The brilliance of the flowers is enhanced by bold illumination which rakes across the bouquet, picking out highlights and casting dark shadows in the niche.

Jacob Marrel was trained in the still-life genre in his native Germany under the Frankfurt master Georg Flegel (1566-1638).[2] In its delicacy and detail the present painting attests to Flegel's influence; however, it also bespeaks the early developments in seventeenth-century Dutch still-life painting which took place in Middelburg and later in Utrecht. Marrel was living in Utrecht as early as 1634 and remained there until 1649.[3] Many of his paintings from this period, including the present one and his *Bouquet in a Niche with Cherries, Shells, and a Lizard*, also in the Weldon Collection (no. 30), demonstrate a conception of flower painting which evolved through the innovations of the Bosschaert dynasty, native to Middelburg and relocated to Utrecht, and those of Roelandt Saverij (1578-1639), the Bosschaerts' associate who lived in the same city from 1618 until his death. The *Bouquet on a Ledge with Landscape Vista*, 1624 (no. 2), by Balthasar van der Ast (c. 1593/4-1657), who was related to the Bosschaert family by marriage, represents the classic Bosschaert formulation of flower painting.[4] The strict symmetry of the present composition and its clarity and detail of rendering are characteristic of the type. Marrel's work has been likened especially to still lifes by

Ambrosius Bosschaert the Younger (1609-1645).[5] One of Saverij's apparent legacies to the Bosschaert tradition, and to Marrel in particular, is the format of the bouquet in the stone niche employed in the present composition and seen in Savery's earlier painting dated 1603, *Flowers with Lizards, Shells, and Insects in a Niche*, Centraal Museum, Utrecht.[6]

There are several flower paintings by Marrel which feature bouquets in a niche, and the inventory of his belongings compiled in 1649 includes two paintings described as *Romer*, probably references to similar *roemer* vase arrangements.[7] Nonetheless, the small size of the copper support and the highly refined technique in the Weldon painting are relatively rare in the artist's *oeuvre*. A close parallel is found in Marrel's *Flowers in a Glass Vase with a Lizard and Cherries*, private collection, which is also painted on copper and is only marginally larger,[8] and where the niche setting and the lighting recur almost exactly. While the flowers, container, and insects are varied, the relative disposition and size of the bouquet are similar. Likewise, the fine technique corresponds to the minute detail and the scale and support of the work. Although this painting is also undated, it has recently been associated with the period of the artist's arrival in Utrecht.[9] A date of c. 1635 is consistent with the relatively conservative style of the painting and Marrel's early Utrecht *oeuvre* which was influenced by the Bosschaert dynasty and Saverij as discussed above.[10]

The Marrel bouquets in the Weldon collection feature hallmarks of the artist. The dominant tulips of each bouquet relate to the magnificent watercolor illustrations of the sought-after species from the artist's *Tulip Book* dating from 1637 to 1645.[11] The sand lizard of the larger painting is a frequent visitor in Marrel's flower pieces and is probably borrowed from Saverij.[12] Finally, each painting bears the "signature" of the morello cherries, a feature which Segal has interpreted as the artist's reference to his own name.[13]
NTM

1 Rummer, a type of glass often featured as a vase in Dutch seventeenth-century flower paintings. They are also shown as drinking vessels in still-life and genre paintings.

2 Bott 1966, p. 86, states that Marrel began to study under Flegel in 1627. For comparably fine and diminutive flower paintings by Flegel, see his *Flower Still Life*, panel, 22.5 x 15 cm., Henry R. Broughton Collection, and the *Flower Still Life with Pokal*, private collection, both illustrated and catalogued in Frankfurt 1993-94, nos. 24 and 42, respectively.

3 Bott 1966, pp. 86-87.

4 On the Bosschaert tradition, see the entry on van der Ast's *Bouquet on a Ledge with Landscape Vista*, cat. 2.

5 Bott 1966, pp. 90-91. The influence of Ambrosius the Younger is most evident in Marrel's *Bouquet in a Niche with Cherries, Shells, and a Lizard*, cat. 30, in the present collection, especially in the round glass vase with reflections from a window.

6 The painting, on copper, 29 x 19 cm., is reproduced and catalogued by Segal in Osaka/Tokyo/Sydney 1990, no. 24. Bol 1960, p. 29, has cited Saverij as the innovator of the niche and bouquet composition, rather than the Bosschaerts. Bott 1966, p. 92, also relates Saverij's niche type of composition to Marrel's work.

7 See, for example Bott 1966, no. 5, 10, and London 1976, no. 258. The inventory is published in Bredius 1915-22, vol. 1, 1915, pp. 112-19.

8 20 x 14 cm. Catalogued by Seifertová and illustrated in Frankfurt 1993-94, no. 140.

9 Frankfurt 1993-94, no. 140. However, in Osaka/Tokyo/Sydney, no. 39, Segal related the painting to a larger composition by the artist, dated 1650.

10 A painting dated 1635, entitled *Bouquet with Fruit, Insects, and a Lizard*, private collection, though larger and painted on panel, illustrated and catalogued in London 1976, no. 258, shows the same general format and style. The Weldon *Bouquet in a Niche with Cherries, Insects, and a Lizard*, cat. 28, is probably also datable to the artist's early Utrecht years, since it exhibits the Bosschaert/Saverij characteristics discussed above. Furthermore, it closely resembles the painting dated 1635, listed above.

11 The *Tulip Book*, Rijksprentenkabinet, Amsterdam, consists of parchment sheets with precise botanical representations of many different types of striped tulips.

12 The type of lizard is identified by Segal in Osaka/Tokyo/Sydney 1990, no. 195, the entry on the small copper panel *Flowers in a Glass Vase with a Lizard and Cherries*, discussed above.

13 Ibid.

(detail)

28   Jacob Marrel (Jacobus Marellus)
(Frankenthal 1613/14 - Frankfurt am Main 1681)

Bouquet in a Niche with Cherries, Shells, and a Lizard

c. 1635
oil on panel
42.4 x 34.2 cm.

PROVENANCE:
Sale, London, Christie's, May 19-20, 1926, no. 235 (as A. Bosschaert, to Lepper);
Lady E. Bird, Solihull, U. K.; Private collection.

EXHIBITIONS:
Providence 1964, no. 15 (ill.); New York 1965, no. 69; New York 1966, no. 22;
Birmingham 1995, no 11 (ill.); New Orleans 1997, no. 30 (ill.).

Please refer to entry no. 27 for a brief discussion of this painting.

29 Jacob Marrel (Jacobus Marrellus)
(Frankenthal 1613/4 - Frankfurt am Main 1681)

Flowers Resting on a Ledge

1669
oil on panel
36.2 x 43.8 cm.
Inscribed lower right: *J. Marrell. f 1669*

PROVENANCE:
French private collection.

See the Introduction for a brief discussion of this recent acquisition.

30 Jan Miense Molenaer

(Haarlem c. 1610 - Haarlem 1668)

Violinist

c. 1630-35
oil on panel
24.1 x 21.6 cm.
Inscribed, upper right: *IML* [in monogram]

PROVENANCE:
R. T. Paget Collection; G. H. Edgar Collection, Hambledon, Henley-on-Thames; Leonard L. Koetser Gallery, London (by 1966); Private collection, U.K., Private collection.

EXHIBITIONS:
London, Leonard L. Koetser Gallery, 1966, no. 2; Haarlem/Worcester 1993, no. 32 (ill.), and cited p. 84; New Orleans 1997, no. 31 (ill.).

Molenaer's high-spirited violinist strikes a characteristically playful note in this small painting which probably dates from the beginning of the artist's career. The musician, depicted in three-quarter profile to the waist, directly engages the viewer with his twinkling gaze and his broad, open-lipped smile which suggests laughter or a song. His attire is traditional, consistent with the fashions of contemporary portraiture — a black cape over his left shoulder, a black jacket and a lace-trimmed collar — except for the bright red hat which partially covers his blond curls, its raised, slashed brim jauntily framing his forehead. His glistening violin rests beneath his chin and faces downwards according to musical practice, yet his bow does not seem to make contact with the strings.[1] The vibrant technique, incorporating lively brushwork and local colors with marked highlights, evokes the mood of *staccato* string music.

Molenaer's presentation of his subject is a response to the contemporary tradition of depictions of musicians in his native city of Haarlem. In the 1620's his elder and probable model Frans Hals (c. 1582/3-1666) evolved a type, exemplified by his *Merry Lute Player*, c. 1626, Harold Samuel Collection, London, which in turn was developed from the musician paintings of the Utrecht Caravaggists such as *The Merry Fiddler*, 1623, Rijksmuseum, Amsterdam, of Gerrit van Honthorst (1590-1656). The musician paintings by Hals and his followers, like the present one, tend to feature young, jovial sitters, sometimes children, in bust or three-quarter-length view with simple settings and strong light effects.

The violinist was a favorite motif, his instrument being the most common in low-life genre paintings.[2] Indeed, the theme recurs in Molenaer's paintings of individual musicians and groups, in those of his wife, Judith Leyster (1609-1660) and in those of Frans Hals. In Leyster's *Self-Portrait*, c. 1630, National Gallery, Washington, she chose to depict herself painting a merry violinist.[3] Molenaer's own dependence on the instrument as a painter's prop is underscored by the presence of a violin among the objects listed in his inventory.[4] The contemporary adage of the musical theorist Praetorius, that the violin was the "king of instruments," seems to have prevailed also in artistic circles in Haarlem.[5]

In Molenaer's *oeuvre* there are several representations of violin players which relate to the present painting. The closest work, known only in reproduction, is another version of the Weldon painting but with minor variations in costume and in the placement of the musician's hands,[6] featuring the same sitter in an almost identical composition.[7] There is a third painting by the artist entitled *Boy Playing Violin*, comparable both in composition and scale, which shows a younger sitter, who looks up rather than out.[8] Molenaer's group in *Children Making Music*, Wawel Castle, Kracow, also includes a youthful violinist in a pose which combines elements of the latter boy and the musician of the Weldon painting.[9]

While the Weldon panel is undated, as are all of the related violinist paintings, Biesboer has placed it early in the artist's *oeuvre* for stylistic reasons, prior to 1630.[10] Characteristics associated with the beginning of the artist's career, such as the simple composition and the use of bright

71

local color, are evident in the painting. More specifically, Biesboer has identified the technical influence of Dirck Hals (1591-1656), combined with that of his older brother Frans, as characteristic of this phase of Molenaer's career. While the overall impression of dash and bravado derives from Frans, as in the quick brush-work of the lace, in the highlights on the face and the contrasting flesh tones, the particulars of technique do resemble Dirck. As with the younger Hals' manner, the flickering brush strokes are smaller and the paint surface thinner than is usually seen in the work of Frans.[11]

The recent interpretation of the Weldon painting notes that the musician is not actually playing his instrument. Rather, he flourishes his bow in a gesture that has been seen as an allusion to sexual prowess instead of musical skill. While contemporary literary and artistic references to the playing of the instrument support this view, with the bow as the symbol of the man and the violin as the woman,[12] other possible associations are suggested by the image.

In many still-life paintings of the period, the concept of *vanitas*, or the fleeting pleasure of earthly existence, is signaled by the presence of a musical instrument, frequently a violin, based upon the temporal ephemerality of music.[13] Images of youthful musicians playing are likewise viewed as allegories for the vain pursuits of humankind.[14] In the Weldon painting, the aimlessness of the bow and the frivolous expression of the musician may suggest a *vanitas* theme.

Finally, it is possible that the painting may represent a personification of the sanguine temperament or humor. This interpretation has been offered for a similar image, the *Self-Portrait as Lutenist*, c. 1663-65, by Jan Steen, Fundación Colección Thyssen-Bornemisza, Madrid.[15] Molenaer's younger colleague Jan Steen (1626-1679) was in Haarlem when he painted the self-portrait which shares a number of characteristics with the present painting, notably the red slashed hat, the extreme joviality of the sitter, and the playing of a stringed instrument. The hat in the present work, incongruous in juxtaposition with the relatively sober costume, is comparable to the type seen in several of Steen's paintings in which it has been identified with the theater, specifically the character of the fool or jester from contemporary dramatic and literary rhetorician's societies.[16] Such an attribute would indeed befit the personification of a jovial temperament. Moreover, elements of the type from Cesare Ripa's *Iconologia*, a widely read anthology of personifications translated into Dutch in 1644, offer a literary counterpart to Molenaer's *Violinist* and describe the "sanguine or high-spirited complexion" as follows:

> A jovial laughing young man ... [with] blond hair, with red and white color mixed in his face, playing on a lute...the sanguine temperament is pictured this way because from among those ruled by temperate and perfect blood come the liveliest, sharpest wits of the day, from whom laughter and merriment come forth...[and who] are entertaining and jocular and love acting and singing.[17]

NTM

1 On the particulars of contemporary musical practice as they relate to the pose of the Weldon violinist, see the entry for the painting by van Thiel-Stroman in Haarlem/Worcester 1993, no. 32.

2 Ibid., p. 370.

3 The self-portrait is catalogued and reproduced in Wheelock 1995, no. 1949.6.1, where he associates the violinist painting on the easel with Leyster's *Merry Company*, c. 1629-31, private collection, which features the same figure incorporated into a trio.

4 Haarlem/Worcester 1993, p. 73.

5 As cited in ibid., 1993, p. 370. Michael Praetorius (1571-1621) was a German composer and theorist. He classified ancient and contemporary instruments in his *Syntagma musicum*, 1614-20.

6 *Violinist*, present location unknown, panel, 27 x 21 cm., reproduced in ibid., no. 32 (entry on the Weldon painting), fig. 32a, where a close comparison is drawn.

7 The man also appears in *The Lute Player*, present location unknown, as cited and illustrated in ibid.

8 Panel, 29 x 24.3 cm., present location unknown, illustrated in ibid., p. 372, fig. 42d.

9 Illustrated in ibid., p. 370, no. 42b.

10 Ibid., p. 84. The artist's earliest dated works are from the year 1629, as stated in Philadelphia/Berlin/London 1984, p. 261. Some of the 1629 paintings are listed and discussed in Haarlem/Worcester 1993, pp. 82-83.

11 Compare, for example, the small, nervous strokes in Dirck's *Seated Woman with a Letter*, 1633, John G. Johnson Collection, Philadelphia Museum of Art. For a similar painting by Frans of comparable dimensions which appears to achieve the same effects as seen in the Weldon panel but actually employs a broader, freer technique, see *A Young Man in a Large Hat*, c. 1626-9, panel, 29.3 x 23.2 cm., National Gallery, Washington.

12 This reading is posited by van Thiel-Stroman in the entry on the painting in Haarlem/Worcester 1993, no. 32.

13 As stated, with further references to the subject in Philadelphia/Berlin/London 1984, p. 209.

14 Ibid., where such an interpretation is suggested for Frans Hals' *Singing Boy With a Flute*, c. 1627, Gemäldegalerie, Berlin, and other examples are cited.

15 As catalogued by Perry Chapman in Washington/Amsterdam 1996-97, no. 25.

16 As, for example, in Steen's *Rhetoricians at a Window*, 1662-66, John G. Johnson Collection, Philadelphia Museum of Art, in the entry in Philadelphia/Berlin/London 1984, no. 106.

17 Ripa's *Iconologia* was first published in Rome in 1593. The above passage is excerpted from the section of Ripa 1644, pp. 75-76, as it was translated by Perry Chapman in Washington/Amsterdam 1996-97, p. 182, where it is discussed in relation to Steen's *Self-Portrait as a Lutenist*.

31 **Emanuel Murant**

(Amsterdam 1622 - Leeuwarden c. 1700)

Village Road

oil on canvas
31.5 x 41 cm.
Inscribed, bottom right: *EM*

PROVENANCE:
Private collection.

EXHIBITIONS:
London 1961, no. 56; New York 1966, no 24; New Orleans 1997, no. 32 (ill.).

32 Aert van der Neer

(Amsterdam 1603/4 - Amsterdam 1677)

Moonlit Landscape with Wooden Raft on a Canal

oil on canvas
55.3 x 71.8 cm.
Inscribed, lower right: *AVN.* [with first two initials in monogram ligature]

PROVENANCE:
F. Kleinberger, Paris; Paul Cassirer, Berlin; Private collection, U.S.A.

EXHIBITIONS:
London 1961, no. 39; Providence 1964, no. 16 (ill.); New York 1966, no. 25;
Birmingham 1995, no. 12 (ill.); New Orleans 1997, no. 33 (ill.).

LITERATURE:
Hofstede de Groot 1907-28, vol. 7, 1923, no. 257; *Burlington Magazine* 103 (April
1961) p. 154; *Apollo* 74 (April 1961) pp. 114-115 (ill.).

(actual size)

33   **Eglon van der Neer**
(Amsterdam 1634 - Düsseldorf 1703)

Pastoral Landscape

c. 1690
oil on copper
11.8 x 16 cm.
Inscribed, bottom left: *E. H. van....*[?]

PROVENANCE:
Private collection.

EXHIBITION:
New Orleans 1997, no. 34 (ill.).

34   Adriaen van Ostade
(Haarlem 1610 - Haarlem 1685)

Peasants Playing Cards

c. 1660-65
oil on panel
27.5 x 21.75 cm.
Inscribed; bottom left: *AV. O* . [first two initials in monogram ligature]

PROVENANCE:
T. Emmerson, London (by 1842); Comte R. de Corneliessen, Brussels (Sale, May 11, 1857, no. 57); Sale, Paris, Gilkinet, April 18, 1863, no. 33 (for frs. 7,700); Sale, Paris, J. A. Tardieu, May 10-11, 1867, no. 41 (for frs. 6,000); Lippmann von Lissingen, Vienna (Sale, Paris, March 16, 1876, no. 32 (ill.), for frs. 28,100); B. Field, London (by 1888); Sale, G. Field, London, June 10, 1893, no. 30; M. Colnaghi, London; C. Sedelmeyer, Paris (by 1894); Sale, Amsterdam, J. Monchen, and others, April 30, 1907, no. 136 (for fl. 2750); Sale, Paris, Georges Petit, A. Lehman Collection, June 12-13, 1925, no. 274 (ill.); H. Becker, Dortmund; Private collection.

EXHIBITIONS:
Vienna 1873, no. 171; London 1888, no. 115; Dortmund 1954, no. 45 (ill.); London 1958A, no. 36; Providence 1964, no. 17 (ill.); Allentown 1965, no. 54 (ill.); New York 1966, no. 27; Birmingham 1995, no. 14 (ill.); New Orleans 1997, no. 35 (ill.).

LITERATURE:
Smith 1829-42, Supplement, 1842, no. 111; Paris 1894, no. 27 (ill.); Hofstede de Groot 1907-28, vol. 3, 1910, no. 850; *Der Cicerone* 17 (1925), p. 152.

Adriaen van Ostade's eighteenth-century biographer, Arnold Houbraken, reserved his highest praise for the artist's peasant interiors, Ostade's favorite theme, exemplified by this small panel. The author described "domestic interiors with all their ramshackle furnishings" and "the figures in their costumes doing all sorts of activities, so naturally peasantlike and witty."[1] This humble scene of three figures grouped around a table, two men and a woman conversing while smoking, drinking, and playing cards, vividly conveys the quiet pleasures of whiling away the hours. The man at lower left, who appears to command the attention of his companions by speaking, holds an earthenware jug and a clay pipe in his right hand.[2] Standing behind him and bowing slightly as if to listen, a second pipe smoker rests his hand and elbow on a chair back. A seated woman also leans toward the speaker, her absorption indicated by her tilted glass of beer. Facial expressions of slight amusement and mildly caricatured physiognomies lend a subtly humorous note.

Houbraken's life of Ostade recounts that he was the pupil of Frans Hals (c. 1582/3-1666) in Haarlem along with Adriaen Brouwer (1606-1638), the Flemish painter who resided there intermittently from the late 1620s until 1631.[3] Although there is no documentary evidence to support these claims, the early peasant paintings of Ostade certainly reveal Brouwer's influence. The work of both artists from this period illustrates the development of the low-life interior, a subject which was to preoccupy Ostade and other genre painters through the century.[4] Ostade's fascination with the peasant subject of a group gaming, drinking and/or smoking lasted throughout his career. His earliest dated painting, from the year 1633,[5] bears the same title as the present work and his significant *oeuvre* of over eight hundred paintings, many watercolors and drawings, and approximately fifty etchings, is filled with related images.[6]

In particular, the threesome in a triangular composition, as in the present painting, appears to have been a favored motif which spans Ostade's *oeuvre*. It occurs in numerous paintings,[7] in prints like *The Concert*, c. 1644, and *The Empty Jug*, c. 1653,[8] and in several drawings, notably the *Two Peasants and Innkeeper* dated to the 1650s and the *Woman and Two Men Reading* from the following decade.[9] With regard to the Weldon panel, close parallels may be drawn with two paintings in Dresden from the mid-1660s, *The Feasting Peasants*, 1663, and *The Smoking Peasants*, 1664.[10] Like the Weldon painting, they feature a triangular composition of seated and standing three-quarter length figures, one woman and two men, situated in the corner of a restricted space.

Ostade often employed stock figure types for different subjects. For example, the woman with lopsided features in the Weldon panel may be seen with minor variations in physiognomy and attire in two works with amorous themes: the painting entitled *A Peasant Courting an Elderly Woman*, 1653, National Gallery, London, and *La Tendresse Villageoise*, an etching of about 1667.[11]

Although the artist repeated his peasant subjects, his *oeuvre* is characterized by a shift in the tenor of his low-life depictions accompanied by an increasing refinement in technique. Both of these developments are illustrated by the present painting. By the 1660s Ostade's peasants, while

still rustic, are far better-behaved than the raucous Brouwer-like ruffians of his early paintings.[12] Indeed, the threesome of the Weldon panel pursue their vices with quiet respectability. From a technical point of view, the painting shows the artist's later preference for brighter, local colors and finer brushwork, over his early choice of dark tones and a rougher touch. The relatively presentable clothing of the peasants in the Weldon painting is enhanced by the pleasing color effects, as in the blue-green tunic and pink sleeves of the talker and the fine delineation and description of all the garments.[13] The presence of these technical characteristics, the geniality of the scene and the resemblance the painting bears to the dated Dresden works of the mid-1660s all suggest a similar date for this panel.[14]

The idle pursuits of smoking, drinking and card playing were sometimes depicted with moralizing, even chastising intent by Ostade's contemporaries. Seventeenth-century Dutch literature and imagery are replete with chiding references to these pursuits.[15] The vices of smoking and drinking are likened in Bredero's expression "tobacco-drinkers," used to describe smokers in his farce of 1613.[16] Another common contemporary view of smoking which underscores the theme of vanity is expressed in the inscription on a print of a lone pipe smoker: "Verinas [tobacco] finely cut I smoke with all my might/And oftentimes I think: So doth the world take flight."[17] Likewise, playing at cards and gambling were variously interpreted as wasteful, dishonest and sinful pursuits.[18] Ostade's benign portrayal of these pastimes in the present painting, in which the players seem happily, rather than perilously engaged, at the very most suggests a gentle and even an affectionate admonition.
NTM

1 Houbraken 1718-21, vol. 1, 1718, pp. 347-48 (excerpted from the passage cited and translated by Robinson in Philadelphia/Berlin/London 1984, p. 284).

2 He holds up a white object in his other hand in a gesture which appears to elaborate on his speech. While Smith and Houbraken (see Literature above) identified this object as a coin, it seems to have a soft texture and an irregular shape. It may represent a piece of chalk, an object sometimes seen in paintings of card players usually in conjunction with a board and used as a means to keep score; see, for example, Jan Steen's *The Cardplayers*, c. 1660, private collection, illustrated and catalogued in Washington/Amsterdam 1996-97, no. 14.

3 Houbraken 1718-21, vol. 1, pp. 347-49, as cited by Wheelock 1995, pp. 184-85.

4 Philadelphia/Berlin/London 1984, p. 166.

5 Hermitage, Saint Petersburg, as stated in Philadelphia/Berlin/London 1984, p. 282.

6 On the paintings, see Rosenberg 1900, and Hofstede de Groot 1907-28, vol. 3, 1910, pp. 140-436, and Schnackenburg 1970. On the prints and drawings, see Godefroy 1990 and Schnackenburg 1981, respectively.

7 Dated paintings occur throughout; see, for example Hofstede de Groot 1907-28, vol. 3, 1910, nos. 848 (1639), 345 (1640), 327 (1647), 341 (1649), 374 (1650), 326 and 351 (1661), 236 (1663), 237 and 355 (1664), 846 (1674).

8 Godefroy 1990, nos. 30 and 15, respectively.

9 Schnackenburg 1981, nos. 95 and 148, respectively.

10 Gemäldegalerie, Dresden. These paintings are illustrated in Rosenberg 1900, figs. 62-63 and they are included in the chronological list above, note 7, nos. 236- 237.

11 On the painting, see Brown/MacLaren 1992, no. 2542, and on the print, Godefroy 1990, no. 11. Her type appears in several other works as well.

12 As described in Wheelock 1995, p. 187. Compare, for example, the mayhem in Ostade's *Drinking Figures and Crying Children*, 1634, Sarah Campbell Blaffer Foundation, Houston; illustrated in Philadelphia/Berlin/London 1984, no. 89.

13 These technical innovations are taken further in Ostade's *Man with Pince-Nez, Reading Notices*, c. 1670-75, in the Weldon collection; see cat. 35.

14 No date appears with the signature in the present painting. When it was exhibited in 1954 it was characterized as a late work; see Dortmund 1954, no. 45.

15 For a still life which features smoking accessories, see Jan Fris's *Still Life with Pipe and Jug* in the Weldon collection, cat. 18.

16 From A. Bredero's *Klucht van de Molenaer*, 1613, cited in Haarlem/Worcester 1993, no. 21, pp. 248, 250, note 8. On interpretations of images of smokers, see the entry just cited, and for further information, see Brongers 1964.

17 The engraving *A Man Smoking* is by Hendrick Bary. It is illustrated with the above-quoted and translated inscription in Auckland 1982, p. 102.

18 On the perceived sinfulness of gambling, see Philadelphia/Berlin/London 1984, no. 37. On the parallel significance of the games of cards and love, see Washington/Amsterdam 1996-97, no. 14.

(actual size)

35 Adriaen van Ostade

(Haarlem 1610 - Haarlem 1685)

A Man with Pince-Nez, Reading Notices

c. 1670-75
oil on panel
15.25 x 11 cm.
Inscribed, bottom left: *AvOstade 16* [the last two digits of the
date are obscured]

PROVENANCE:
R. de Saint-Victor, Paris (Sale, November 26, 1822, for frs. 850); Sale comte Pourtalès, London, Phillips, May 18, 1826, no. 39 (for £ 47); Miss S. Seymour, Salisbury; A. Peek, The Hague, 1927; W. J. R. Dreesmann, Amsterdam; W. Dreesmann, 1940-80; R. Dreesmann, 1980; Private collection.

EXHIBITIONS:
Amsterdam 1929, no. 28; Delft 1952-53, no. 108; Birmingham 1995, no. 13 (ill.); Washington, National Gallery of Art, Dutch Cabinet Galleries, temporary loan, April 1-September 15, 1996; New Orleans 1997, no. 36 (ill.).

LITERATURE:
Smith 1829-42, vol. 1, 1829, no. 169; Hofstede de Groot 1907-28, vol. 3, 1910, no. 90l.

Late in his career, Adriaen van Ostade demonstrated a fondness for finely crafted images with simple subjects, often single figures, as in the present small panel. A curious villager rocks back on his heels as he lifts his head, holds his *pince-nez* at the end of his long nose and attempts to decipher the notices high on the wall before him. His dapper yet old-fashioned attire is carefully articulated – knickers, short cape, crisp white ruff and black hat – more a costume than mere clothing. The bricks, timber, and window of the wall are minutely described, as are the colorful chicken strutting on the ground and the vine clinging to the corner of the archway behind the figure. A view beyond leads to three figures, a building and a patch of blue sky.

As Ostade grew older, his artistic vision sharpened, and the Weldon panel is a fine example of his last manner which is characterized by crisp definition and coloristic clarity.[2] When Smith catalogued the work in 1829, he summed up his description with a simple statement which seemingly alluded to its immaculate technique and pristine condition, readily visible to this day: "This is a picture of very good quality."[3] The luminous effect of this painting is similar to that of Ostade's watercolors of the same period which were highly prized as independent, finished works of art by his contemporaries and by subsequent collectors.[4]

Along with his refinement of technique, Ostade nuanced his typical peasant subject matter, lending greater dignity and respectability to the figures in his late works. The present man, more solid *burger* than shiftless *boer*,[5] typifies this tendency. He appears to be an elaboration on the theme of the single figure which occupied Ostade in earlier studies and became an autonomous subject in subsequent watercolors and oils. Two drawings of hurdy-gurdy players dated to the 1650s feature musicians wearing the same attire as the bespectacled man in the Weldon panel.[6] The series of watercolors of single peasants which are placed in the artist's final decades also relate to the present painting, as vignettes of lone figures, although they revert to the low-life theme.[7] Oil paintings like *The Doctor in his Study*, 1665, Gemäldegalerie, Berlin, and *The Woman at the Window*, c. 1665, Kunsthistorisches Museum, Vienna, similarly focus on the anecdotal potential of a solitary figure.

Ostade's slightly comical depiction of an older man struggling to see, placing his glasses as far down his nose as possible, and craning toward the distant fine print, may be an allusion to the sense of sight. His painting *Sight*, The Hermitage, Saint Petersburg, one of a series representing his recurrent theme of the five senses, is evidence of his interest in the subject.[8] Moreover, he highlights the feature of eyeglasses in his watercolor of the *Spectacle Seller*, 1673, Boijmans Van Beuningen Museum, Rotterdam, by focusing on the narrative of an elderly woman sampling the *pince-nez* from a pedlar's box, a subject which he had treated earlier in his career in an etching from the late 1640s.[9] NTM

1 Except for the hat the costume is very close to that of the stock figure of the hurdy-gurdy player in Netherlandish art. See note 6 below.

2 For a description of his earlier technique, see the entry on the *Peasants Playing Cards*, also in the Weldon collection, cat. 35.

3 Smith 1829-1842, vol. 1, 1829, no. 169.

4 On the watercolors, which span the period of 1672-80 and number over fifty, see Schnackenburg 1981, nos. 217-73. For an introduction to the collecting of these works, see Broos in The Hague/San Francisco 1990-91, pp. 358-59.

5 *Burger*/citizen or commoner, *boer*/peasant or farmer.

6 *Hurdy-Gurdy Player Walking to the Left*, location unknown, illustrated and catalogued in Schnackenburg 1981, no. 112, and *Hurdy-Gurdy Player from the Front*, Rijksprentenkabinet, Amsterdam, illustrated and catalogued, ibid., no. 118. The hurdy-gurdy player type in seventeenth-century Dutch art tends to be dressed in this way. On conventions of depictions hurdy-gurdy players, see the entry on van de Venne's *Poverty Leads to Cunning* in this catalogue, no. 57.

7 Schnackenburg 1981, nos. 291-359.

8 Hofstede de Groot 1908-28, vol. 3, 1910, no. 15. Each panel of the series, nos. 14-19, which the author dates c. 1681, has notably small dimensions, c. 13 x 9 cm., which are comparable to the Weldon panel. Ostade painted other sense series. For all of the sense paintings in Hofstede de Groot, see nos. 6-27.

9 The watercolor is illustrated and catalogued in Schnackenburg 1981, no. 223. There is a preparatory drawing for it in a private collection, reproduced and discussed, no. 224. The earlier etching, of the same title, dated to c. 1646, is reproduced in Godefroy 1990, no. 29.

The theme of reading recurs in the artist's *oeuvre*. See Hofstede de Groot 1907-28, vol. 3, nos. 83-96b. On the subject of reading in Dutch seventeenth-century art, see Frankfurt 1993. NTM

36   Isack van Ostade

(Haarlem 1621 - Haarlem 1649)

Frozen Canal with Cottage, Bridge, and Horse-Drawn Sledge

c. 1645
oil on panel
37.1 x 33. cm.
Inscribed, bottom left: *Isack van Ostade*

PROVENANCE:
Possibly Godarts-Desmarets Collection; Lebeuf de Montgermont Collection, Paris; Dr. M. Wassermann, Paris; F. Kleinberger, Paris; A. de Ridder, Frankfurt-am-Main (by 1910); J. Goudstikker, Amsterdam (by 1932); Private collection.

EXHIBITIONS:
Amsterdam 1932, no. 69 (ill.); Delft 1952-53, no. 56; New Orleans 1997, no. 37 (ill.).

LITERATURE:
Hofstede de Groot 1908-27, vol. 3, 1910, no. 287; Bode 1913, p. 12; 45, pl. 45.

In this small winter scene Isack van Ostade excels both as a landscapist and as an observer of rural life. A rustic cottage and a timber bridge, occupied by two onlookers, dominate a narrow, icy canal which teems with activity. At the center a boy pushes a sledge laden with timber while three figures across from him appear to linger and converse around another sledge. A white horse labors up a ramp leading to the cottage, hauling a larger sledge, its driver and a keg. The ice leads out beneath the bridge to the horizon where distant skaters all but disappear. A cool winter sky, warmed by patches of sun, backlights the cottage, a barren tree, and the bridge.

This close-up, rustic portrayal of labor and leisure is characteristic of the type of winter landscape that was Isack's specialty. There are approximately two dozen extant examples.[1] True to the artist's training with his older brother Adriaen (1610-1685), a genre painter, Isack gives his figures prominence, often employing anecdote.[2] In the scale of his staffage and the low, close viewpoint, his winter landscapes differ from those of his predecessors Hendrik Averkamp (1585-1635), Esaias van de Velde (1587-1630), and Jan van Goyen (1596-1656).[3]

A comparison of Isack's canal view with that of Adriaen van de Venne's *Winter Pleasures* (no. 56), c. 1615, also in the present collection, demonstrates how the genre had evolved from the Flemish world landscape type of the early 1600s to a more typically Dutch topography by mid-century. Nonetheless, Isack's landscape retains some of the pictorial conventions of the older type such as the pattern of the tree branches against the sky and the distant horizon vista.

The dated winter landscapes in Isack's *oeuvre* span the years 1639-47,[4] a considerable period in the artist's lamentably short life which ended in 1649 at the age of 28. Many feature the subject of a halt before an inn, for which the artist usually employed a larger horizontal format. The Weldon painting is a more intimate variation on that theme. The building depicted may simply be a cottage rather than an inn, as the artist often identified the latter with a sign. While the motif of the white horse drawing a sledge is characteristic of many of the artist's winter paintings, the pose and cargo usually differ.

Of all the winter landscapes, the painter's *Winter Scene, with an Inn by a Frozen Stream*, National Gallery, London, appears to bear the strongest resemblance to the Weldon painting. Although slightly larger, it is also in a vertical panel format and it shows a similar general composition in reverse: a narrow canal, a white horse drawing a sledge, a tumble-down building with a bare tree behind and a bridge. Each of these elements is varied, however, and the staffage is also changed.[5] The right half of a larger horizontal panel, *A Frozen Canal with Skaters*, Musée du Louvre, Paris, features virtually the same composition as the Weldon painting, albeit with characteristic variations. The painting has recently been dated c. 1644-47.[6]

With regard to technique, the Weldon painting appears to be consistent with the later winter landscapes in which the artist employed a diverse palette with strong accents of local color and a meticulous touch.[7] Bode characterized the manner in the present panel as follows: "The color laid on with vigor and somewhat thickly, the tone warm, the colouring effective. From the excellent drawing we may conclude that it was painted during the artist's last and best period."[8] Indeed the paint surface is lively and fresh, especially in the cottage where rich brushstrokes describe the textures of snow, straw, vines, brick and timber. While the artist's boldness is visible in such passages, we may discern minor *pentimenti* in other more thinly painted areas, as in the hat of the figure to the right on the bridge, designating where the painter changed his mind.

It has been observed that none of the artist's many drawings appear to have functioned as studies for his landscapes. They have, however, been posited as "points of departure" for ideas worked up in his paintings.[9] The motif of a figure peering over a bridge spanning a canal, seen in one of Ostade's contemporaneous drawings, may well have been the inspiration for the engaging observers on the bridge in the present painting.[10] NTM

1 Sutton in New York 1995, p. 79. Hofstede de Groot 1907-28, vol. 3, 1910, listed over fifty winter landscapes.
2 For paintings by Adriaen van Ostade in the present collection, see cats. 34, 35.
3 Sutton in New York 1995, p. 79.
4 Ibid.
5 The painting is undated and it measures 48.4 x 40 cm., as described and illustrated in Brown/MacLaren 1992, no. 848. In Hofstede de Groot 1907-28, vol. 3, 1910, no. 262d, the description of *A River Scene in Winter*, panel, 36.8 x 34.3 cm., formerly collection of Jan Maul, Leiden, also closely parallels the present painting.
6 As illustrated, dated and described by Sutton in Amsterdam/ Boston/Philadelphia 1987-88, no. 63.

7   Ibid., in which the author states that the earlier paintings show the stronger influence of Jan van Goyen in their darker tonality and freer brushwork.

8   Bode 1913, p. 12.

9   Wheelock 1995, p. 192.

10   *Canal Landscape with Bridge*, c. 1644-49, Staatliche Museen Preußischer Kulturbesitz, Kupferstichkabinett, Berlin, as described, dated and illustrated in Schnackenburg 1981, no. 559, recto.

37 Cornelis van Poelenburgh
(Utrecht c. 1594/5 - Utrecht 1667)

*Italianate Landscape with Sleeping Venus and
Spying Satyrs*

c. 1640-50
oil on panel
23.8 x 34 cm.
Inscribed, below Venus's lower leg: *C.P.*

PROVENANCE:
Private collection.

EXHIBITION:
New Orleans 1997, no. 40 (ill.).

Cornelis van Poelenburgh excelled at depictions of female nudes cast in mythological roles and set in Italianate landscapes, a genre that was highly coveted by aristocratic patrons. On a rocky outcropping the naked figure of Venus reclines in sleep with her son, Cupid, before her and silken drapery at her head. Two satyrs observe her at close proximity from behind. The leafy backdrop to the scene gives way to a panoramic view with distant, misted mountains and a golden horizon. A bright blue, nearly cloudless sky completes the idyllic landscape.

As the popularity of landscape painting grew in the Dutch Republic during the seventeenth century, the genre of the Italianate scene with mythological figures became the most costly, and those by Poelenburgh fetched some of the highest prices.[1] They were collected by Prince Frederik Hendrik in The Hague,[2] by King Charles I in London, for whom Poelenburgh worked intermittently from 1637-41[3] and later c. 1640s-50s, and by his most fervent patron from his native Utrecht, Baron van Wyttenhorst, who owned twenty-three.[4] The combination of mythological subject matter and an Arcadian setting in paintings like the Weldon panel reflected the tastes of the classically educated, Italophile aristocracy of northern Europe.[5] Furthermore, the inevitably sunny landscapes held a particular appeal for the inhabitants of meaner climates.[6]

As Sluijter has noted, many of Poelenburgh's mythological paintings are scarcely narrative, and they feature an "abundance of nude females."[7] While the present panel does portray an episode from the story of Venus, it resembles Poelenburgh's numerous nymph paintings in which nude women are arrayed throughout idyllic landscapes for the viewer's delectation. Like Poelenburgh's "anonymous nymphs,"[8] the Venus in the Weldon painting, appears and appeals more for the sake of her naked self than any narrative role she might fulfill.

The motif of the voluptuous female nude observed by male onlookers, personified in this work by Venus and the satyrs, recurs in Poelenburgh's *oeuvre* in many depictions of the stories of Diana at her bath, and of Cimon and Iphigenia.[9] Sluijter has traced this type of imagery from the erotic Mannerist nudes of Hendrik Goltzius of the early 1600s to the mid-century representations of academic painters, stressing the primacy of the element of voyeuristic titillation over any possible moralizing intent on the part of the artist.[10] Indeed, in the present painting, the peacefully sleeping nudes bathed in sunshine and the rapt onlookers convey a note of delight rather than admonition.

While the theme of the nude in the Italianate landscape occurs in Poelenburgh's *oeuvre* as early as the mid-1620s, the present painting most closely resembles a later work, the *Cimon and Iphigenia*, dated c. 1640-1650.[11] The nude figure of Iphigenia is strikingly similar to the Venus of the Weldon painting. She is presented to the viewer sleeping on her side with slight variations in her pose. The details of the face, even the headband, are virtually identical, and although the Iphigenia is rendered on copper in a smaller scale than the Venus of the Weldon panel, the brushwork in both displays the same level of refinement. Further parallels with the Weldon panel are seen in the stony, forested backdrop to Iphigenia and in the position of her onlooker, who is depicted behind her on a lower plane, albeit at a greater distance. In

summation, the Iphigenia painting gives the appearance of a detail of the lower right quadrant of the present work, as if the artist had isolated the narrative and virtually eliminated the landscape.[12] Although the subject of Venus occurs in at least two paintings and one drawing by Poelenburgh, none of these represents the same narrative, nor do they feature motifs similar to those of the Weldon painting.[13]

The distant view of faraway mountains shown to the left of the figures is reminiscent of aspects of Poelenburgh's early Italian landscapes, and it probably derives from the style of Adam Elsheimer (d. 1610).[14] However, in the Weldon painting the vista has expanded, and the landscape itself has taken on a more important role. In this regard it contrasts with Poelenburgh's "Forum pieces," painted in the early 1620s when he lived in Rome, as represented in the present collection by his *Peasants Before Roman Ruins* and *Bakery in the Cave of Erigeria* (nos. 38, 39).[15] The bakery painting in particular displays the flat topography and relatively close-up view associated with many of the ruin pictures. Both paintings also feature the brilliant light and high contrasts of Poelenburgh's early period. The softer, golden atmosphere of the Venus panel places it in a later moment in the development of Italianate landscape painting, and its esthetic influenced the succeeding generation of landscapists, most notably Jan Both (no. 6) with whom Poelenburgh collaborated.[16] NTM

1 Chong, "The Market for Landscape Painting in Seventeenth-Century Holland," pp. 116, table 2 and 117, table 3, in Amsterdam/Boston/Philadelphia 1987-88, pp. 104-120.

2 Ibid., pp. 105, 119, note 11, where the author indicates that eleven paintings by the artist hung in the Noordeinde Palace by 1632, two of which were landscapes.

3 On some of the landscapes by Poelenburgh in the collection of Charles I, as well as those belonging to later British royal patrons of the artist, see White 1982, p. 92. See also his introductory essay in the same catalogue, xi-lxxii, for the royal patronage of Poelenburgh.

4 Chong in Amsterdam/Boston/Philadelphia 1987-88, p. 110, where the author states that the Baron also owned a number of portraits and religious paintings by Poelenburgh in a significant collection, which encompassed the work of many artists, especially Italianate landscapists. On the van Wyttenhorst inventory, see de Jonge 1932. For a detailed description of van Wyttenhorst's Poelenburghs, his collwction in general and Utrecht patronage, see B.O. Meierink and A. Bakker. "The Utrecht Elite as Patrons and Collectors," in San Francisco/Baltimore/London 1997-98, pp. 72-85.

5 Montias 1991, p. 335. On the similar patronage of the related landscape genre of the pastoral, see McNeil Kettering 1983, pp. 16-17, 123. For the style, subject matter, and patronage of Poelenburgh's arcadian paintings done in Utrecht, see recently Spicer in San Francisco/Baltimore/London 1997-98, pp. 40-1, nos. 54-55.

6 Ibid., p. 18, where the author describes the "painted pastoral garden" as a *Lusthof*.

7 Sluijter 1986, p. 578.

8 This expression is used by Sutton in Amsterdam/Boston/Philadelphia 1987-88, p. 31.

9 On the Diana paintings, see Sluijter-Seijfert 1984, pp. 134 ff., and nos. 9-13, and for the theme of Cimon and Iphigenia, see pp. 97-98 and nos. 35-39.

10 On Goltzius's *Venus and Adonis*, 1614, Rijksmuseum, Amsterdam, his *Jupiter and Antiope*, 1612, Rijksdienst Beeldende Kunsten, The Hague, and other similar paintings, see Sluijter 1986, pp. 41-42. On the voyeuristic eroticism of the academic painters, ibid., p. 159, and p. 280, on the lack of moralizing content in representations of *Cimon and Iphigenia*. On the erotic content in the pastoral genre, see also Sluijter's article in Utrecht 1993, pp. 33-57.

11 For an early example, see *Nymphs and Satyrs in a Hilly Landscape*, 1624[7?], Collection of Queen Elizabeth II (illustrated and discussed in White 1982, no. 142). The *Cimon and Iphigenia*

painting is in the Musée d'Art et d'Histoire, Geneva, and it is illustrated and discussed in Basel 1987, no. 72. It is painted on copper and measures 13.5 x 17.5 cm.

12 An analogous depiction of a nude and a similar composition are seen in the painting of *Jupiter and Antiope* by Poelenburgh's student François Verwilt (c. 1620-1691), Dulwich Picture Gallery, London.

13 The paintings are both representations of the theme of *Sine Cerere et Baccho Friget Venus* (Venus is Ice without Ceres and Bacchus). One dates to the 1630s, Gemäldegalerie der Akademie der Bildenden Künste, Vienna (illustrated and discussed in Vienna 1982, pp. 17-19). The second painting is at the Musée des Beaux-Arts, Lille. They are catalogued in Sluijter-Seijfert 1984 as nos. 7 and 8. See also her discussion of the Venus theme on p. 133. The drawing is of a standing *Venus and Cupid*, Rijksmuseum, Amsterdam, as discussed and illustrated in Chong 1987, no. 73. Jan Gerritsz van Bronkhorst (c. 1600-1661) made an etching dated 1636 after Poelenburgh's drawing. It is illustrated in Bartsch 1978- , vol. 5, 1979, p. 76. There is a second print by Bronkhorst which is closer to the Weldon painting. It is the *Nymph Asleep in a Grotto*, ibid., p. 77, based on a lost drawing by Poelenburgh, showing a nude sleeping Venus set in a grotto and observed by a satyr.

14 As discussed by Sutton in Amsterdam/Boston/Philadelphia 1987-88, p. 407, regarding Poelenburgh's *Flight into Egypt*, 1615, Centraal Museum, Utrecht, which he associates with Elsheimer's *Aurora*, Herzog Anton Ulrich-Museum, Braunschweig. Another artist who is frequently cited as an influence during Poelenburgh's Roman period is Paul Bril (1554-1626).

15 While the site of the bakery painting may be identified as the cave of Erigeria, from a drawing attributed to Poelenburgh which is dated c. 1624 , in Roethlisberger 1969, no. 5, the setting of the second painting is not specific. There are no extant dated paintings by the artist beyond the year 1625, an occurrence which Sluijter-Seijfert 1984, p. 283, describes as prohibitive to the establishment of a chronology for the work of the later period, c. 1625-1667.

16 On a number of occasions, Poelenburgh painted staffage for Both, his younger Utrecht colleague. He also painted Both's portrait, c. 1648, *Portrait of Jan Both*, Freiherr von Fürstenberg Collection, Herdringen (illustrated in Amsterdam/Boston/Philadelphia 1987-88, p. 276).

(detail)

38 Cornelis van Poelenburgh

(Utrecht c. 1594/5 - Utrecht 1667)

Peasants Before Roman Ruins

c. 1620-25
oil on copper
16 x 18 cm.

PROVENANCE:
Nijstad Antiquairs N. V., The Hague; Private collection.

EXHIBITIONS:
Delft 1963; London 1963, no. 15; Providence 1964, no. 19 (ill.); New York 1966,
no. 32; New Orleans 1997, no. 38 (ill.).

Please refer to entry no. 37 for a brief discussion of this painting.

39   Cornelis van Poelenburgh
(Utrecht c. 1594/5 - Utrecht 1667)

Bakery in the Cave of Erigeria

c. 1624
oil on copper
13.5 x 16.5 cm.

PROVENANCE:
Private collection.

EXHIBITIONS:
Providence 1964, no. 18 (ill.); New York 1966, no. 31; Birmingham 1995, no. 15
(ill.); New Orleans 1997, no. 39 (ill.).

Please refer to entry no. 37 for a brief discussion of this painting.

40 Frans Post
(Leiden c. 1612 - Haarlem 1680)

Brazilian Landscape with Laborers, an Armadillo and an Anteater

c. 1665
oil on panel
35.4 x 41.2 cm.
Inscribed, bottom, left of center: *F. POST.*

PROVENANCE:
Privatgesellschaft patriotischer Kunstfreunde, Prague (1815); National Gallery, Prague (1948-after 1961); Private collection.

EXHIBITIONS:
New Brunswick 1983, no. 101 (ill.); Basel/Tübingen 1990, p. 76 and ill. opposite; Zurich 1990, no. 2 (ill.); Birmingham 1995, no. 16 (ill.); New Orleans 1997, no. 41 (ill.).

LITERATURE:
Prague 1835, no. 558; Prague 1889, no. 558; Smith 1938, no. 42; Guimarães 1957, no. 221 (ill.); Síp 1961, no. 54 (ill.); Larsen 1962, no. 69; De Sousa-Leão 1973, no. 94 (ill.).

Frans Post made the Brazilian landscape his specialty in images much like this which juxtapose minutely observed *flora* and *fauna* with an idealized setting. He typically incorporated ruins and plantation buildings in a vision of the local topography adapted to the conventions of his native Haarlem school of landscape painting. A distant view of water, jungle, and mountains is bracketed by banks of lush vegetation which in turn shelter a group of workers at foreground right, and opposite them, an armadillo and an anteater. In a brightly lit clearing beyond, additional figures are placed near a hut. Other small buildings appear at a greater distance, and ruins are scattered from the leafy bank at the right through to the far trees at the left. While the foreground is relatively dark, the landscape is well lit and the windless blue sky is filled with serene white clouds.

In 1637 when Governor-General Johan Maurits of Nassau-Siegen embarked on his mission to the territory of Brazil, newly won by the Dutch from the Portuguese, he was accompanied by a team of scientists and artists. Frans Post was among them and for the duration of Maurits' expedition, which lasted until 1644, he recorded the sights of Brazil in drawings and paintings.[1] Although there are only about ten extant paintings which have been identified with Post's Brazilian residency,[2] virtually all of the surviving works from his subsequent Dutch period are based on the rich experiences of his Brazilian sojourn. Approximately 130 paintings are attributed to his Haarlem years (1644-1680), of which about half are dated from 1647 through to 1669.[3] While these paintings all exhibit Post's highly individual style, they are variations on recurrent themes. De Sousa-Leão has aptly described the artist's method:

To avoid repetition Post scrambled his subjects like a jigsaw puzzle, dismantling and regrouping buildings and churches... rearranging animals, trees, prospects of mountains and water, and bringing in as many human, zoological, and botanical novelties as possible.[4]

The Weldon panel probably dates from the final years of the artist's Haarlem activity, his most prolific phase, described as his "culminating" period.[5] The marked blue hue of the horizon and the stratification of the landscape into three color zones, recalling the earlier Flemish tradition, are characteristic of his paintings of 1665-69.[6] The devices of the elaborate screen of foliage against the sky, as defined by the palm tree and bushes to the right of the present painting, and the leafy repoussoirs occur most frequently in the paintings of the 1660s.[7] The foliage in these works has been associated with the influence of the Haarlem artist Cornelis Vroom (c. 1591-1661).[8]

After Post left Brazil he seems to have abandoned precise topographical views in favor of imagined scenes which exhibit more conventions of the Dutch landscape tradition.[9] Nonetheless, he retained the specificity of detail from his early paintings, using it to great effect to animate and lend realism to his composite views. De Sousa-Leão has described the botanical elements of his Brazil period paintings as having been "rendered with the precision of an herbal."[10] This approach is in keeping with the scientific nature of Johan Maurits' interest in Brazil and the endeavors of his team of researchers and recorders. Post's sustained interest in depicting the specific *flora* and *fauna* of Brazil is evident in the Weldon painting, exemplified notably by the exotic armadil-

lo and anteater in the lower left quadrant.[11] In a Dutch report from Brazil dated 1640, the chronicler van der Dussen offered definitions of these seemingly fantastic creatures, likening aspects of their strange physiologies to familiar beasts: "the tatu (armadillos), are of the size of a young pig...their skin is covered in scales...they lift their heads from their armor like turtles...their meat is delicious; the tamandua (anteaters) have bodies like sheep, a long and thin muzzle and large flat feet."[12] The armadillo was the most commonly collected quadruped in seventeenth-century curiosity cabinets, probably because of its preternatural appearance.[13]

Although many of Post's paintings include Brazilian creatures, his primary role on the expedition of Johan Maurits seems to have been as a topographic artist. However, the work of Post's colleague Albert Eckhout (c. 1607-1665) suggests that he was employed specifically to record the native population and the *flora* and *fauna* of Brazil. In particular, Eckhout produced a collection of nearly 1,500 folios, oil sketches, watercolors and drawings, mostly of plants and animals, known as the *Theatrum rerum naturalium Brasiliae*.[14] Among Eckhout's illustrations, there is a drawing of an anteater which was probably rendered from life, possibly at Johan Maurits' menagerie at Recife.[15] Eckhout's anteater is very close to its cousin in the present painting. While it cannot be conclusively identified as the model, Joppien has posited that Post might have used Eckhout's sketches for his paintings citing specifically the similarities between the artists' depictions of anteaters and armadillos.[16]

After Johan Maurits returned to The Hague, he continued to patronize Post, and the artist's Brazilian scenes were also acquired by the Stadholder Frederik Hendrik who exhibited them in his palaces.[17] Post's paintings fetched good prices,[18] and merchant-class Dutch collectors with imperialist interests such as sea captains and investors in Brazil have been proposed as his audience.[19] In addition to providing sunny, exotic vistas, Post's serene and lush landscapes of the Dutch territory surely evoked the Dutch Republic's political might and economic hegemony. NTM

1 Joppien 1979, pp. 297-376.
2 Ibid., p. 299, note 11. While six of the paintings are listed by de Sousa-Leão 1973, nos. 1-6, two other paintings which date from the Brazil years, Smith 1938, nos. 6 and 10, are not included in de Sousa-Leão's catalogue raisonné. Two more paintings recently appeared on the art market.
3 De Sousa-Leão 1973, pp. 18, 32. Although Post lived until 1680, his latest extant dated painting is from 1669, *Varzea Landscape*, Kunstmuseum, Düsseldorf. De Sousa-Leão, pp. 28, 32, cites a letter of Jacob Cohen, financial agent of Johan Maurits, written in 1679, where the artist is described as having become shaky and fallen to drinking, as an explanation for the absence of paintings from the last decade of the artist's life.
4 Ibid., p. 28.
5 Ibid. Larsen 1962, no. 69, dated the Weldon painting "after 1660." A securely dated painting which closely resembles the Weldon panel is the *Rural Landscape*, 1664, panel, 34.2 x 41 cm., John and Mable Ringling Museum, Sarasota, de Sousa-Leão 1973, no. 40.
6 Ibid., p. 28.
7 On these motifs, see Sutton's entry on Post's *Brazilian Landscape with Native Figures*, 1666, H. Samuel Collection, London, in London 1992, no. 55. This painting, which is dated, shares many characteristics with the Weldon panel.
8 Ibid. In addition, see Chong in Amsterdam/Boston/Philadelphia 1987-88, p. 412, where he also discusses the influence of Pieter Post's (1608-1669) work on his brother Frans. Furthermore, he corrects the misconception that Post was specifically influenced by the Haarlem school of panoramic painters, except in the most "general of terms." Chong favors the "sharper, crisper pictorialism" of Pieter Post and Vroom as having influenced Frans.

9 Ibid., p. 414, where Chong describes the Dutch conventions of the use of repoussoirs, the distancing of figures and the framing devices.
10 De Sousa-Leão 1973, p. 23.
11 These species recur in his composite Brazilian views.
12 Van der Dussen 1640, as excerpted and translated into French in Larsen 1962, p. 279 (English translation by present author).
13 Ashworth in Hanover/Raleigh/Houston/Atlanta 1991-93, p. 121.
14 On the history of this collection of works on paper, see Joppien 1979, pp. 311-317. The works were lost, from the Second World War until the 1970s, when they were rediscovered at the Jagiellonian Library, Cracow. Although the works are known through photographs, they were unavailable for study when Joppien published his article in 1979.
15 Ibid., p. 313. The drawing is on folio 95 of volume 3. A photograph of it from the collection of the Deutsche Staatsbibliothek is reproduced in van den Boogaart 1979, p. 465.
16 Joppien 1979, p. 337. However, he states that he cannot be definitive about this question without having studied the original works from the *Theatrum* (see note 14 above). This matter is further complicated by the fact that the *Theatrum* would not have been readily available to Post after Johan Maurits sold it to the Elector of Brandenburg in 1652. This does not preclude the possibility that Post might have made copies from it before it left the collection of Johan Maurits.
17 Joppien 1979, p. 336.
18 Chong in Amsterdam/Boston/Philadelphia 1987-88, pp. 116, 118.
19 Joppien 1979, p. 336.

41   **Adam Pynacker**
(Schiedam 1620 - Amsterdam 1673)

The Annunciation to the Shepherds

c. 1670
oil on panel
19 x 23 cm.
Inscribed, middle ground right, along horizontal board of stable:
APynacke [r]   [first two initials in monogram ligature]
bottom right: *APynacke[r]* [probably spurious]
[first two initials in monogram ligature]

PROVENANCE:
Probably J. van der Marck, Amsterdam (Sale, H. de Winter, Amsterdam, August 25, 1773, no. 252, for fl. 62, to Hellein); R. Geeland, Antwerp (until 1888); E. Huybrechts, Antwerp (Sale, M. E. Le Roy, Antwerp, May 12-15, 1902, no. 119, for frs. 90, to Maes); Maes Collection, Lucerne; Speyr-Jselin Collection, Basel; Private collection.

EXHIBITIONS:
Zurich, David Koetser Gallery, 1995; Washington, National Gallery of Art, Dutch Cabinet Galleries, temporary loan, April 1-September 15, 1996; New Orleans 1997, no. 42 (ill.).

LITERATURE:
Hofstede de Groot 1907-1928, vol. 9, 1926, no. 3; Harwood 1988, no. D2 (unseen, as a lost painting, known from sales catalogues).

In this small painting, Pynacker presents the full drama and mystery of the story of the Annunciation to the shepherds. The bright, celestial light rending the darkness of night conveys the divine message to the figures who shield themselves and cower below: "and the Glory of the Lord shone round about them, and they were sore afraid."[1] Even the white goat and the standing cow in the foreground appear to be agitated. Opposite them in the lower right corner, a dark, tumble-down stable provides a foil to the brilliance of the sky. A black, barren tree, which diagonally bisects the painting, further strengthens the impact of the light behind it, and its twisted form echoes the turbulence of the moment.

The narrative of the Annunciation to the shepherds was taken up by Dutch artists and its iconography widely disseminated in prints. The treatment of the story by Abraham Bloemaert (1566-1651), as reproduced in an engraving by Jan Saenredam (1565-1607) of 1599, features elements which were common to subsequent representations, including Pynacker's painting: a shelter repoussoir, prominent livestock, and a turbulent sky.[2] Rembrandt's (1606-1669) conception of the story as represented in his etching of 1634, *The Angel Appearing to the Shepherds*, enhances the drama of the moment, focusing on the scattering shepherds and their livestock and strengthening the effect of chiaroscuro. While the print could not be construed as a direct precedent for the present painting, aspects of Rembrandt's rendering were a legacy to succeeding artists,[3] notably the marked contrast of divine light and the surrounding darkness, and the stunning impact of the apparition on the shepherds and their beasts.

Depictions of the narrative are rare in Pynacker's *oeuvre*. There is only one other extant painting which may be attributable to Pynacker that also represents the subject, *The Annunciation to the Shepherds*, Fine Arts Museums of San Francisco (fig. 1). In Harwood's catalogue raisonné of the artist's *oeuvre*, she has categorized it as an unresolved work.[4] While there are two published inventory records of paintings by Pynacker describing three works as *Kersnacht* or *Christmas Night*, possibly referring to the subject of the Annunciation to the shepherds, they date from the years 1652-54, a period in

Pynacker's *oeuvre* which predates the relatively broad technique of both the present painting and the San Francisco panel.[5]

The Weldon painting does indeed resemble the San Francisco *Annunciation*, the chief differences being that it omits the feature of the heralding angel, and it is about half the size.[6] However, it appears that the Weldon panel has been cut down from its original format, and formerly may have included the angel.[7] Prior to its probable reduction, the composition would have extended further into the sky above and along the left margin.

While Harwood has expressed doubt about the broad handling of the San Francisco painting, a technique which the Weldon panel seems to share, she has noted a loosening in the brushstrokes in a number of works which she associates with the artist's late years, c. 1670. She describes the artist's return to cabinet-sized pictures from his larger format of the 1660s, accompanied by a "more impressionistic representation of nature caught in some passages by sharp, spiky brushstrokes."[8] This approach may be seen in the artist's *Landscape with Trees*, c. 1670, private collection, and it recalls a loose technique which he occasionally employed during the 1650s.[9] The broad appearance of the paint application in the Weldon painting should further be considered as a consequence of its reduction in size. In its original larger format, the scale of brushstroke to surface would certainly have been perceived differently.[10]

A characteristic that Harwood has noted in the works dated from 1670-73, which corresponds to the freer technique and which may also be discerned in the present painting, is the relative decline in the depiction of minute details, in comparison to the works of the 1660s where the artist featured near-microscopic representations of foreground foliage and bark.[11] The Weldon painting does include vegetation at foreground right which is consistent with this simplifying tendency.[12]

The element of light is crucial to the success of the narrative in this painting and its rendering also may be placed within the context of the artist's *oeuvre*. While the San Francisco painting is the only point of reference for another nocturnal scene, the high contrast and drama of the illumination of the Weldon panel is characteristic of Pynacker. Skies with marked contrasts and brilliantly lit clouds appear in a number of paintings with increasing frequency during the late 1660s.[13] In the Weldon painting the overwhelming impact of the light is combined with the refined description of the shafts penetrating the darkness and the finely crafted highlights, like the tiny speck which glimmers off the cow's left horn.[14]

The depiction of the two principal animals in the Weldon painting is also typical of Pynacker.[15] The shaggy white goat is familiar from the artist's paintings of about 1665, and the standing cow is a close variation on the bulls in works from the same period.[16]

It is likely that this small panel was owned by Johan van der Marck (1695-1770) during the eighteenth century. Along with six other works attributed to Pynacker, it was probably included in the sale of van der Marck's celebrated collection in 1773 which numbered nearly five hundred paintings. Van der Marck was an honored citizen as well as an esteemed collector. He was burgomaster of Leiden at least four times, and he was also a governor of the West Indies company in Amsterdam.[17] NTM

1 Excerpted from Luke 2: 8-10.

2 The print is catalogued and reproduced in Roethlisberger/Bok 1993, no. 51.

3 The print is reproduced and catalogued by Welzel in Berlin/Amsterdam/London 1991-92A, no. 9, where the author discusses its precedents, including the Saenredam engraving after Bloemaert, as well as its impact on later representations. Examples of paintings are by Govaert Flinck (1615-1660), Musée du Louvre, Paris; Nicolaes Berchem (1620-1683), Musée du Louvre, Paris; Adriaen van Ostade (1610-1685), Herzog Anton Ulrich-Museum, Braunschweig.

4 Harwood 1988, no. B6, oil on panel, 38.5 x 48.2 cm. While the author recognizes elements of the painting as characteristic of Pynacker's work around 1665, i.e. the rough fencing, the broken branches, and the long-haired white goat, she dissociates the broad, impressionistic technique from Pynacker's style. Harwood does not accept the proposed attribution to Abraham Hondius (1625-1695) for this painting, given in Berkeley 1966, no. 52.14, which indeed seems unlikely.

5 On the inventories, see Harwood 1988, p. 17, and notes 25- 27, and p. 188. In her entry for the San Francisco painting, B6, note 1, Harwood notes that the apparent style of the 1660s precludes an identification with the inventory entries from the early 1650s.

6 For the size of the San Francisco painting, see note 4 above. Harwood knows the Weldon panel in reproduction only, and she has noted the resemblance of the two Annunciation paintings in her letter, November 4, 1996 (followed by a conversation, January 5, 1997), in which she described them as "unresolved works". (In her catalogue raisonné, she includes the Weldon painting as a lost work, see "Literature" above). While Harwood states that she is "very much handicapped by not seeing the painting itself," she questions elements of the style and

composition, i.e., the intensity of the light in a nocturnal scene, for which she regrets there is no secure point of comparison in the artist's *oeuvre*. I would like to thank Dr. Harwood for offering her assistance and her opinion. While she reserves final judgment on the present painting until she has seen it, E. Haverkamp-Begemann accepts the attribution to Pynacker and A. Wheelock exhibited the painting under the artist's name at the National Gallery of Art, Washington (see "Exhibitions" above). The painting also bears a signature on the horizontal log of the stable, to the right of the center, which is previously unrecorded (see "Signature" above), and which corresponds to the facsimile version of the artist's signature in Harwood 1988, p. 177, shown at the top of the first column. This signature, unlike the previously noted one at bottom right, is very fine, and it seems doubtful that a forger would make a signature as small and inconspicuous as this if he were trying to identify the painting with the artist's name.

7 A. Wheelock, in a letter, July 31, 1996, first noted the absence of beveling on two margins of the reverse of the panel. The cuts in the panel correspond to the left side and top of the painting as we now know it. The cuts occurred prior to the sale of 1773, since the dimensions given in the catalogue (see "Provenance" above) correspond to the present ones.

8 In Williamstown/Sarasota 1994-95, pp. 36, 68.

9 Illustrated and discussed in Harwood 1988, no. 95.

10 This observation was made by E. Haverkamp-Begemann in conversation, January 10, 1997.

11 Williamstown/Sarasota 1994-95, pp. 36, 66. On the relative lack of detail, see, for example, Pynacker's *An Italianate Mountainous and Wooded Landscape*, private collection, no. 66, in that exhibition.

12 However, it should be noted that although this feature is far less detailed than the vegetation seen in his larger, earlier paintings, its appearance has probably been altered as the greens have darkened over time and sunk into the background.

13 Harwood 1988, nos. 19, 47, 73, 75, 83. 84. For an outstanding example, see *Landscape with Thunderclouds*, c. 1665, Brussels, Musée Communal; Harwood 1988, no. 73.

14 Harwood drew my attention to this detail (in conversation, January 5, 1997). While she expressed reservations about Pynacker's authorship of the present work (see note 6 above) pending a viewing of the painting which she knows only in reproduction, she described such details as characteristic of the artist.

15 This was confirmed by Harwood (in conversation, January 5, 1997).

16 For an example of this type of goat, see *Landscape in the Apennines*, c. 1665, Rijksmuseum, Amsterdam; Harwood 1988, no. 76. For the bull paintings, featuring an animal that is close to the cow in the Weldon panel, see *Boatmen Moored on the Shore of an Italian Lake*, c. 1665, Rijksmuseum, Amsterdam and *Landscape with Enraged Ox*, c. 1665, collection of S. P. Steinberg, New York; Harwood 1988, nos.74, 75.

17 The entry for the painting which seems to describe the Weldon *Annunciation* appears in the van der Marck sales catalogue as no. 252 "De boodschap der Engelen aan de Herders, op Paneel, h. 7 1/2 b. 9 duim." The above information on van der Marck and his collection was taken from the sales catalogue (see Provenance above) and The Hague/San Francisco 1990-91, p. 199.

Fig. 1 Adam Pynacker, attributed to *The Annunciation to the Shepherds*, c. 1670 Fine Arts Museums of San Francisco, Gift of Mr. and Mrs. Robert Neuhaus, in memory of Louise Anne Neuhaus, 52.14

42 Peter Paul Rubens
(Siegen 1577 - Antwerp 1640)

Jan Brueghel the Younger
(Antwerp 1601 - Antwerp 1678)

Landscape with Pan and Syrinx

c. 1625-30
oil on panel
58 x 94 cm.

The back of the panel bears the mark of the Antwerp panel maker Michiel Vriendt.[1]

PROVENANCE:
Counts Schönborn, Schloss Weissenstein, Pommersfelden (Sale, Hôtel Drouot, Paris, A.M. Le Comte de Schönborn, May 17-18, 1867, no. 210, for frs. 7000); Salomon Goldschmidt (Sale, Georges Petit, Paris, M.G..., March 14-17, 1898, no. 95 (ill.), to Max for frs. 9,200); Baron Rothschild, Vienna; Kunstsalon Franke, Leipzig, 1933; Rosenberg & Stiebel, New York (c. 1960); B. Jenks, Astbury Hall, Shropshire; Edward Speelman, London (1979-80); British Rail Pension Fund Collection (Sale, Sotheby's, London, July 5, 1995, no. 42, ill.).

EXHIBITIONS:
London 1984, no. 3 (ill.); London, National Gallery, loan, 1980-88; Leeds Castle, loan, 1988-1995; Boston/Toledo 1993-94, no. 17 (ill.); New Orleans 1997, no. 43 (ill., as by Rubens and Jan Brueghel the Younger, attributed to).

LITERATURE:
Possibly, Campori 1870, p. 191 (approximate description in inventory of C. and F. Muselli Collection, Verona, 1622, as by Rubens and "Breughel" [sic]); Possibly, Denucé 1934, p. 142 (approximate description in ongoing estate sale of Jan Brueghel the Elder, 1626-27, as by Rubens and the Elder), p. 147 (approximate description in journal of Jan Brueghel the Younger, as by Rubens and the Younger);2 Pigler 1956, vol. 2, p. 191 (as by Rubens and Jan Brueghel the Elder); Jaffé 1967, p. 100, note 16, fig. 5 (as by Rubens and Jan Brueghel the Elder); Müller Hofstede 1968, p. 231 (as by Rubens and suggesting a co-attribution to Jan Brueghel the Younger); Jaffé 1977, pp. 23, 106, note 50 (as by Rubens and Jan Brueghel the Elder); Ertz 1979, pp. 417, 420, 622-23, no. 384a (ill.) (as by Rubens and Jan Brueghel the Elder); *Burlington Magazine* 122 (September, 1980) p. 664, fig. 63 (as by Rubens and "Jan Brueghel"); Ertz 1984, pp. 70, 81, 417-18, no. 256 (ill.) (as by Rubens and Jan Brueghel the Younger); Jaffé 1989, no. 442 (ill.) (as by Rubens and Jan Brueghel the Elder); Boston/Toledo 1993-94, pp. 35, 221 and no. 17 (ill.) (as by Rubens and Jan Brueghel the Elder); Balis 1994, p. 53, no. 17 (as by Rubens and Jan Brueghel the Younger).

The half-naked figure of Syrinx flees from the pursuing Pan, who embraces a bundle of reeds in her stead. The tumult of the figures is contrasted with the peaceful and lushly abundant riverscape enveloping them. The bank is bordered by sheltering reeds and rushes and decorated by a variety of brightly colored, finely delineated flowers: yellow and blue irises, forget-me-nots, lilies, and aquatic specimens. The plenitude and refinement of the botanical elements is matched by the numerous water fowl animating the river which meanders into a distant pastoral landscape.

The story of Pan and Syrinx is taken from Ovid's *Metamorphoses*, a classical source whose popularity in artistic circles in the Netherlands is underscored by the analysis of the work by the theorist and painter Karel van Mander (1548-1606) in his Schilder-boeck of 1604, and the profusion of copiously illustrated translations.[3] Representations of Ovidian themes proliferated in northern painting during the ensuing century. The present painting tells the tale of Pan's pursuit of the nymph Syrinx, a particularly popular narrative among Netherlandish artists.[4] The chosen moment shows the satyr-like figure of Pan, with shaggy goat-legs and pointed ears, as he grasps the reeds and Syrinx seemingly escapes him. In Ovid's telling, however, Syrinx elects to become the reeds themselves rather than succumb to Pan. He, in turn, entranced by the song of the wind as it rushes through the reeds, cuts and waxes them together, making a pipe which he names after Syrinx, and through which he figuratively keeps her: "You and I shall stay in unison."[5] In this representation Rubens, who is responsible for the figural elements in the painting, has actually conflated two phases of the

narrative thereby creating a simultaneous image. Pan is shown grasping the reeds that Syrinx has become, while she is depicted just prior to the moment of her metamorphosis.

The subject was variously treated by Rubens throughout his career. There is a drawing attributed to him, *Pan and Syrinx*, c. 1615, British Museum, London, which is after a presumably lost work by Raphael engraved by Marcantonio Raimondi in which Syrinx is shown seated, combing her long locks as a lustful Pan observes from behind a bush.[6] A painting which probably dates from the period of the Weldon panel, attributed to Rubens and workshop and Jan Brueghel the Younger, *Pan and Syrinx*, present location unknown, depicts the same narrative as the present work with simultaneous episodes, albeit with larger, stiller figures in a diminished landscape.[7] Rubens returned to the subject in at least two instances during the following decade. In his *Pan and Syrinx*, Collection of Queen Elizabeth II, Buckingham Palace, a collaborative effort dated to the 1630s, with the landscape attributed to Jan Wildens (1585/6-1653), the figures of the fleeing nymph and her pursuer are larger than those in the Weldon painting and their direction is reversed, yet the narrative moment is the same.[8] Finally, in 1636 Rubens painted an oil sketch of *Pan and Syrinx*, Bayonne, Musée Bonnat, for a larger version, now lost, showing a similar view of the protagonists. However, the story has changed. Syrinx sprouts shoots from her fingertips: her transformation has begun.[9] While the present painting features reeds, which very nearly spring from the fingers of Syrinx's left hand and possibly allude to her metamorphosis, the vegetal and human forms are not quite merged as in the sketch.

Rubens' figures from the Pan and Syrinx compositions resemble his work from the large-scale mythological paintings of the 1620s and 1630s. The figure of the Weldon Syrinx is similar to the nude Hilaeira from *The Rape of the Daughters of Leucippus*, Alte Pinakothek, Munich, c. 1620, whose upper torso with outstretched arms and turned head seems to anticipate the pose and manner of the present nymph. In the Weldon panel as in other collaborative works in which Rubens' figures are smaller than in his independent compositions, his characteristically broad and vigorous brushwork has been modified somewhat to suit the smaller format. Nonetheless, his seemingly rapid technique contrasts with the meticulously described surroundings and still-life-like details of his probable collaborator, Jan Brueghel the Younger.

While the landscape element of the painting has been attributed to Jan Brueghel the Elder — and it was certainly painted in his manner — it is likely the work of his son and follower Jan Brueghel the Younger. In Ertz's catalogue of the father's *oeuvre*, he initially published the painting as a collaboration between the Elder and Rubens, dated c. 1623. However, as Ertz noted, he only knew the painting in reproduction at the time.[10] Ertz has subsequently catalogued the painting in his book on Jan Brueghel the Younger as the work of the son and Rubens, dating it to the end of the 1620s and likening its background to the landscape elements in the Pan and Syrinx, present location unknown, which he attributed to the same artists.[11] While Sutton reverted to the attribution to the Elder when the painting was exhibited in 1993-94, his entry on the work addressed neither the related debate nor issues of technique, focusing rather on inventory evidence.[12] Balis' review of the exhibition noted Sutton's return of the landscape to the hand of the father and he re-ascribed it the son. Most recently, the painting was sold at auction under the name of Rubens and Jan Brueghel the Younger.[13]

Unfortunately, although inventory evidence from the estate of the Elder Brueghel and the daybook of his son offers citations of Pan and Syrinx paintings, no conclusions can be drawn regarding the attribution of the present work. When the father died in 1625, his son Jan took over his estate and his workshop, selling his paintings and finishing and disposing of

works that had been left incomplete.[14] A *Pan and Syrinx*, described as the work of Rubens and Jan the Elder, appears in the records of the estate sale of 1626-27 and another work of the same subject is recorded in the son's production list for the year 1626 as a collaboration between Rubens and himself.[15] It is conceivable that the present work may have been begun as an effort of Rubens and the father and that it was completed by the son.

The flowers and birds in the immediate foreground of the Weldon painting exhibit the refinement of technique that one might associate with Brueghel the Elder. Indeed, the son's particular expertise at painting flowers, to the point of being nearly indistinguishable from those of his father, is illustrated in many of his still-life paintings which are copies or variations on the work of the Elder. However, the foliage of the tree at foreground right and the distant landscape are more generalized than comparable features in paintings that are securely attributed to the father. The vista of the river leading into the landscape and its accompanying flora and fauna in fact closely resemble a similar, though reversed, view in Jan the Younger's *Duck Hunters*, private collection.[16]

The fact that the son followed his father's work and successfully approximated his style tends to confuse the issue of attribution. In paintings in which the Younger is known to have imitated his father's famous example, such as his *Entry into Noah's Ark*, Prado, Madrid, which is a copy of the painting of the same subject by Jan the Elder, 1613, J. Paul Getty Museum, Malibu, the difference is apparent.[17] While the son recreates the image, his rendering is slightly harder than his father's. An understanding of Brueghel workshop practices is further complicated by the issue of autograph copies. As was his frequent practice, Jan the Younger apparently made a close variant of the present painting in which the figures, attributed by Ertz to Rubens and studio, are nearly identical to those of the Weldon painting, and the landscape view is reversed.[18]

Jan the Younger most probably painted the Weldon panel shortly after his father's death in 1625 when he was successfully filling a demand for work in his famous manner and the output was of the highest quality. NTM

1   As cited in the entry for the painting in the sales catalogue, Sotheby's, London, July 5, 1995, no. 42. The type of mark, which appears as the initials *MV* in monogram ligature, with the Antwerp coat of arms, is described and illustrated in van Damme 1990.

2   The collections corresponding to these inventory notations are not listed in the "Provenance" section above as the evidence is inconclusive. However, the reverse of the panel does bear a collector's mark which may eventually help to trace it to the Brueghel the Elder estate inventory and/or the Younger's journal. The mark appears in large black letters and reads: . *I* [or J]. *B* . *R*., with the latter two initials superimposed.

3   Van Mander 1604. On the rise of mythological subjects in Netherlandish painting and the importance of Ovid's *Metamorphoses*, see Sluijter 1986.

4   Pigler 1956, vol. 2, pp. 190-92, lists over forty representations by Netherlandish artists.

5   Ovid, *Metamorphoses*, 1: 686-715, trans. Melville, Oxford/New York, 1986, pp. 21-22, cited in Boston/Toledo 1993-94, pp. 260, 262, note 1.

6   The drawing is discussed and illustrated in Jaffé 1977, p. 23.

7   The painting is catalogued and illustrated in Ertz 1984, no. 253, where the author dates it to the end of the 1620s and attributes the figures to Rubens and workshop. It is on panel with approximate dimensions of 39 x 60 cm., sold, Christie's, London, March 23, 1973. It is also discussed in Held 1976, pp. 42-43, and Held 1980, vol. 2, p. 290. In both instances, Held attributes the work to Rubens and Jan Brueghel the Elder.

Ertz also elaborates on his Rubens attribution for the present painting, describing it as Rubens und Atelier, noting that the drapery lacks the touch of the master. The complicated issue of the Rubens workshop cannot be addressed here, and indeed there appears to be enough of Rubens in the figures of Pan and Syrinx to render the point moot in this instance.

8   The painting is on canvas and it measures 61 x 88 cm. It is illustrated and discussed in Ertz 1979, pp. 417-18, and Boston/Toledo 1993-94, pp. 261-62, in conjunction with the present painting and other related works.

9   The sketch, painted on panel, 27.8 x 27.7 cm., a design for the larger painting (now lost) created as a part of the Torre de la Parada decorations, is illustrated and catalogued in Alpers 1971, no. 47a and Held 1980, no. 207.

10   Ertz 1979, no. 384a.

11   Ertz 1984, no. 256, for the entry on the Weldon painting, and on the lost painting, no. 253, oil on panel, 39 x 60 cm. It is discussed above with regard to the attribution to Rubens, and in note 7.

12   Boston/Toledo 1993-94, no. 17. In the "Literature" section of the entry although the Ertz 1979, no. 384a citation for the painting is given, the Ertz 1984 citation, reattributing the landscape to Jan Brueghel the Younger, is omitted.

13   Sotheby's, London, July 5, 1995, no. 42.

14   Ertz 1984, p. 18.

15   The contents of the estate sale are listed in the daybook of Jan the Younger, Ertz 1984, pp. 523-25, where the painting by the Elder and Rubens is listed as number 54 and where the Rubens/Brueghel the Younger painting appears on page 526, no. 14. The prices recorded for each, 142 and 120 guilders respectively, show less of a range than one might expect.

16   Ertz 1984, no. 326a, panel, 58 x 84 cm., dated there to the 1640s.

(detail)

17   The copy is catalogued in Ertz 1984, no. 97, and dated to the 1630s, and the Getty painting by Jan the Elder is published in Ertz 1979, no. 273.

18   *Pan and Syrinx*, panel, 51.5 x 85.6 cm., Staatliches Museum, Schwerin, catalogued in Ertz 1984, no. 255 (illustration is reversed), and dated to the end of the 1620s. The painting is correctly reproduced in Boston/Toledo 1993-94, p. 262, fig. 1. There are also copies which are non- autograph: a horizontal version is in the Pinacoteca di Brera, Milan, reproduced in Ertz 1979, fig. 503, and a second one was sold at Sotheby's, New York, November 5, 1986, no. 13. The second copy was cited in Boston/Toledo 1993-94, p. 261, 262, note 8.

43 Jacob van Ruisdael

(Haarlem c. 1628/29 - Amsterdam 1682)

Cascade Landscape with Mother and Child

c. 1670
oil on canvas
40.3 x 50.28 cm.
Inscribed, lower left, on rock: *Ruïsda[el]*

PROVENANCE:
Sale, Roos, Amsterdam, Jurriaans Collection, August 28, 1817, no. 56 (to de Lelie, for fl. 950); Sale, van Cleef, The Hague, W.A. Verbrugge Collection, September 27, 1831, no. 47 (to Hagens, for fl. 915); Chaplin (dealer), U. K. (by 1836); S. Hodgson, London; E. H. Lawrence, London; Charles Sedelmeyer (dealer), Paris (by 1898); Rodolph Kann, Paris; Duveen Bros., Paris (by 1907); Thos. Agnew & Sons, London (c. 1926); Kunsthandel J. Borghouts, Utrecht; J.C.H. Heldring, Oosterbeek (by 1955); Col. S.J.L. Hardie, Ballethie, Scotland; Leonard Koetser, London (by 1970); Private collection, U.K. (1970-1992).

EXHIBITIONS:
Arnhem, Gemeente Museum, 1958, no. 25 (ill.); Utrecht, Centraal Museum, 1960, no. 30; London 1970, no. 9; Birmingham 1995, no. 17(ill.); New Orleans 1997, no. 44 (ill.).

LITERATURE:
Possibly Smith 1829-42, vol. 6, 1835, no. 246, and Supplement, vol. 9, 1842, no. 33; Paris 1898, no. 188 (ill.); Paris 1907, p. ix and no. 78 (ill.); Hofstede de Groot, 1907-1928, vol. 4, 1912, no. 270; Valentiner 1919, pp. 351-2; Rosenberg 1928, no. 192; Hannema 1955, no. 25 (ill.); Birmingham 1995A, cover ill.

Jacob van Ruisdael presents a benign view of nature in this portrayal of a cascade and its sheltering banks. A smooth river gives way to the frothy waters of a rocky ledge and becomes a rushing stream. The right bank is dominated by splendid oaks, beneath which a thatched hovel conceals a man and shelters a seated mother and child. A shepherd watches his flock on the hillside above and a low mountain range is visible in the distance. While the sky is filled with massive cumulus clouds, a warm golden light infuses the landscape, suggesting autumn and the end of day.

The motif of the waterfall recurs in Ruisdael's *oeuvre* from its first appearance in the early 1660s, through the following decade. In the early depictions, he tended to favor a more torrential and dramatic chute and a vertical format as seen in his *Waterfall with Castle and a Hut*, c. 1665, Fogg Art Museum, Harvard University, Cambridge.[1] These works appear to have been influenced by the waterfall paintings of Allart van Everdingen (1621-1675), his Amsterdam colleague who, unlike Ruisdael, actually traveled to Scandinavia where such phenomena exist.[2] The torrents of Roelandt Saverij (no. 48a), which inspired Everdingen, have also been cited as likely precedents for Ruisdael's vertical waterfall paintings.[3] Ruisdael transformed the monumental motif of the torrent, reducing its height and taming the turbulence by rendering it in a horizontal rather than vertical format as seen in his *Waterfall*, Rijksmuseum, Amsterdam. In a group of analogous works, dated around 1670, the artist lends serenity and softness to the waterfall and its surrounding landscape.[4]

The Weldon painting reflects this development, taking the transformation of the waterfall even further by lowering its height, diminishing its movement and reducing it to a cascade. In this regard it closely resembles two of the artist's paintings in Florence and Washington, both dated c. 1670.[5] Furthermore, the three paintings share a relatively intimate scale and correspondingly delicate brushwork, particularly in the foliage and the white water. The artist's depictions of water earned high praise from his early biographer Houbraken: "He could depict water splashing and foaming as it dashed upon the rocks, so naturally, delicately and transparently that it appears to be real."[6] While the Weldon painting appears to belong chronologically with works from the early 1670s, Ruisdael's later *oeuvre* is difficult to place.[7] The present canvas has also been dated to the artist's younger years by at least one scholar.[8]

Ruisdael's paintings have been the subject of considerable debate regarding interpretation and meaning in Dutch seventeenth-century landscape. Wiegand, Walford, and Bruyn have found *vanitas* significance in his landscape forms, a tendency culminating in the interpretation of his late cemetery paintings which unquestionably function at some symbolic level.[9] Wiegand also ascribes *vanitas* meaning to Ruisdael's water paintings, particularly the early vertical waterfalls, which are likened to contemporary literature that equates fleeting human life to rushing water.[10] Bruyn suggests a similar "religio-literary" reading of a group of Ruisdael's horizontal waterfall paintings that include the motif of a small church on the horizon, comparing the hostile waterscape to the life of challenge that must be traveled to reach salvation (the church).[11]

While the landscape of the present painting may not lend itself entirely to a scriptural reading, as Wiegand and others might advocate, it appears to be the setting for an important Christian narrative.

The presence of the nursing mother, the man in the shed and the shepherd indicate that the artist may have intended to represent the subject of the rest on the flight into Egypt, as first noted by Bode in 1907 and later elaborated by Valentiner.[12] Given the scale of the figures and the magnificence of the landscape, it is not surprising that the subject would have been lost on Smith, Hofstede de Groot, and others who first catalogued it. In the nineteenth century Rembrandt's painting of the same subject, which is similar in both scale and a dominant landscape, was variously described as "Two Gypsies by moonlight" and "a company of travelers," temporarily losing its narrative and religious significance.[13]

If a "flight" depiction was not uppermost in the artist's mind when he conceived the present painting, he would certainly have been aware of the Christian associations that would have been stirred by his imagery of mother and child. Moreover, he blessed his domestic scene with a sheltering, protective landscape.[14]
NTM

1 On this painting, see The Hague/Cambridge 1981-82, no. 34, and Amsterdam/Boston/Philadelphia 1987-88, no. 85.

2 Davies 1978, pp. 217-29, reviews the sources on the relationship between the two painters.

3 Simon 1927, p. 64, as cited by Giltay in Amsterdam/Boston/Philadelphia 1987-88, p. 451.

4 Walford 1981, p. 210, characterizes the later paintings as follows: "They differ from his earlier waterfalls: cornfields and pastures replace wild, mountainous landscape; logs rest inert over languid waters; the trees are more decorous, and the pastoral element is more pronounced than ever." Walford's 1981 dissertation has been revised and published as a book, Walford 1991, in which he describes the more peaceful late waterfall paintings on pp. 141-46, 174-76. In The Hague/Cambridge 1981-82, p. 107, Slive describes the late, horizontal waterfall paintings as heralding the "idyllic mood" of Ruisdael's "final phase." He refers in particular to the Amsterdam, *Waterfall*, fig. 48, as well as the *Waterfall with a Steep Hill and Cottages*, private collection, cat. 35; the *Waterfall*, Wallace Collection, London, fig. 49; and *A Waterfall in a Hilly Landscape*, The Hermitage, St. Petersburg, fig. 50.

5 *A Waterfall with a Low Wooded Hill*, Uffizi, Florence, in The Hague/Cambridge 1981-82, no. 50, and *Landscape*, National Gallery of Art, Washington, in Wheelock 1995, no. 1961.9.85. For Saverij's origination of the thundering alpine waterfall as a subject in European art, see Spicer 1997.

6 Houbraken 1718-21, vol. 3, 1721, pp. 65-66, as cited and translated in Amsterdam/Boston/Philadelphia 1987-88, p. 452.

7 While many of the paintings are dated for the period of 1646-53, few are dated after that (ibid., p. 438).

8 In Paris 1907, p. ix, Bode dates the painting to the "end of his [Ruisdael's] first period," and Hannema 1955, no. 25, dates it c. 1655. For a painting, dated by Slive and Sutton to the mid 1650s, which appears to depict a landscape similar to that of the Weldon canvas, see *A Rushing Stream in a Mountain Landscape*, private collection, in Boston 1992, no. 126. Although the motif is similar, the technique in the *Rushing Stream* painting, described as a "thick application of paint," is not analogous to the present work.

9 The paintings in question are both entitled *The Jewish Cemetery*, c. 1668-72, Detroit Institute of Arts and Staatliche Kunstsammlungen, Dresden. For a review of the scholarship on the interpretation of these paintings, see the entry on the Detroit canvas in Amsterdam/Boston/Philadelphia 1987-88, no. 86, and the discussion of both paintings in The Hague/Cambridge 1981-82, nos. 20, 21.

10 On the symbolism of water, see Wiegand 1971, pp. 87 ff.

11 From Bruyn's article "Toward a Scriptural Reading of Seventeenth-Century Dutch Landscape Painting," in Amsterdam/Boston/Philadelphia 1987-88, pp. 99-100.

12 Paris 1907, no. 78, where Bode also notes the presence of a donkey under the shelter. The donkey, which is a telling iconographic motif in depictions of the flight, is no longer clearly discernible in the painting, nor is it visible in the plate which illustrated the painting in the 1907 catalogue. Valentiner 1919, pp. 351-52, also interprets the scene as a Flight into Egypt, citing the observations of Wilhelm Meister. In his discussion of the iconography of the painting, he also described the motif of the donkey. Hannema 1955, p. 44, citing Valentiner, posited the same hypothesis.

13 *Landscape with the Rest on the Flight into Egypt*, 1647, National Gallery of Ireland, Dublin. The descriptions were given by Waagen in 1854 and Smith in 1836, as cited in Amsterdam/Boston/Philadelphia 1987-88, no. 78, p. 433. Rembrandt's painting is also illustrated and discussed in Berlin/Amsterdam/London 1991-92, no. 38, and Schneider 1990, no. 8.

14 In this regard, his setting differs from the view of nature given in Rembrandt's nocturnal *Landscape with the Rest on the Flight into Egypt*, which has been interpreted as a setting imbued with "disquiet and an uncertain mood," and symbolic of a "world that is hostile towards the child [Christ];" see Kelch in Berlin/Amsterdam/London 1991-92, pp. 238, 241.

44 Jacob van Ruisdael, circle of

(Jacob van Ruisdael, Haarlem c. 1628/29 - Amsterdam 1682)

Wooded Landscape with Waterfall

oil on canvas
100.5 x 83 cm.

PROVENANCE:
Leuchtenberg-Romanoff, St. Petersburg; Leuchtenberg, Paris; A. Popoff, Paris;
Dr. Benedict, Paris;1 Private collection.

EXHIBITIONS:
London 1963, no. 18 (as Claes Molenaer); Providence 1964, no. 20 (ill., as Jacob
van Ruisdael); New York 1966, no. 34 (as Jacob van Ruisdael); New Orleans 1997,
no. 45 (as Jacob van Ruisdael, circle of).

1 Provenance, as given by the owner at the time of purchase. The early provenance cannot be confirmed at the present time.

45 Rachel Ruysch
(Amsterdam 1664 - Amsterdam 1750)

Nosegay of Roses, Marigolds, and Larkspur, with Insects and Bumblebee

1695
oil on canvas
32 x 25.5 cm.
Inscribed, bottom right: *Rachel Ruysch/1695*

PROVENANCE:
Collection of Princess Arthur of Connaught, Duchess of Fife, Scotland; Private collection.

EXHIBITIONS:
Berlin 1988, no. 93 (ill.); Birmingham 1995, no. 18 (ill.); New Orleans 1997, no. 46 (ill.).

LITERATURE:
Parnass (1992), 8, p. 59; London 1993, p. 36, fig. 6; Alabama Art Monthly 2 (Sept. 1995) p. 8 (ill.).

Ruysch's distinction as one of the Netherlands' last great classical flower painters is fully evident in this refined still life. A lush nosegay of one white and several pink roses, marigolds, and blue and white larkspur overlaps a stone ledge, spilling toward the viewer. The flowers are brilliantly lit against a dark ground. The fullness of the bouquet is most apparent in the roses whose petals, unfolding in various states of maturity, are skillfully layered and modeled. The nosegay is host to an array of creatures, from the minute ants who explore the unfurling white rose, to the green dragonfly, a fat, fuzzy bee and the delicate white moth perched on an upper leaf.

As a student of the celebrated flower painter Willem van Aelst (c. 1626-c. 1683)[1] and the daughter of the distinguished Amsterdam botanist and anatomist Frederick Ruysch (1638-1731), Rachel was exposed to the classical tradition of floral still life with the benefit of an intimate knowledge of science. These legacies of her training are apparent in the present painting.

The nosegay or posy composition was an innovation of Ruysch's teacher, van Aelst, as seen for example in his *Group of Flowers on a Ledge*, 1675, Fitzwilliam Museum, Cambridge,[2] painted just a few years before his brilliant student joined him in 1679. Ruysch exploited the motif in many paintings, a fact which suggests that it was a successful composition.[3] As in the Weldon nosegay, Ruysch's renderings tend to favor a lighter palette and have a more decorative effect than those of van Aelst. A pair of Ruysch's nosegay paintings in London closely approximates the present work in motif and format, albeit with different specimens of flowers and insects.[4] It is possible that the Weldon nosegay might have also been one of a pair.

Síp has likened Ruysch's less floral and more animal still lifes to the scientific renderings in the illustrations from her father's publications, stating that such works originated in collectors' cabinets.[5] Indeed Ruysch did execute a number of forest-floor pieces, in the manner of van Schrieck's *Still Life of Thistle and Frog Before Woodland Waterfall* in the present collection (no. 49), which demonstrate a strong interest in *naturalia*.[6] While the present painting is more decorative than those works and is principally a flower piece, its insect and moth population, numbering twelve, illustrates the artist's knowledge of nature's minutest forms. It also recalls the current wonder evoked by God's tiniest creations brought to light by the microscope. The collector and secretary to the Stadholder Constantin Huygens (1596-1687) was both awed by the spectacle that magnification revealed to him and humbled by the powers of creation: "In the most minute and disdained of creatures, [we] meet with the same careful labor of the great architect, everywhere an equally indescribable majesty."[7]

Ruysch's characteristically meticulous brush lingers in the task of refined description in the present still life. The veining of leaves and insect wings reveals exquisite delicacy, be it in the fine brown wings of the dragonfly, the gossamer pair of the bumblebee, or the chameleon-like silken green, white, and black bearers of the moth. As the nineteenth-century cataloguer Smith concluded in his brief description of Ruysch: "[she] attained such extraordinary perfection, that no successful imitator of her best works has hitherto appeared."[8]

Ruysch was well compensated and recognized for her skill. From 1708-1716, she was court painter to the Elector Palatine Johann Wilhelm in Düsseldorf. She continued to paint into her eighties, and before her death she was honored in a collection of poems written by her peers.[9]
NTM

1 Van Aelst is represented in the present exhibition by an early fruit piece, *Peaches, a Plum, and Grapes on a Ledge*, 1646, cat. 1.

2 The painting, on canvas, 31.1 x 25.4 cm., is virtually the same size as the present work. It is catalogued and illustrated in Auckland 1982, no. 26, where it is likened to a similar painting by Ruysch, *Study of Flowers*, Victoria and Albert Museum, which is discussed in this entry.

3 In Grant 1956, which is the catalogue raisonné on the *oeuvre*, approximately eighteen nosegay paintings are listed. Grant's catalogue includes many paintings only known from sales and inventory descriptions. It includes a total of 230 paintings. In Síp 1968, p. 157, the extant *oeuvre* is estimated at one hundred paintings.

4 These paintings, both entitled *Study of Flowers*, are on canvas, approximately 33.5 x 28 cm., belong to the Victoria and Albert Museum. They are nos. 192 and 193 in Grant 1956, and one of them is illustrated in Auckland 1982, p. 150. They are also catalogued and illustrated in Kauffmann 1973, nos. 314-15.

5 Síp 1968, p 160. Her father published two illustrated anthologies of *naturalia*, the *Thesaurus animalium*, Amsterdam 1700, and the *Thesaurus anatomicum*, Amsterdam, 1714.

6 See the entry on Schrieck for a discussion of the parallel developments in science and art during the period. On Ruysch's early career and the scientific aspect of her paintings, see Berardi 1998.

7 From Huygens's *Autobiography*, 1629-31, as cited and translated in Hanover/Raleigh/Houston/Atlanta 1991-93, p. 38.

8 Smith 1829-42, vol. 6, 1835, p. 502.

9 These details of her life are taken from Segal's biography in Osaka/Tokyo/Sydney 1990, p. 235. The poetry collection entitled *Dichtlovers voor de uitmuntende schilderesse mejuffrouwe Rachel Ruisch...*, was published in 1750.

46   Salomon van Ruysdael
(Naarden c. 1600/03 - Haarlem 1670)

Riverview with Boats and Liesvelt Castle Tower

1641
oil on panel
55 x 78 cm.
Inscribed, lower right: *.v [R]ysd[?]/1641*

PROVENANCE:
F. Lugt, Blaricum; A. N. Nienhuys-Versteegh, Aerdenhout; by descent to J. W. N. Nienhuys, Bloemendael; Sale, P. Brandt, Amsterdam, May 11, 1971, no. 7 (for fl. 132,000); R. Smith, Washington; Private collection.

EXHIBITIONS:
Haarlem, Frans Halsmuseum, December-January 1926-27; Amsterdam 1936, no. 17; Birmingham 1995, no. 19 (ill.); New Orleans 1997, no. 47 (ill.).

LITERATURE:
Stechow 1975, no. 331, and p. 21; Niemeyer 1959, p. 52-3, fig. 6; London 1992, p. 177.1.

This broad, serene riverscape represents the type of painting for which Salomon van Ruysdael is most recognized and admired. The wide sweep of the river gives way to the horizon at left and an immense sky filled with billowing clouds. The right bank, defined by stands of trees, periodic landmarks, and staffage, slopes towards the glassy water where sailing, fishing, and ferry boats go about their business.

Painted in 1641, one decade after the riverscape first appeared in the artist's *oeuvre*, this panel dates from the mature tonalist phase of Ruysdael's career.[2] Stechow has characterized the early 1640s as the painter's period of "gold/yellow splendor and brilliance" and he has described the Weldon painting as being "permeated" with gold.[3] Much like the dune setting in van Goyen's smaller landscape of 1651, also in the present collection (no. 20), the subject of the sky and the river and its bank is particularly suited to a tonalist rendering, where the depiction of atmospheric conditions is as important as the definition of forms.

From the late 1620s through the mid-1640s van Goyen and Ruysdael appear to have developed concurrently, and perhaps cooperatively, the river landscape type and the tonalist technique.[4] A technical analysis of a sampling of paintings by the two artists has revealed that they frequently chose a similar monochrome range of pigments, mostly earth colors for the foreground, and that they combined a thin layering of paint with the slightly exposed grain and hue of the wood panel in order to unify the composition. Moreover, monochrome paintings that were once perceived as degraded and dulled shadows of their former polychrome selves are now seen to be the result of deliberate choices and workshop practices on the part of these artists who sought "inexpensive supplies and efficient painting techniques."[5] These findings are consistent with the considerable productivity of both painters — Ruysdael's extant *oeuvre* numbers over 600 paintings and van Goyen's surpasses 1200.

Montias has set the development of the tonalist technique within a larger socioeconomic context. He considers the evolution of style, from mannerist to painterly, to be a response to an increased demand for private art in the wake of the destruction and intolerance of religious imagery during and after the Iconclasm. Landscape painting largely filled the demand, and Montias believes that it was the genre where "supply-cost reduction began."[6]

Innovations that may be termed tonalist are evident in the present painting. The artist's use of the panel and a pinkish ground as a coloristic unifier may be seen in the exposed lines describing the waves in the foreground and in the thinner clouds in the sky. In the details of the boats, figures, and bank in the lower right quadrant a method may be discerned which is consistent with the description of his painting technique:[7] a workup from a thin, brown, roughed-in design, with exposed sections left as shadows and midtones, and definition by means of color layers, outlines and highlights.

It is unclear how Ruysdael devised his compositions. Since there are no extant drawings attributed to him, evidence of his draftsmanship has been sought in the underdrawings of his paintings. While an examination using infrared technology has revealed extensive charcoal sketches in Ruysdael's first riverscape of 1631, in which the drafting technique was described as "deft, fragmented strokes," his *View of Rhenen*, 1648, shows no evidence of underdrawings.[8] In the present painting no drawn lines are visible beneath transparent passages of paint, whereas another panel, dated 1641, featuring a similar composition offers ample evidence of underdrawings.[9] It is possible that the composition of the Weldon panel was entirely crafted in the paint layers, *alla prima*, rather than drawn beneath. In the sailboat to the left, this technique is visible in the hull and sails which are created in the buildup and incised definition of the paint.

While aspects of Ruysdael's technique remain unknown to us, the architectural landmark of the solid turret and the general site shown in the Weldon painting have been identified. Niemeyer has established that the Weldon panel and three other works by Ruysdael represent the castle of Liesvelt on the Lek River near the town of Groot-Ammers in the southern part of the province of Holland.[10] His identification was made using prints of the site by Anthonie Waterloo (1609-1690) and Abraham Rademaker (1675-1735), where Niemeyer specifically likened the representation of the castle structure in the present painting to a northern view in a print by Rademaker.[11] Although the print was not published until 1725 when it appeared in Rademaker's series entitled *Kabinet van Nederlandse Outheden en Gezichten*, the inscribed date of 1631 suggests that it was modeled on an earlier representation which precedes the Weldon painting by ten years.[12] While the substantial turret of the castle recurs in several paintings by Ruysdael, the surrounding landscape has been manipulated to suit his artistic ends,[13] indicating that his interest lay in the picturesque potential of the tower rather than in the precise rendering of the topography. NTM

1 As "formerly in the Smith collection," with incorrect illustration, fig. 4, which is actually of Stechow 1975, no. 395.

2 Stechow 1975 identified the artist's first dated riverscape as the *River Landscape*, 1631, National Gallery, London (catalogue raisonné, no. 435).

3 Ibid., p. 21 (present author's translation from the original German).

4 Los Angeles/Boston/New York 1981-82, p. 88. Their developments of the river motif and tonalist technique were based at least in part on the example of their elders Esaias van de Velde (1587-1630) and Pieter de Molijn (1595-1661). For an example of an early tonalist river painting by van Goyen, see his *Cottages and Fishermen by a River*, 1631, Museums and Art Gallery, Glasgow; Beck 1973, no. 441. The exact circumstances of the relationship between van Goyen and Ruysdael are unknown; however, archival evidence records van Goyen's presence in the house of Salomon's brother, the art dealer Isaack van Ruysdael, in The Hague in 1634, where van Goyen was painting (as discussed in Amsterdam/Boston/Philadelphia 1987-88, p. 318).

5 Gifford 1983, p. 44, and pp. 40-44.

6 Montias 1987, p. 459.

7 Gifford 1983, p. 44, describes the artist's layering technique.

8 Bomford "Technique of the Early Dutch Landscape Painters," in London 1986, p. 54, and figs. 8, 9, for illustrations of the reflectograms of the 1631 painting, and pp. 53-54, and no. 57 for the *View of Rhenen*, National Gallery, London. For the full citation of the 1631 painting, see note 2 above.

9 The Weldon painting has not been examined using infrared technology. The second 1641 panel is the *View of the River Lek with Boats and Liesvelt Castle*, 1641, H. Samuel Collection, London. In Sutton's catalogue entry on the Samuel painting in London 1992, no. 60, he includes information on the underdrawings, suggesting that they are visible to the naked eye and that the painting was not examined by special means.

10 Niemeyer 1959. The other three paintings are *View of the River Lek with Boats and Liesvelt Castle*, 1641, H. Samuel Collection, London, *Two Fishing Boats*, 1642, Alte Pinakothek, Munich, and *Castle with Round Tower*, c. 1660, formerly David Koetser Gallery, Zurich. The above paintings are, respectively, Stechow 1975, nos. 333, 447, 395. For a recent discussion of the Samuel Collection painting which includes specific references on the castle, see Sutton in London 1992, no. 60.

11 Niemeyer 1959, pp. 52-53.

12 Ibid., p. 52.

13 Ibid., pp. 54-55.

(detail)

47 Cornelis Saftleven

(Gorinchem 1607 – Rotterdam 1681)

Interior with Vegetable Still Life

oil on canvas
39 x 29.5 cm.

PROVENANCE:
Kunsthandel Gebr. Douwes, Amsterdam; Private collection.

EXHIBITIONS:
London 1959, no. 6; Providence 1964, no. 2 (ill.); New York 1965, no. 80; New York 1966, no. 36; Birmingham 1995, no. 20 (ill.); New Orleans 1997, no. 48 (ill.).

LITERATURE:
Schulz 1978, no. 709.

Cornelis Saftleven was one of the Rotterdam painters in the mid seventeenth century who, along with David Teniers the Younger in Antwerp, popularized the idea of large vegetables as still-life motifs.[1] For example, his *Barn Interior with a Peasant Woman Feeding Chickens*, Gemäldegalerie, Dresden,[2] features an immense cabbage. Such still lives with vegetables remained popular into the eighteenth century. Indeed the present still life of vegetables in a rustic interior has recently been attributed to the Flemish eighteenth-century still life painter Pieter Snijers (1681-1752) who painted both elaborate allegories featuring vegetables and handsome close up studies of just a few cabbages, cauliflowers, and turnips, perhaps by a wicker basket.[3] The studies of vegetables used to compose the Weldon still life were used as well for other still lives of vegetables by Snijers.[4] There does not appear to be any exact correspondence with individual vegetables in paintings by Saftleven. The signature "*C. Saftleven* f." described at the upper left in earlier Weldon collection catalogues and taken over in Schulz 1978[5] could not be confirmed by Minty in 1997. JS

1 Rotterdam 1994-95.
2 Schulz 1978, no. 673; Bernt 1970, no. 1022, ill.
3 Fred Meijer, in a letter to the author, including the comparisons in the following note.
4 For example, *Still Life with Cabbage, Cauliflower and Other Vegetables*, Noortman Gallery, London, in 1991; *Allegory of November*, Christies, New York, January 11, 1995, lot 5, ill.; *Cabbage, Cauliflowers and Other Vegetables Spilling from a Wicker Basket before a Balustrade*, Christies, London, May 23, 1986, lot 4, ill.
5 Schulz apparently did not examine the painting himself.

48a **Roelandt Saverij**
(Courtrai 1576 - Utrecht 1639)

Alpine Landscape with Torrent and Hunter
(Pendant to cat. 48b)

c. 1608
oil on copper
22.3 x 16.5 cm.
Inscribed, lower left, on rock face: *[R.] SAVERY/FE*

48b   **Roelandt Saverij**
(Courtrai 1576 - Utrecht 1639)

Alpine Landscape with Hunter
(Pendant to cat. 49a)

c. 1608
oil on copper
22 x 17.2 cm.

In 1675 Saverij's biographer, Joachim von Sandrart, relayed the story of the young painter's Tyrol journey under the employ of Emperor Rudolf II who had engaged the artist to record the "curious marvels of nature." Saverij's drawings from his travels became the models for his later landscape paintings.[1] This pair of dramatic mountain views featuring a torrent, myriad deciduous and coniferous trees, fantastic rock formations, and a variety of flora and fauna are doubtless the fruit of Saverij's early sketches. The paintings are linked with two other pairs, both dated 1608, and at least two drawings associated with the alpine excursion.[2] This body of work is recognized for the artist's direct portrayal of nature, as opposed to his later more mannered style.[3] Moreover, Saverij's depictions of waterfalls in many of these alpine scenes are unique among the landscapes of both his Netherlandish predecessors and contemporaries.[4]

In scale, refinement and natural detail this pair of paintings on copper is related to the small landscapes in this collection by Jan Brueghel the Elder (nos. 8, 9). Brueghel's influence is evident in both the landscape and still-life work of Saverij; the artists may even have met at the court of Rudolf II in Prague, just a few years prior to Saverij's execution of these paintings.[5] As in Brueghel's landscapes, Saverij demonstrates a fondness for nature's particulars. He has carefully rendered and differentiated the types of foliage, the reeds, grasses and broken, twisting trunks, and the birdlife and deer in both paintings. Kaufmann has posited that Saverij was first called to Rudolf's court to succeed the miniaturist Georg Hoefnagel (d. 1600) as a "naturalist" painter.[6] The approach to landscape illustrated by this pair of paintings, as well as by the artist's nearly microscopic presentation of nature in his early still lifes, supports this view. Saverij's nascent interest in birds and deer in the Weldon pair is notable since these particular motifs appear frequently in his later paintings, for example in *Landscape with Birds*, 1622, National Gallery, Prague, and *Landscape with Stags and Deer*, 1624, University Museum, Göttingen.[7]

A series of large chalk drawings which are dated to 1606-08 attests to Saverij's work in the alps. Of these drawings, Erasmus has identified the *Wooded Swamp with Hunters*, 1608, Fondation Custodia, Paris (fig. 1) as a model for an engraving of 1609 made by Aegidius Sadeler (c. 1570-1629).[8] The Weldon swamp painting is remarkably close to the Paris drawing,

Fig. 1 Roelant Saverij, *Wooded Swamp with Hunters*, 1608
black chalk and watercolor on paper, Collection Frits Lugt, Institut
Neérlandais, Paris.

particularly in the details of the left side where the same outcropping and surrounding trees support three hunters in similar poses. Spicer has also cited the drawing of the *Rainbow over a Mountainside*, Vienna, Nationalbibliothek, as a possible study for the Hannover Waterfall, especially in the motif of the rocky grottoes.[9] The drawing may well have provided elements and ideas for the Weldon *Torrent* pendant as well.

The difference between the Hannover paintings, the other New York pair, and the present pendants resides mainly in the depiction of staffage.[10] While the Weldon versions feature a single hunter in the *Torrent* and a group of three hunters in the pendant, none of the other depictions includes hunters. The landscapes from the two pairs which correspond to the Weldon *Alpine Landscape with Three Hunters* include a hermitage, and each torrent painting shows peasant figures rather than the lone hunter of the Weldon composition. That Saverij made several variations on a theme is not unusual and may suggest simply that he was exploiting a pleasing subject. Sadeler's publication of a print that closely reflected the Weldon painting of the three hunters further suggests that the composition was popular.

The theme of the deer hunt runs through Saverij's *oeuvre*. It is the subject of his earliest dated forest landscape of 1604 and it recurs in his later paintings.[11] Hunting was a courtly pursuit throughout Europe and records from the household of Rudolf II indicate that he kept deer on the grounds of his Prague palace.[12] While Saverij is unexceptional in his choice of subject given this context, his frequent depiction of commoners or peasants, rather than noblemen, as hunters sets him apart from many of his contemporaries.[13]

Saverij's dramatic landscapes have been interpreted expressionistically. Kaufmann has suggested that the artist's depiction of natural phenomena in the Hannover paintings may reveal the artist's philosophy of nature's destructive and regenerative forces, with the cascading water and the alternately fallen and burgeoning vegetation as the signifiers.[14] While such an interpretation may be apt for a painting that includes a hermitage with a cross on its roof as seen in the Hannover pendant, it is less applicable to the Weldon hunting scenes which, in their casual atmosphere of woodland pleasures, may be likened to the bucolic peasant paintings of Saverij's predecessor, Pieter Bruegel the Elder (c. 1525/30-1569).[15] NTM

1 Sandrart 1675-80, p. 305. Spicer has noted that Saverij's alpine views feature inhospitable landscapes rather than pleasant vistas (as cited by Kaufmann 1988, p. 85.).

2 *Woodland Landscape with Hermitage*, signed and dated 1608, and *Landscape with Mountain Waterfall*, signed and dated 1608, copper, 20 x 16 cm., Niedersächsische Landesgalerie, Hannover. The second pair is *Woodland Landscape with Hermitage*, signed and dated 1608, and *Landscape with Mountain Waterfall*, signed and dated 1608, copper, 23 x 17 cm., private collection, New York. Both of these pairs are illustrated in Kaufmann 1988, nos. 19-20 to 19-23. There is also a related painting, *Travelers Near a Mountain Stream*, signed and dated 1607, copper, which is lost and was apparently cut in two. Kaufmann 1988, no. 19-14, describes it as the "first clear evidence of Saverij's journey to the Alps." For the drawings, see text below and note 8.

3 Sutton, "Introduction," p. 22, in Amsterdam/Boston/Philadephia 1987-88. The author refers specifically to the drawings and the Hannover paintings (see note 2 above).

4 For a discussion of Saverij's conception of the alpine landscape, as it differed from that of other Netherlandish artists, particularly Pieter Bruegel the Elder, see Spicer 1983, pp. 62-65.

5 Brueghel was at Rudolf's court in 1604 (Ertz 1979, p. 14) the same year that Savery 's presence is first documented in Prague (as discussed by Bok in Amsterdam 1993-94, p. 315). For an example of Brueghel's influence on Saverij's conception of landscape, see Saverij's *Mountain Landscape with Peddlars*, 1609, Vienna, Kunsthistorisches Museum, in Kaufmann 1988, no. 19-37.

6 Kaufmann 1988, p. 228 (under no. 19-1).

7 On the role of these animal motifs in Saverij's *oeuvre*, see Müllenmeister 1988, pp. 113-116.

8 Erasmus 1908, p. 190, first published this finding, as cited and reiterated by Hasselt in London/Paris/Bern/Brussels 1972, no. 89 and Spicer 1983, no. C 44 F46, where she also notes the resemblance to the Hannover pendant of the *Woodland Landscape with Hermitage*. In her subsequent entry for the Hannover painting in Essen 1988, no. 144, she stressed the primacy of the role of the Paris drawing as a model for the Sadeler print rather than for the Saverij painting. The print was one of a series of six made after mountain landscapes by Saverij. They are published without illustrations as nos. 225-230, in de Hoop Scheffer 1980. For a recent overview of Sadeler, see Limouze 1990.

9 Spicer in Essen 1988, p. 260.

10 The copper support is common to all three pairs and the size varies only slightly. For dimensions, see note 2 above.

11 The early painting is the *Forest with Deer Hunters*, 1604, Vienna, Kunsthistorisches Museum. An example of a later work is the *Deerhunt*, c. 1620, Koninklijk Museum, Brussels. On the theme of hunting in Saverij's paintings, see Müllenmeister 1988, pp. 92-98.

12 Kaufmann 1988, p. 230.

13 Ibid., p. 230.

14 Ibid., p. 274, citing M.L. Hendrix's unpublished article, "Codex Naturae: Research in Landscape Painting at the Court of Rudolf II," as his source.

15 Rudolf II owned a number of paintings by Pieter Bruegel the Elder and his influence on Saverij is evident in many of the latter's paintings, as well as his series of eighty "naer het leven" peasant drawings, dated from 1603 to 1609, and contemporaneous to the Weldon landscapes. On this series of drawings, long attributed to Bruegel, and only relatively recently reattributed to Saverij, see Spicer 1983, chapter 4.

49 Otto Marseus van Schrieck
(Nijmegen 1619/20 - Amsterdam 1678)

Still Life with Thistle and Frog Before Woodland Waterfall

c. 1670
oil on canvas
58.8 x 47.3 cm.
Inscribed, bottom right: *OMar fec.*

PROVENANCE:
Galerie Abraham Fontanel, Montpellier; Sold to J. J. de Boussairolles, Montpellier, February 10, 1805, for frs. 240; Comte de Saporta, domaine du Moulin Blanc, Aix-en-Provence; Sale, Sotheby's, New York, January 11, 1996, no. 72 (ill.).

EXHIBITION:
New Orleans 1997, no. 50 (ill.).

LITERATURE:
L'Etat des Tableaux dressé par J. J. de Boussairolles à la fin de sa vie, no. 19; Chevalier 1984, no. 61.

Otto Marseus van Schrieck's characteristic forest-floor fantasy demonstrates the aptness of his nickname *Snuffelaer*, or *Ferreter*. A thistle with a single glowing pink flower dominates the still life which is set against a backdrop of a woodland waterfall. The plant, which rises from a bed of moss and fungi, is surrounded by creatures: a tiny white spider and a yellow moth hover about a snail creeping along a leaf; a second moth flits further off to the right, and a third flies near the base of the thistle; the frog on the moss appears ready to leap, and a dragonfly near the flower is in a vertical descent. Van Schrieck's tableau teems with life, small beings made large by the worm's-eye perspective and luminous by the eerie light.

The forest-floor still life, whose principal Dutch innovator was van Schrieck, became a popular genre in the Dutch Republic during the 1660s, when it was also taken up by the master's followers Willem van Aelst (c. 1626-c. 1683), Matthias Withoos (1627-1703), and Rachel Ruysch (1664-1750).[1] A consideration of contemporary cultural and scientific developments in conjunction with the events of van Schrieck's life clarifies his interest in the genre as well as its general appeal to collectors.

From 1648 until the late 1650s, van Schrieck was in Florence, along with Withoos, where he worked for the Grand Duke Ferdinand II de Medici. His works which remain in Florentine public collections suggest that he served there principally as a painter of animal still lifes featuring insects and reptiles.[2] Since the Medici Grand Dukes were avid collectors of animal specimens, living and dead, as well as painted and drawn faunal representations, van Schrieck's subject matter is

fitting.[3] Their interests in *naturalia* were consistent with the rising curiosity among collectors. Menageries were increasingly common at the courts of Europe, including at the palace Het Loo of the Dutch Stadholder Willem III. They have been characterized as the living counterpart to the *Wunderkammern* or curiosity cabinets of preserved specimens that were equally popular.[4]

This collecting activity reflects the general excitement of the period with regard to developments in the natural sciences. The innovation of the microscope miraculously opened eyes to the unknown, in the words of the English scientist Robert Hooke (1635-1703), "producing new Worlds and Terra Incognitas to our view."[5] In the Dutch Republic Anthonie van Leeuwenhoek's (1632-1723) work with the microscope led to the discovery of "animalcules."[6] The Dutchman Swammerdam (1637-80) applied the magnifying approach to insects in his detailed and enlarged illustrations for his *Historia Insectorum*, published in Leiden in 1685.

Van Schrieck's characteristically close-up and minute view of nature, illustrated by the myriad details of the present painting, notably the tiny spider, appears to reflect some of these developments. Furthermore, the events of his life amply demonstrate his committed interest in nature. Houbraken's biography of the artist provides the origin for the nickname allegedly accorded him by his Dutch colleagues in Rome: "Snuffelaar [sic]; because he was snuffling all about after strangely colored or speckled snakes, lizards, caterpillars, spiders, spinnerets, and odd plants and herbs." Houbraken also records the artist's widow's account of her husband's menagerie which included

snakes.[7] This is corroborated by the Frenchman de Monconys' description of the artist's country home Waterijck, where he bred snakes and reptiles.[8] The artist's inventory also indicates that he collected preserved specimens as well as illustrated botanical and zoological books.[9]

The thistle still life was a preferred subject of van Schrieck as suggested by the many extant examples in addition to the presence of over a dozen such compositions in his inventory.[10] A painting entitled *Nature Scene*, Heinz Collection, Washington, one of a pair dated 1671, exhibits the thistle motif and features the same style and format as the Weldon canvas.[11] It is likely that the present painting was executed during this period, and it too may originally have been one of a pair.[12]

Van Schrieck's distinctive technique serves his subject well: it fulfills the demands of scientific realism in the detail, while it underlines the strange and exotic in the use of color and lighting. The artist depicts textures, lending a tactile quality as in the moss, probably rendered with a sponge, and the tiny spider whose form is built up in white paint.[13] Along with the generally minute description of *naturalia*, this feature contributes to the illusionistic effect. By contrast, the luminous palette of the silvery leaves, the bright flower and highlights of other features combined with the unearthly glow denote a supernatural realm. NTM

1 This type of painting remained popular through the 1680s, and the above-mentioned artists are only some of its practitioners. For introductions to the genre, see Taylor 1995, pp. 172 ff., and Bol 1982, pp. 317 ff.

2 On van Schrieck's work in Florence, and the general scientific milieu, see Franchini Guelfi 1977. Without exception, his paintings in the Uffizi are still lifes of creatures in landscapes.

3 On the Medici animal collections, both natural and representative, which date back to the sixteenth century, see New York /Coral Gables 1986.

4 Hanover/Raleigh/Houston/Atlanta 1991-93, p. 349. This catalogue includes chapters devoted to the phenomena of the *Wunderkammern* and menageries, in addition to an abundance of information about the scientific and cultural developments resulting from the exploration of the natural world.

5 From the preface to his *Micrographia; or, Some Physiological Descriptions of Minute Bodies Made by Magnifying Glasses*, London, 1665, cited in ibid., p. 38.

6 Microscopic forms of life which he found in water samples. Ibid., p. 139. See also the following pages therein under the heading "Microscopic Marvels."

7 Houbraken 1718-21, vol. 1, 1718, p. 357 (present author's translation).

8 De Monconys 1666, pp. 109-113, cited in Bol 1982, p. 317.

9 The inventory of the artist's possessions, made following his death in 1678, is published in Bredius 1915-22, vol. 2, pp. 697-707.

10 Ibid. The inventory includes at least fifteen items which were probably thistle paintings.

11 The painting is illustrated and discussed in Washington/Boston 1989, p. 126, fig. 1, in the entry on the pendant with recorded dimensions of 59 x 47 cm.

12 In the catalogue entry for Weldon painting, Sotheby's, New York, January 11, 1996, a date of 1671 is recorded with the signature. The painting has since been cleaned, and while the signature is intact, the date is not. Nonetheless this recorded date is entirely consistent with the artist's stylistic chronology.

13 The sponged-moss technique is described in Taylor 1995, p. 173, where the author discusses other distinctive characteristics of the painter's method.

50 **Pieter Sion**
(Antwerp ?, 1624 - Antwerp 1695)

Vanitas Still Life with Flowers and Fruit

oil on canvas
77 x 62.2 cm.
Inscribed, on page: *IN HOC MOMENTO/PENDET - ETERNITAS*

PROVENANCE:
Private collection.

EXHIBITION:
New Orleans 1997, no. 51 (ill.).

51 Hendrick van Steenwijck the Younger

(Antwerp? c. 1580 - London? before 1649)

Prison Interior with Sleeping Guards and the Deliverance of Saint Peter

oil on copper
35 x 41 cm.
Inscribed, lower left, on pilaster: *H. V. S./16[?]7*

PROVENANCE:
Collection of J. P. Larsson, Stockholm, c. 1949; Sale, Christie's, London, December 8, 1995, no. 29 (ill.); Private collection, U.S.A.

EXHIBITIONS:
Stockholm, Nationalmuseum; New Orleans 1997, no. 52 (ill.).

The architectural painter Hendrick van Steenwijk the Younger[1] was born about 1580, probably in Antwerp where his father the architectural painter Hendrick van Steenwijk the Elder (1550-1603) had entered the painters' guild in 1577. Since by 1586 the elder Steenwijk had moved to Frankfurt, known for its Flemish emigre community, the younger Steenwijk would have received his father's artistic instruction there. The reference to the younger Steenwijk by Carel van Mander in his "Lives of the Illustrious Netherlandish and German Painters," published as part of his *Schilder-Boeck* in 1604, implies that the younger Steenwijk was then working as a painter of architectural views in the same town as had his recently deceased father, thus in Frankfurt.[2] Indeed, though he is thought of as an Antwerp artist, apparently no evidence has been uncovered of his actually working there.[3] In any case, by late 1617 he was living in London.

Steenwijk seems to have flourished in London. Besides painting independent architectural fantasies—of which Charles I owned perhaps a dozen[4]—within a few years of his arrival he began to supply stately architectural vistas for court portraits, including adding such views to two Holbein portraits in Charles' collection.[5] If the Weldon *Prison Interior* was painted in 1627, as the date seems to read, then it is contemporary with the full-length standing *Portrait of Charles I* (Turin, Galerie Sabauda)[6], jointly signed by Steenwijk in 1626, responsible for the architectural elements, and by the Antwerp-born, court portrait painter Daniel Mijtens in 1627.[7] Mijtens' rigid portraits lacked the "up to date" appeal of those of Gerard van Honthorst (who visited in 1628), Rubens (1629), and Anthony van Dyck (who set-

tled in England in 1632), and Mijtens' move in 1634 to The Hague with its court fashioned on the English model may have precipitated the move to The Hague of his colleague Steenwijk around 1637/38. Though Steenwijk remained active until his death in 1649,[8] the great productivity of the London years was at an end.

Steenwijk is chiefly known today for his imaginary church interiors, entertaining images of fanciful pavilions and courtyards surrounded with palatial buildings, or equally fanciful interiors. These grand spaces and their elegant inhabitants, exemplified by the *Imaginary City Square* dated 1614 in the Mauritshuis,[9] are composed around the comprehensive and obvious use of a perspective system, usually with a clear vanishing point, articulated through elaborate architectural detail. They reflect the work of Steenwijk's father and of Hans Vredeman de Vries (1527-before1609), a widely traveled Dutch architect and painter of architectural fantasies. In 1604 de Vries published an enormously influential book of engravings of his perspective inventions as models for painters entitled *Perspective* and another entitled *Architectura*, one engraving of which has been shown to be a source for the 1614 *Imaginary City Square*.[10]

Along with these light-filled, decorative pieces with easily-mastered visual rewards, already in 1604[11] he had began exploring a more sophisticated approach to the problem of intriguing the eye with a play of architecturally defined spaces. The theme chosen as the vehicle of this was the darkened prison interior, most often as the setting for the Biblical narrative of the miraculous liberation of St. Peter. These prison interiors deserve more attention.[12] They are the most haunting representations of prisons before Piranesi's magnifi-

cent *Carceri d'Invenzione* etchings (1746-61), and one of the finest is that in the Weldon collection.

Although the variations are myriad, the known examples are composed around intersecting, broad, vaulted passageways of unadorned granite masonry marked by massive stone columns at the turning points. With a satisfying shiver we mentally explore the receding passageways plunged in nocturnal darkness except for the warm light of a torch or dying embers of a fire, the latter often partially blocked from our view by a column. The yellow light slides across the flat grey stones, lodging in the crevises, and edges the vaults, columns, and sleeping guards with its reflected glow. The lines of recession created by the blocks of stone and rhythmic marking of the piers in the Weldon painting as elsewhere suddenly disappear into shadow long before they reach into the deep recesses of space from which emerge the tiny figures of St. Peter and his angelic deliverer. The artist cleverly persuades us to try to accustom our eyes to the darkness so as to penetrate the shadows and complete the recessional pattern. Steenwijk's mastery of the perspectival projection of these vaulted spaces is ultimately indebted to Vredeman de Vries' publications, as seen for example in *Perspective*, pl. 26 or 27 ; however here that mastery is underplayed. If the complexities of space and recession in his daylight scenes are intended to beguile through an obvious show of virtuosity in handling an elaborate, but easy-to-follow perspective, railroad tracks that invite the eye to "ride the rails," here they engage the viewer with the subtle fascination of finding a way through the gloom at the point where the tracks break off. Steenwijk makes us work for our visual reward.

The drawings that Steenwijk included in his "little boock of Prosspectives," cited in the collection of Charles I but no longer identifiable, were probably real perspective studies, in contrast to the artist's more pictorial 1625 drawing of a *Dungeon with Sleeping Guards*, J. Paul Getty Museum, Los Angeles.[13] Both types very likely played a role in his continued rethinking of the prison theme, the last extant, dated rendering known to the present writer being that from 1633 from the collection of Charles I and now in a Dutch private collection.[14] For example the compositions before about 1619[15] often favor split viewing angles and other mannerist devices which thereafter give way to centrally organized spaces enhanced by glimpses into adjacent passageways.[16] Steenwijk sometimes produced his most successful compositions in more than one version with only small variations in architectural details or the sleeping soldiers. Another signed but undated and probably slightly later version of the present 1627 composition, but with fewer sleeping soldiers, is in the collection of Mallory Factor, New York.[17]

The story represented here of the apostle Peter's liberation from prison is told in Acts of the Apostles 12.3-11. Herod Agrippa I, grandson of Herod the great (ruled 41-44), carried out persecutions of the Christians including the execution of some leaders of the church in Jerusalem as a gesture to the Jews. Peter was put in prison "with four squads of soldiers to guard him." The night before he was to be presented for judgment,

> Peter was sleeping between two soldiers, bound with two chains, and sentries before the door were guarding the prison; and ... an angel of the Lord appeared, and a light shone in the cell; and he

struck Peter on the side and woke him, saying, 'get up quickly.' And the chains fell from off his hand.... And he went out and followed him; he did not know that what was done by the angel was real, but thought he was seeing a vision. When they had passed the first and the second guard, they came to the iron gate leading into the city. It opened to them of its own accord, and they went out passed on through one street; and immediately the angel left him.

Given that the deliverance took place under cover of night—with the opportunity for the dramatic play of light and shadow inherent in the story—it is not surprising that the finest interpretations of the story among Steenwijk's contemporaries are those by the Utrecht Caravaggisti Gerard van Honthorst and Hendrick ter Brugghen.[18] However, for these artists the drama that attracts them is not the prison escape but the awakening of the apostle. JS

1   For Steenwijk in general see Jantzen 1910, pp. 33, and more recently Liedtke 1991, pp. 31-35; Rotterdam 1991, pp. 70-75; Boston/Toledo 1993-94, pp. 444-47; London 1996, no. 142-43.

2   Van Mander 1604, p. 261v.

3   In the *Age of Rubens* (Boston/Toledo 1993), Steenwijk is included with a work dated 1614 (no. 76); the biography proposes that "Steenwijk was probably in Antwerp during the first decades of the seventeenth century, and may have resided there for a period in the 1590s as well, although there is no firm documentary evidence for either stay and he was never enrolled in the artists' guild in that city (p.444)."

4   Millar 1960, p. 243; MacGregor 1989, p. 416.

5   Liedtke 1991, p. 33.

6   Rotterdam 1991, p. 30, ill.

7   Kelly 1920; London 1996, under no. 142.

8   It has been suggested that the artist died in London (Rotterdam 1991, p. 71); however it seems more likely that he died in The Hague, as Liedtke (1991, p. 33) has suggested. Steenwijk is referred to as living in The Hague in the inscription on the print after van Dyck's portrait of him in the *Iconography*, no works associated with England are known after 1637, and his wife was referred to as his widow in late 1649, at which point she was living in Leiden.

9   Rotterdam 1991, no. 6; Boston 1993, no. 76.

10   Rotterdam 1991, no. 6. For Hans Vredeman de Vries, see Rotterdam 1991, pp. 53-56; Briels 1987 pp. 270-72.

11   Vienna, Kunsthistorisches Museum, inv. 723, oil on panel, 37 x 47 cm., 1973 catalogue, p. 168.

12   The primary discussion of these paintings remains Jantzten 1910, p. 39; more recently see for example London 1996, no. 143.

13   *Getty Museum Journal*, 14 (1986) fig. 150.

14   Formerly in the Willem Russell collection, Amsterdam (Amsterdam 1970, no. 84, ill.), Janzten 1910, p. 39, cites one dated 1649, then in the depot of the Berlin museum (destroyed in World War II).

15   For example, the same basic composition with a split view: dated 1617, Sothebys, London, December 11, 1985, lot 178; dated 1617, Christies, London, June 28, 1974, lot 23; dated 1618, Sothebys, London, July 10, 1974, lot 112.

16   For example: 1619, Her Majesty the Queen, London 1996, no. 143; dated 1626, Fitzwilliam Museum, Cambridge.

17   Oil on panel, 71.2 x 106.8 cm., formerly with Rafael Valls, London.

18   See for example San Francisco/ Baltimore/London 1997-98, p. 22 and no. 11.

52   David Teniers the Younger
(Antwerp 1610 - Brussels 1690)

River Landscape with Rainbow

c. 1645-55
oil on panel
27.3 x 38.4 cm.
Inscribed: *D. TENIERS*

PROVENANCE:
Chevalier Le Roque, his sale Paris, Gersaint, April, 1745; Newhouse Galleries, New York, 1959; Thomas Mellon Evans, New York; Private collection.

LITERATURE:
Smith 1831, p. 271, no. 41.

David Teniers the Younger[1] is best known for his scenes of peasant life and representations of collectors' cabinets of paintings, especially that of the Spanish governor of the Southern Netherlands, Archduke Leopold Wilhelm, whose service he entered in 1647. Nevertheless, in the 1640s Teniers began exploring the Flemish landscape as a subject in itself and not just as a backdrop to peasant revels. He was increasingly interested in the effects of inclement weather, including feathery, darkened clouds, rays of light breaking through them, rain, and the rainbow.

In contrast to earlier artists who only depicted rainbows in the context of an allusion to a biblical, mythological, or emblematic text, Teniers was one of the seventeenth-century painters who began to celebrate the rainbow as a wonderful natural phenomenon that could bring atmospheric subtlety to a landscape. Teniers' *Three Fishermen Setting Out Their Nets,* collection of Dr. Manuel R. Espirito Santo Silva,[2] with its striking rainbow, dates from the same years as the Weldon panel. The importance of the soft coloristic effects is brought home by comparison of these paintings with the black and white engravings made after them a century later by J. P. Le Bas.[3]   JS

1   For the best comprehensive treatment of Teniers, see Antwerp 1991 (catalogue by Margaret Klinge), and for his artistic environment, see Boston/Toledo 1993-94.
2   Antwerp 1991, no. 54.
3   See the engraving after *Three Fishermen* in Antwerp 1991, fig. 54a.

53 Lucas van Uden
(Antwerp 1595 - Antwerp c. 1672/3)

Woodland Road with Wayfarers and Distant View

oil on copper
13 x 16.6 cm.

PROVENANCE:
Private collection.

EXHIBITIONS:
Providence 1964, no. 23 (ill.); New York 1966, no. 38; New Orleans 1997, no. 53
(ill.).

54 Wallerand Vaillant

(Lille 1623 - Amsterdam 1677)

Trompe l'Oeil of Landscape Prints on a Letter-Rack

1671
oil on canvas
61 x 45 cm.
Inscribed, on letter, at top on either side of wax seal: 16/71
above date: *Monsieu/Monsieur Louis/A Pa* [resembling partial
address]
on topmost landscape sheet, bottom left: *ALEGESIS DVRE-*
bottom right: *PINXIT*
on third sheet, bottom right: *PINYT* [sic]

PROVENANCE:
J. Kraus (until 1975); Sale, London, Christie's, July 8, 1994, no. 70 (ill.).

EXHIBITION:
New Orleans 1997, no. 55 (ill.).

LITERATURE:
Faré 1974, pp. 162-3 (ill.).

55 Esaias van de Velde

(Amsterdam 1587 - The Hague 1630)

Farm beside a Frozen River with Skaters

oil on panel
33 cm. in diam.
Inscribed, lower right: *E. WELDE 1616*

PROVENANCE:
Paget collection?; Mrs. Holbrooke, Bladon Castle, Burton-on-Trent (sold London, Christies, February 17, 1939, no. 153, ill.); Private collection, France; Private collection.

LITERATURE:
Keyes 1984, no. 101, ill.

Farm Beside a Frozen River with Skaters dated 1616 was painted by Esaias van de Velde during the years that the artist was working in Haarlem; it beautifully exemplifies the artist's critical role at that time in the development of a new focus on portraying the indigenous, Dutch landscape, rather than the woodland fantasies beloved by the previous generation.

Van de Velde was born in Amsterdam where he may have received some initial training from one of the leading landscapists there, either Gillis van Coninxloo (1554-1607) or David Vinckboons (1576-c. 1632).[1] In 1609 he was in Haarlem, where he joined the painters' guild in 1612. In 1618 he moved to The Hague, working there until his death in 1630.

In the words of Wolfgang Stechow, winter landscapes are "the Dutch seventeenth-century landscape par excellence."[2] In contrast, van de Velde's contemporaries in other countries, especially in Italy and France, found little aesthetic merit in winter's harsh realities and reduced palette. The predilection for winter or ice scenes found in van de Velde's *oeuvre* and especially in his earliest paintings is remarkable. For example, three of the four identified landscapes bearing the date 1614,[3] the first year for which George Keyes has identified dated works by the artist, are winter or ice scenes, as are half of the landscapes dated 1614–17 from the years in Haarlem.[4] The only Amsterdam or Haarlem artist to share this preoccupation was Hendrick Avercamp (1585-1634), whose early skating scenes van de Velde may well have seen before he left Amsterdam. However, van de Velde views his subject as a winter landscape animated by a few skaters on the ice, while for Avercamp, the bustle of human activity is just as important as the frozen canals. An even more striking difference in approach can be found in a comparison of van de Velde's landscape with the lively evocation of *Winter Pleasures* (no. 56) from just the same years by the Middelburg master Adriaen van de Venne.

Very likely *Farm Beside a Frozen River with Skaters* originally represented "Winter" in a pairing with a scene of the countryside representing "Summer." At least two of van de Velde's other early winterscapes were part of such decorative pairings,[5] and the round format was often used in the early part of the century for companion compositions. As Minty has proposed, van de Venne's rondel *Winter Pleasures* was surely conceived with a similar companion piece.

Keyes has identified a second, slightly different, version of the present composition dated 1618.[6] JS

1 For van de Velde see Keyes 1984.
2 Stechow 1966, p. 82, at the beginning of his chapter on the *Winter Landscape.*
3 Winter landscapes dated 1614 catalogued by Keyes 1984: his no. 71 (Fitzwilliam Museum, Cambridge), no. 73 (private collection, Cologne), no. 89 (North Carolina Museum of Art, Raleigh). See also two further paintings Keyes dates to c. 1614: his no. 93 and 102 (location unknown).
4 Besides the Weldon painting of 1616, see Keyes 1984, no. 70 (1617), 75 (1615), and 82 (1615).
5 Keyes no. 14 (c. 1612/13), 75 (1615), 90 (round format; proposed by Keyes as possibly the companion of a scene of haymaking, dated 1616, his no. 130).
6 Keyes 1984, no. 103.

56   Adriaen van de Venne

(Delft 1589 - The Hague 1662)

Winter Pleasures

c. 1615
oil on panel
21 cm. diameter

PROVENANCE:
Private collection.

EXHIBITIONS:
London 1961A, no. 60; Providence 1964, no. 24;
New York 1966, no. 40; Birmingham 1995, no. 22.;
New Orleans 1997, no. 56 (ill.).

LITERATURE:
Apollo (September 1961), cover illustration.

Van de Venne's animated *Winter Pleasures* evokes a merry afternoon on a frozen canal and recreates the subtle tonalities of the northern winter landscape. While the viewer is treated to an icy and picturesque vista framed by barren, craggy trees, the eye is immediately drawn to the elegantly clad skaters and revelers in the foreground, and further along the canal by the lively rhythm of the crowd. At this early date in the artist's career, c. 1615, his potential as a figure painter is evident. He fulfilled this promise in both the caricatures of his later genre grisailles (nos. 57 and 58) and his chronicles of the pursuits and fashions of the court in his album of miniatures made for Frederik Hendrik, Prince of Orange.[1] The foreground group of well-dressed onlookers and skaters, complete with the women's elaborate millstone collars, is enlivened by the anecdote of the couple at the right; the poised, muff-bearing lady is being gently pushed from behind by her companion. Just beyond to their left, a more robust man spins with one foot in the air, prefiguring the whirling, dancing peasants of the grisailles. Van de Venne received early training in the miniature technique, a fact which is borne out by the small scale of this roundel in which dozens of finely-rendered figures populate a fantastic yet viable landscape.[2]

While the staffage in this work announces van de Venne's promise as an innovative genre painter, the landscape type and its roundel format situate the artist within the context of his early seventeenth-century Middleburg colleagues, Mattheus Molanus (c. 1590-1645), Jacob van Geel (c. 1584-5 - c. 1638) and Christoffel van den Berghe (c. 1590-after 1642).[3] These artists maintained conventions of the Flemish tradition, especially

those established by the Bruegel dynasty, namely the high viewpoint of the "world landscape" and the tripartite color scheme of brown for the foreground, green for the middleground, and blue for the distance, features evident in the Weldon roundel where the colors are somewhat muted to suit the season. The tree *repoussoir* at left, animated by the varied bird-life as is typical of the artist, is another Flemish element.[3] The roundel format, also seen in Brueghel's *Fantastic Forest Scene*, c. 1600 (no. 8), and van Goyen's *Summer Landscape*, 1620, in the present collection (no. 19), may be traced back to Flemish print precedents, notably those of Hans Bol (1534-1593).[4]

Van de Venne has aptly been characterized as an important figure in the transmission and transformation of the Flemish landscape idiom in the Dutch Republic.[5] However, his possible relationship to Hendrik Averkamp (1585-1635), another transitional and slightly older Dutch landscape artist and a pioneer of winterscape painting, has yet to be fully explored.[6] Averkamp's relevance to van de Venne is striking with regard to the present painting when one considers his roundel *Winter Scene with Skaters near a Castle*, before 1610, National Gallery, London.[7]

It is likely that the present panel was conceived as one of a pair of paintings representing winter and summer, or possibly even a foursome of all the seasons, a tradition which dates back to medieval illuminations of the months. Although van de Venne's *Winter Pleasures* does not literally allegorize the season depicted as many earlier representations do, it appears to borrow from precedents featuring the personification of winter or February, typically shown warming itself by a fire, seen

here in the detail of the shrouded figure in the left foreground. There are a number of seasonal landscape groups in the artist's *oeuvre*, mostly of rectangular format. His earliest dated landscapes are a summer/winter pair of 1614, and in 1615 he painted a foursome which may have belonged to Constantin Huygens, the secretary to Prince Frederik Hendrik of Orange. A later group of four seasons, dated 1625, remains intact at the Rijksmuseum, Amsterdam.[8] While the winter paintings of these pairs or groups share many of the characteristics of the Weldon panel, there is a roundel belonging to a summer/winter pair in a German private collection which most closely resembles the present painting. From a similar bird's-eye perspective, the artist has rendered an icy canal teeming with activity and bordered by trees and frozen fairy-tale architecture.[9] Both of these paintings seem to date from an early moment in the artist's career, c. 1615, when the figures, though animated and numerous, still maintain a miniature quality in the fantastic, panoramic landscape.[10]
NTM

1 A fine overview of van de Venne's *oeuvre* is Bol 1989. For specialized studies on his *grisailles* and his miniature album, see Plokker 1984 and Royalton-Kisch 1988, respectively. The album, British Museum, which dates from the mid 1620s and includes 102 miniatures, is not solely concentrated on the upper classes. It is composed of sections devoted to the Prince of Orange and his entourage, the merchant class, and the peasant class, combining elements of political allegory and social satire.

2 An early source on van de Venne is de Bie 1661, p. 234, who records that one of the painter's teachers was the goldsmith Simon de Valck of Leiden, who instructed him in "drawing and illumination," as cited in van Suchtelen's biography of van de Venne in Amsterdam 1993-94, p. 321. For a similar technique and approach in terms of scale and detail, see Jan Brueghel the Elder's *Woodland Road with Wagons and Travelers*, cat. 9, and note 1, where Brueghel's possible training as a miniaturist is discussed.

3 Bol 1989, pp.15-20.

4 See also Brueghel's *Woodland Road with Wagons and Travelers*, cat. 9, for a discussion of Flemish landscape conventions.

5 Examples of Bol's round landscape prints, featuring biblical narratives, may be found in Hollstein 1949- , vol. 3, pp. 36-41.

6 Sutton in Amsterdam/Boston/Philadelphia 1987-88, p. 503.

7 De Bruyn Kops, in ibid., p. 320, who also states that Averkamp may have been the first Dutch artist to use the roundel format for landscape.

8 On this painting, see Welcker 1979, no. S54 and Brown/MacLaren 1992, no. 1346, pp. 3-4.

9 *Winter Landscape* and *Summer Landscape*, 1614, Gemäldegalerie, Berlin. *Spring* and *Summer*, 1615, J. Paul Getty Museum, Malibu, *Autumn*, 1615, private collection, Switzerland, and *Winter*, 1615, Worcester Art Museum. On this group of paintings, see van Suchtelen's catalogue entry in Amsterdam 1993-94, no. 328. *Spring, Summer, Autumn* and *Winter*, 1625, Rijksmuseum, Amsterdam.

10 *Winter* and *Summer* undated, unsigned, 18.5 cm., in Bol 1989, figs. 5A, 5B, p. 20, where the author does not date the paintings. For another winter roundel, see *Winter Landscape*, private collection, dated c. 1614-15 by Royalton-Kisch 1988, fig. 11, p. 48. In later landscapes, i.e., the *Winter Landscape*, 1620, private collection, England, in Bol 1989, p. 18, fig. 6, and especially the Amsterdam foursome (see note 9 above) the horizon is lowered, the landscape diminished, and the figures are enlarged.

57   **Adriaen van de Venne**

(Delft 1589 - The Hague 1662)

Poverty Leads to Cunning /Armoe' soeckt list

c. 1630-35
oil on panel
38 x 30.5 cm.
Inscribed, bottom right: *A V. Ven[ne]*

PROVENANCE:
Possibly, Sale, Haarlem, Enschedé Collection, March 30, 1786, no. 49, to Jan Valter; Princes Bariatinsky; F. Meazza, Milan (Sale, Milan, April 15-23, 1884, no. 90 ill.); G. Stroganoff, Rome; Gray Collection; Mrs. A. Vroeg, London (Sale, Sotheby's, London, May 14, 1958, no. 131); Private collection.

EXHIBITIONS:
London 1958A, no. 33 (as Pseudo van de Venne); Providence 1964, no. 26 (ill.); New York 1966, no. 42; New York, Metropolitan Museum of Art, temporary loan, 1972; Birmingham 1995, no. 24 (ill.); Washington, National Gallery of Art, Dutch Cabinet Galleries, temporary loan, April 1-September 15, 1996; New Orleans 1997, no. 57 (ill.).

LITERATURE:
Possibly Franken 1878, no. 22; Muñoz/Pollack 1912, vol. 2, p. 72, plate 53; Plokker 1984, no. 19 (ill.), p. 207; van Thiel 1986, p. 70; Royalton-Kisch 1988, pp. 122, note 100, 136, note 226; Hollstein 1949- , vol. 25, 1990, p. 21.

Adriaen van de Venne unleashes his sense of irony and demonstrates his technical brilliance in this genre *grisaille* with inscription, a type of painting which he pioneered and perfected in his later career in The Hague. An elderly, seemingly blind couple, voluminously clad in tattered rags, hobbles along making music. The bearded man, whose progress is impeded by one wooden leg, turns the crank of his hurdy-gurdy with gnarled and massive fingers, while his female companion, also ham-fisted, plays the rommel-pot. Her poverty is underscored by the bits of straw spilling from her clogs – insulation against the cold.[1] While the twosome is indeed outwardly pathetic, van de Venne's satirical purpose is announced by the inscription in the banderole at the base of the image: "Poverty leads to cunning." There are other telling details: The man's blindness may be feigned because his right eye is fully opened. The "guide dog," who leads both musicians by a thin chain, appears to smile, and the figure standing on his head beyond them alludes allegorically to a world upside down in which things are not necessarily as they appear.[2]

Van de Venne began his career in Middelburg, chiefly as a painter of landscapes (see no. 56) and political allegories in the highly detailed, refined, and colorful manner of Jan Brueghel the Elder (1568-1625).[3] He focused much of his later production from the period of his residency in The Hague, c. 1625-1662, on *grisaille* paintings which feature social satire.[4] These paintings reflect elements of the artist's youthful training and experiences. According to the seventeenth-century biographer de Bie, one of van de Venne's teachers had been the grisaille painter Hieronymus van Diest, whose works are regrettably unknown to us.[5] Furthermore, the artist's illustrations of the 1620s for the poems of Jacob Cats and others in addition to his own poetry, such as his *Tafereel van Sinne-Mal/Picture of Foolish Sense*, 1623, are evidence of his early exposure to, and interest in, literary and pictorial satire.[6] In his *grisailles* van de Venne evolved the satirical genre, often incorporating image and inscription and making it his own particular specialization.

The Weldon panel exemplifies van de Venne's mature variety of the genre *grisaille* in its iconography, composition, and technique. In the dozens of extant *gri-*

sailles the artist often caricatures the indigent, mendicant underclass.[7] Variations on certain types are characteristic of these paintings, such as the bearded man of the present painting who is reinvented as the bearer of the lame figure in *Every Gift Helps*, also in the Weldon Collection (no. 58), and who reappears with a recorder in *The Beautiful and the Ugly*, private collection.[8] The majority of these representations includes inscriptions (banderoles with gothic lettering), mostly puns and mottoes relating to the artist's poetry and/or contemporary emblems.[9]

The artist developed a rapid monochrome technique for this genre, referred to as *grisaille* when executed in gray tones and more specifically as *brunaille* when in brown as in the Weldon painting.[10] Bol has generally described the artist's working method which is illustrated by the present painting, a masterfully executed and well-preserved example of the type. The design was drawn onto the prepared panel in charcoal or graphite with fluid, large gestures. A first layer of darker paint loosely defined the design, while it often varied the specific outlines of the underdrawing. The surface was further refined and articulated by the means of highlights, applied last.[11] The lively underdrawing and the artist's deviations from its outlines in the subsequent paint layers are easily discerned in the Weldon panel as in the ragged drawn line of the woman's apron hem which is evened out in the paint. The effective use of highlights is illustrated in the articulation of her facial features where the artist crafts an expressive likeness with judicious touches.

The meaning of the present painting is illuminated by the artist's own verses from his narrative peasant epic *Tafereel van de Belacchende Werelt/Picture of the Ridiculous World*, published in 1635. In the story the two protagonists visit a *kermis* and the author details their account, including a description of the forty-two types of beggars seen. Among these are the *Platschierers*/Fleecers "...blind singers and players of stringed instruments, who...play in the streets, twaddling numerous deceptions, fabricating silly lies about the causes of their ill-fated blindness."[12] In the same book, the motto of the painting is elaborated: "Poverty leads to cunning/As no wealth grows from it./Much is plotted to make a living, livelihood is unequally earned/The one on water, the other on land,/ The one with honour, the other with disgrace."[13] These lines are qualified by a statement in the margin: "In order to withstand hunger/The human race becomes accustomed to many guiles."[14] The duplicitous and scurrilous nature of van de Venne's musicians in the present painting is conveyed in the details of the allegedly blind man's open and seeing eyes and the sheathed knife which swings from the woman's apron strings.

While the Weldon panel is undated, it relates to van de Venne's endeavors of the early 1630s, both literary and artistic. It closely resembles another painting of the same title which is polychrome.[15] This second version is paired with a work entitled *Wealth Leads to Luxury* and they probably were originally part of a series of five illustrations of various mottoes.[16] Both of these paintings have been dated to the 1630s by Bol, and hence they would be roughly contemporary to van de Venne's peasant poem of 1635, *Picture of the Ridiculous World*.

There is a third, undated painting by the artist which features a similar pair of musicians, albeit the woman sings rather than plays an instrument. Although it bears no inscription, a print after it by Adriaen Matham features a telling heading on the woman's broad sheet: "A new song by the old and new cheats."[17]

The northern tradition of representing disreputable beggars, notably the type of the blind hurdy-gurdy player, is part of a continuum which reaches back to Hieronymus Bosch (c. 1450-1516) and Pieter Bruegel the Elder (1528-1569) and forward through Rembrandt (1606-1669) and beyond.[18] Buijsen has traced the motif of the blind couple led by a dog in van de Venne's version of *Poverty Leads to Cunning* in The Hague to an anonymous engraving after Bosch published in 1550.[19] Furthermore, van de Venne's rendering of the hurdy-gurdy player in that painting, as well as in the Weldon panel, follows pictorial conventions of the character as developed from Bosch onwards. He is elderly and bearded, and wears a wide, floppy hat and a tattered cloak.

While many of van de Venne's images of the poor may appear cruelly mocking, they should be considered in the context of the literary and pictorial satire that was a vibrant element of Dutch seventeenth-century culture. Poets, painters, and printmakers spared none, rich nor poor, in their pursuit of humor. In the words of van de Venne himself, from the introduction to his *Picture of the Ridiculous World*: "If you want a good laugh, gather round, [this is] for art-loving beholders, a useful and entertaining Picture, containing in detail human behaviour of the present Golden Age, in peasant guise..."[20] NTM

1   Bol 1989, p. 82.

2   The interpretation of the head-stand figure is taken from van Thiel 1986, pp. 70-71, note 14.

3   An outstanding example of an early allegorical work is van de Venne's *Fishing for Souls*, 1614, Rijksmuseum, Amsterdam, the subject of Knuttel's dissertation, Knuttel 1917, and recently illustrated and catalogued in Amsterdam 1993-94, no. 210. For a discussion of his early *oeuvre*, see the entry on his *Winter Pleasures*, c. 1615, in the present catalogue.

4   While most of van de Venne's *grisailles* date from 1625 on, there are some which precede his move to The Hague and date to 1621, and possibly even earlier. On this, see Royalton-Kisch 1988, pp. 39, and 121-22, notes 95 and 97. For an overview of the genre in van de Venne's work, see Bol 1989, chapter 7. Plokker 1984 focuses only on the images which include banderoles, and she includes polychrome works in her discussion. She does not attempt to establish a chronology for this body of work. Her study is reviewed in van Thiel 1986.

5   De Bie 1661, p. 235 (as cited in the artist's biography by van Suchtelen in Amsterdam 1993-94, p. 321). The other teacher recorded in de Bie 1661 is the goldsmith Simon de Valck of Leiden.

6   Amsterdam 1993-94. p. 321, outlines the artist's career. Royalton-Kisch 1988, pp. 48-57, discusses the genre paintings in conjunction with the artist's literary activities.

7   Plokker 1984, catalogues 107 works; however, her total excludes paintings without inscriptions and includes some polychrome paintings. Van Thiel 1986 discusses the difficulty inherent in categorizing and cataloguing this material.

8   The second painting is illustrated in New York 1995, no page no., in Part 2, under the section on the paintings sold in 1986.

9   For a discussion of the inscriptions, see Royalton-Kisch 1988, pp. 49-52.

10   Bol 1989, p. 80, relates van de Venne's monochrome paintings to the contemporaneous tonalist movement in Dutch landscape painting. Van Thiel 1986, p. 67, describes his *grisailles* as hybrids which combine the graphic means of drawing and printmaking with painting techniques.

11   Bol 1989 describes the technique on p. 89.

12   These passages are cited and translated in The Hague/Antwerp 1994, no. 43, which is Buijsen's catalogue entry on another version of this subject by van de Venne, *Poverty Leads to Cunning*, private collection, The Hague, which will be discussed below. The associations between van de Venne's inscribed *grisailles* and his poems were first explored in Plokker 1984. Her discussion of the Weldon painting, no. 19, includes many of the literary allusions.

13   As cited and translated in The Hague/Antwerp 1994, no. 43.

14   Cited in Plokker 1984, no. 19, p. 67 (present author's translation).

15   Private collection, The Hague. The painting is discussed and illustrated in Bol 1989, pp. 84-85, and it is catalogued in The Hague/Antwerp 1994, no. 43.

16   The other three paintings are lost and known only from copies. As discussed in The Hague/Antwerp 1994, pp. 308, 310, note 12.

There are a number of dated grisailles from the early 1630s which are stylistically and thematically similar to the Weldon painting; see, for example, Plokker 1984, nos. 6 and 75, both dated 1633.

17   The third painting is discussed and illustrated in Plokker 1984, pp. 68-9, fig. 19c, where its location is given as Bodkin Collection, Birmingham. The print which was first noted by Plokker, ibid., is discussed with a transcription of the broadsheet in The Hague/Antwerp 1994, p. 310. There is also an anonymous print, presumably after a lost painting by van de Venne, which shows a similar couple with a dog and which includes the same inscriptions as the Weldon painting and the panel in The Hague. It is illustrated in Hollstein, 1949- , vol. 35, 1990, p. 21. Other paintings of the subject which may be autograph works are Plokker 1984, nos. 20, 21. While the meaning of these works is probably the same as that of the Weldon painting, the compositions are quite different.

18   On this tradition see, among others, Sudek 1931; Winternitz 1943; Jones Hellerstedt 1981; Reinold 1981; Dordrecht 1992-93, no. 63; and The Hague/Antwerp 1994, no. 43. For a discussion which focuses on the representation of the hurdy-gurdy player in French art and which includes Netherlandish examples, see Conisbee in Washington/Fort Worth 1996-97, especially pp. 21-62.

19   The engraving, entitled *The Beggars*, was published by Hieronymus Cock in Antwerp and it is illustrated in The Hague/Antwerp 1994, p. 309, fig. 2. It includes many different vignettes of beggars in addition to the blind couple.

Plokker 1984, p. 69, briefly outlines the tradition and relates it to the Weldon painting.

20   As cited and translated (with the exception of the word Picture, which I have substituted for Buijsen's translation of "Scene" for the word *Tafereel*) in The Hague/Antwerp 1994, pp. 308, 310, note 9. The passage is from the beginning van de Venne's preface, and it appears on an unnumbered page.

58   Adriaen van de Venne

(Delft 1589 - The Hague 1662)

Every Gift Helps/Alle baeten helpen

c. 1630-35
oil on panel
33.5 x 28 cm.
Inscribed, bottom right: *A [?] V. Venne*

PROVENANCE:
Private collection.

EXHIBITIONS:
London 1957; Indianapolis/San Diego 1958, no. 73 (ill.); Providence 1964, no. 25
(ill.); New York 1966, no. 41; Birmingham 1995, no. 23 (ill.); Washington,
National Gallery of Art, Dutch Cabinet Galleries, temporary loan, April 1-
September 15, 1996; New Orleans 1997, no. 58 (ill.).

LITERATURE:
The Connoisseur 156 (July 1964), p. 221 (ill.); Amsterdam 1976, p. 255; Reinold
1981, p. 170, fig. 210; Plokker 1984, no. 3 (ill.), p. 16.

Please refer to entry no. 57 for a brief discussion of this painting.

59 Simon de Vlieger
(Rotterdam c. 1600 - Weesp 1653)

Lightning over Rough Seas with Sailboats

c. 1645
oil on panel
48.3 x 68.8 cm.
Inscribed, bottom left: *S DE VLIGER*

PROVENANCE:
Private collection.

EXHIBITIONS:
Birmingham 1995, no. 25 (ill.); New Orleans 1997,
no. 60 (ill.).

Simon de Vlieger's portrayal of a breaking storm is characteristic of the monochrome seascapes the artist painted in his full maturity, c. 1645. An immense menacing sky is illuminated by bright streaks of lightning that rend the darkness of the clouds and are reflected in the water. The rough, frothy seas are filled with craft that appear to be navigating toward the beacon and jetty to the left. A dory containing two oarsmen nears the jetty, while a small sailboat with leaning mast approaches. To the right a figure in a larger boat lowers the jib and another struggles with the mainsail behind. Sailboats in various states of rigging extend to the horizon.

The subject of this painting, a storm upon an indigenous coastline, and its near monochrome palette place it within the context of the second generation of Dutch seascape painters among whom Simon de Vlieger was a leading figure.[1] While nothing is known about the artist's training, the resemblance of his paintings to those of his predecessor and fellow Rotterdamer Jan Porcellis (c. 1580/84-1632) suggests that he may have been Porcellis' student. The present painting relates to earlier monochrome seascapes by Porcellis, such as his *Pink in the Storm*, c. 1620, and his *Sailboats in a Breeze*, 1629.[2] Its marked brown palette, however, is characteristic of a later phase of tonalism seen in landscape painting and exemplified in the present collection by Jan van Goyen's *Outlook on the Dunes*, 1651 (no. 20).[3] Van Goyen also occasionally painted marines and his *Sailboats in a Thunderstorm*, 1643, is analogous to the present painting both in subject and in its brown monochrome which is even more pronounced.[4] A relationship between the two artists has been posited because of the similarity of their marine, beach, and dune landscapes from this period; opinion is divided, however, on which painter introduced the genre of the storm seascape.[5]

The subject of the thunderstorm is found in several other works by de Vlieger, all dated to the 1640s and painted on panels of the same approximate dimensions.[6] *A Sea Storm*, which is currently lost but known through reproduction, is dated by Kelch to the second half of the decade. It shows a frothy sea with a band of shadow cast across the foreground and a rendering of lightning breaking on the horizon and streaking through the clouds, features also seen in the Weldon painting. It is also dominated by brown and yellow tones.[7] In *Ships in Distress off a Rocky Coast*, Bader Collection, Milwaukee, c. 1645, the artist employs the same pictorial devices for the water and lightning, but the painting is more dramatic and narrative in its portrayal of a shipwreck.

There is another painting by the artist from the late 1640s, *Sailboats in a Stiff Breeze*, Hornstein Collection, Montreal,[8] which depicts craft in strong winds rather than a thunderstorm. In this example the artist repeats the general composition of the Weldon work, reversing the positions of the jetty and the principal boat. Its gray-brown palette also resembles the tonalism of the Weldon painting.

The dating and attribution of de Vlieger's sea storm paintings is problematic since the location of several is currently unknown. The de Vlieger scholar Kelch has stated that the present painting resembles works by Jan Porcellis, while the Porcellis authority Walsh is inclined to accept the attribution to de Vlieger.[9] As discussed above, the Weldon panel is consistent with de Vlieger's accepted storm paintings in terms of style, subject matter, and format. Furthermore, its extreme tonalism would appear to situate it in the

decade after Porcellis' death in 1632. As early as the 1660s, a painting attributed to Porcellis stumped a jury of artists including Allart van Everdingen (1621-1675) and Jacob Ruisdael (1628/9-1682), seascape painters in their own right who could not agree on its authorship.[10] It is therefore unremarkable that opinions might differ today on the present painting.

In a book devoted to the genre of the Dutch seascape, Goedde has put forth an iconographic method of interpretation based upon classical and contemporaneous literary sources on storms thereby ascribing moral significance to the paintings.[11] The author has divided the paintings into subject groups and the present work fits his heading of "Thunderstorms over Local Waters: Humility and Divine Wrath."[12] Goedde suggests an emblematic reading of lightning as "God's warning to and chastisement of the proud and ambitious,"[13] with the fishermen and sailors humbled and retreating. Nature assumes the role of a formidable protagonist, rendering man completely helpless. It is certainly conceivable that seventeenth-century viewers would have seen the present ominous seascape as a meditation on the humility of mankind before divine forces; however, de Vlieger's moral message was much more explicit in his contemporaneous shipwreck painting in which monks are depicted kneeling in prayer and rescuing the survivors on the wave-beaten rocks.[14] NTM

1   These characteristics of the second generation of marine painters are discussed in Bol 1973, pp. 179-80. For de Vlieger see most recently the entries by Kelch in Rotterdam 1997.

2   The first painting is at the Nationalmuseum, Budapest, illustrated and discussed in Bol 1973, fig. 90, p. 94. The 1629 painting is at the Stedelijk Museum de Lakenhal, Leiden, illustrated and discussed in Minneapolis/Toledo/Los Angeles 1990-91, no. 24.

3   For a consideration of tonalism in the present catalogue, see the van Goyen entry as well as the text on Salomon van Ruysdael's *Riverview with Boats and Liesvelt Castle Tower*, cat. 47.

4   Rijksdienst beeldende Kunst, The Hague, illustrated and discussed in Minneapolis/Toledo/Los Angeles 1990- 91, no. 116, where eight other stormscapes by the artist are cited.

5   In Keyes' entry on the van Goyen painting of 1643, ibid., he states that van Goyen was responsible for the marine genre which featured meteorological phenomena in a specifically Dutch setting. Conversely Kelch 1971, p. 86, discusses de Vlieger's leading role as a sea storm painter, while he notes van Goyen's influence over him in the beach and dune landscapes. Bol 1973, p. 177, also stresses de Vlieger's importance in the development of the tonalist sea storm type, claiming that van Goyen came to it relatively late.

6   As listed in Minneapolis/Toledo/Los Angeles 1990-91, no. 46, note 3, four of the paintings are: 1. *Sea Storm*, c. 1645-50, formerly collection of H.M. Cramer, The Hague, discussed in Kelch 1971, p. 84 and no. 44; 2. *Ships in Distress off a Rocky Coast*, c. 1645, collection of Dr. and Mrs. Alfred Bader, Milwaukee; 3. *Ships in a Choppy Sea*, formerly collection of Lord Northbrook, discussed in Kelch 1971, p. 84 and no 41; and, 4. *Sailboats in a Storm*, Sale, van Marle, Rotterdam, May 28-30, 1952, no. 76. See also Kelch 1971, nos. 40, 42-43.

7   *Sea Storm*, c. 1645-50, see note 6 above, number 1. The palette is discussed by Kelch 1971, p. 85, where he characterizes it as a feature of the artist's late work.

8   *Sailboats in a Stiff Breeze*, c. 1645-50, Collection of Mr. and Mrs. Michael Hornstein, Montreal, illustrated and discussed in Minneapolis/Toledo/Los Angeles 1990-91.

9   J. Kelch, in a letter dated May 11, 1987, based on his knowledge of the painting in reproduction only. Kelch wrote his dissertation on de Vlieger, see Kelch 1971. J. Walsh, in a letter dated July 27, 1987, claimed that he was "surprised" by Kelch's opinion, however, he did not contradict him, deferring to his expertise. He did state however that an attribution to Porcellis was incorrect. Walsh wrote his dissertation on Porcellis, see Walsh 1971, and published two articles on him, see Walsh 1971, 1974.

10   As cited in Walsh 1974, p. 654, note 9.

11   Goedde 1989.

12   Ibid., pp. 190-191.

13   Ibid., p. 191.

14   *Ships in Distress off a Rocky Coast*, c. 1645. For a full citation of this painting, see note 6 above.

(detail)

60 Simon de Vlieger
(Rotterdam c. 1600 - Weesp 1653)

A Calm Estuary Scene at Dawn with a Dutch Kaag

oil on panel
38.5 x 58.8 cm.
Inscribed: *S. de Vlieger*

PROVENANCE:
Collection of Bridges-MacDonald of Berniesdale in
the mid-nineteenth century (according to a heraldic
device on the reverse); probably acquired by James
Dunnachie of Glenboig House, Lincolnshire, c. 1920;
Private collection, U.K.

In this calm riverscape with a partly
cloudy sky, a kaag is sailing upriver. The
Dutch kaag is a type of vessel of which
there were scores of variants, designed for
use on inland waterways. The kaag was
used as a ferry for both people and cargo
in the Zuyder Zee and to and from seago-
ing ships in the roastead of Den Helder.[1]
In a way that is characteristic of the artist,
de Vlieger evokes the subtlest of atmospheric conditions, the soft thin sunlight of
a Dutch morning.

Indeed, during the second quarter of
the seventeenth century, de Vlieger and
other contemporary marine painters frequently experimented with monochrome
effects of light and shadow and showed an
increased interest in atmospheric changes.
To achieve this, they typically used a less
colorful, more tonal palette, as compared
to that used by their predecessors earlier
in the century. *The Lighting over Rough
Seas with Sailboats* in the Weldon collection (no. 59) is a good example of de
Vlieger's near monochrome palette in this
period.

Although de Vlieger depicted calm seas
and rivers in the 1620s, the de Vlieger spe-
cialist Jan Kelch has established that in the
following decade he turned more to turbulent seas, only returning to the representation of calm waters around 1645.[2] In
composition the Weldon painting is close
to the artist's *Frigate Firing a Salute and a
Single-Master in a Calm* in the Städelsches
Kunstinstitut, Frankfurt, and his *Ships in
the Roadsteads with Fishermen in a Calm*,
in the Musée des Béaux-Arts, Strassbourg,

which Kelch dates respectively c. 1645-48
and c. 1651-52.[3] In these two marine
paintings as well as in the Weldon riverscape, de Vlieger balances the composition
with vessels prominently placed to the
right and left, creating an open view
towards the low horizon. In the Weldon
painting, the sense of depth is enhanced
by the jetty and riverbank with the farm-
house and trees in the right foreground.
The low viewpoint gives us the impression
that we ourselves are in a boat, following
behind the *kaag*. AvW-TH

1 Rotterdam/Berlin 1997, p. 28.
2 For de Vlieger, see most recently the entries
by Jan Kelch in Rotterdam/Berlin 1997, nos. 32-38.
For other literature, see the previous entry.
3 Jan Kelch in idem, pp. 200-202, no. 38 and
fig, 2.

61   **Jan Wijnants**
(Haarlem ?, c. 1631/2 - Amsterdam 1684)

*Dune Landscape with Hunters and Distant Water
View*

oil on canvas
20.5 x 25.6 cm.
Inscribed, bottom left: *J. W.*

PROVENANCE:
Marquess of Lansdowne, Bowood, U.K.; Possibly Count Czapari, Vienna; Private
collection.

EXHIBITIONS:
London, British Institution, 1839, no. 38; London, Royal Academy, 1903, no. 14;
Providence 1964, no. 29 (ill.); New York 1966, no. 46; New Orleans 1997, no. 61
(ill.).

LITERATURE:
Waagen 1854, vol. 3, p. 164; Hofstede de Groot 1907-28, vol. 8, 1927, no. 673.

62   Philips Wouwerman
(Haarlem 1619 - Haarlem 1668)

The Watering Place

c. 1645-55
oil on canvas
29 x 37 cm.
Inscribed, bottom center, on log: *P.S.W*

PROVENANCE:
Possibly, Sale, Paillet, Paris, December 15, 1777, no. 66 (for frs. 2,000); Baron F. Delessert (by 1842); Sale, Hotel Delessert, Paris, March 15-18, 1869, no. 109 (for frs. 7,500); Sale, Georges Petit, Paris, May 29, 1913, no. 58 (possibly from collection of J. Beer); Sale, Sotheby's, New York, November 4, 1991, no 128 (ill. and attributed to Pieter Wouwerman); Private collection.

EXHIBITIONS:
Birmingham 1995, no. 26 (ill.); New Orleans 1997, no. 62 (ill.).

LITERATURE:
Smith 1829-42, vol. 1, 1829, no. 138 (as on panel), and Supplement, 1842, no. 133; Hofstede de Groot 1907-28, vol. 2, 1908, no. 109; Mireur 1909-12, vol. 7, 1912, p. 554; Zurich 1991-92, no p. no. (ill.). The painting will be included in the catalogue raisonné on Wouwerman, Maier-Preusker/Müller Hofstede, forthcoming.

Wouwerman's reputation as a painter of equestrian subjects is upheld in this fine portrayal of watering horses and bathing boys. A man on a roan mount attempts to lead a riderless piebald horse to the water's edge. The second horse rears in resistance, his pose a mirror-image of the dog at his side, as if he has been frightened by the small adversary. To the right a boy in red sits on the river bank, while his companion undresses to join two other bathers in the water. A mountainous Italianate landscape and blue sky with frothy clouds form the backdrop to the scene.

The subject of the watering place was a favorite of Wouwerman's, and he often included several of the elements seen in the present painting.[1] The pair of horses, one restive and the other obedient, their contrasting colors, the bathers, and an Italianate setting are common to many of his variations on the watering theme.

The rustic quality of the staffage in the Weldon painting, as opposed to some other depictions by Wouwerman which feature more aristocratic figures, derives from the precedents of Wouwerman's fellow townsman, the genre painter Pieter van Laer (1599-after 1642).[2] Van Laer's *Landscape with Bathers* of c. 1640, Kunsthalle, Bremen, (possibly the earliest extant Dutch painting to feature nude bathers in a context that is neither mythological nor allegorical) and other similar representations by him have been cited as probable examples for Wouwerman's figures in the more rustic watering paintings.[3]

Duparc has noted that van Laer's influence is most strongly manifested in Wouwerman's paintings from the late 1640s to the early 1650s. Additional characteristics that he associates with this period of the artist's work, by which Wouwerman eventually distinguished himself from van Laer and others, are displayed in the present painting. The most notable are the superb and relatively naturalistic rendering of the animals and the silver tonality, distinctions which marked the development of Wouwerman's mature style and secured his fame as a painter of horses. By contrast, in Wouwerman's later paintings the brushwork becomes increasingly refined and the style of the horses less naturalistic and more mannered.[4] It is difficult to date the present painting more precisely; although Wouwerman was remarkably prolific, he left most of his works undated and a chronology has been made by Duparc on the basis of stylistic evolution.

The presence of this painting in the collection of Baron Delessert during the nineteenth century is consistent with Wouwerman's overwhelming appeal to French aristocrats beginning in the 1700s.[5] Two lavish editions of prints after his works were published in Paris by Jean Moyreau in 1737 and 1759, a phenomenon which attests to his popularity there and surely increased his renown. The presence of over a dozen paintings attributed to Wouwerman at the Louvre is further evidence of his posthumous fame in France. During the same period in the Netherlands, Prince William V (1748-1806) inherited and acquired ten of Wouwerman's paintings, many of which now belong to the Mauritshuis, The Hague. The collections of The Hermitage, St. Petersburg, and the Gemäldegalerie, Dresden, are also rich in his work because of the courtly taste in those cities during the eighteenth and nineteenth centuries.[6] Wouwerman posthumously fulfilled the expectations inherent in the introduction to Weyerman's 1729 life of the artist, which describes him as "the sparkling diamond from the crown of the noble art of painting."[7] NTM

(detail)

1 Hofstede de Groot 1907-28, vol. 3, 1908 (English edition), lists approximately forty-five paintings which are variations on the watering theme. This is not surprising for an artist whose extant *oeuvre* numbers between 700 and 1000 paintings. Maier-Preusker in Cologne/Utrecht 1991-92, p. 302, estimates the number at 700 and in Duparc 1993, p. 206, the author suggests that it may exceed 1000 paintings. However, as Duparc states, p. 282, the calculation is complicated by the fact that both of the artist's brothers, Pieter and Jan, painted in his manner.

2 For a discussion of the relationship of the works of the two artists and the possibilty that Wouwerman may have owned a coffer of van Laer's studies, as recorded by Houbraken, see Duparc 1993, pp. 262-264.

3 In New York 1985-86, p. 259, Liedtke posited van Laer as a source for the staffage and setting in Wouwerman's *Landscape with Bathers*, Princely Collections of Liechtenstein, Vaduz. In Montreal 1990, p. 273, Duparc/Graif illustrate van Laer's Bremen painting, in their entry on Wouwerman's *River Landscape with Bathers*, private collection,

Montreal, and they discuss van Laer's possible influence on Wouwerman. Broos in The Hague/San Francisco 1990-91, under no. 72, discusses and illustrates van Laer's Bremen painting in relation to Wouwerman's *Merry and Rowdy Peasants at an Inn*, Minneapolis Institute of Arts.

4 Ibid., pp. 276-77.

5 In the Delessert sale of 1869 (see provenance above), there were two other paintings attributed to Wouwerman. In The Hague/Antwerp 1991, pp. 19-20, Sutton provides a summary of the Wouwerman phenomenon in France. He states, for example, that twelve paintings by Wouwerman were included in the sale of the collection of Blondel de Gagny, Paris, December 10, 1776, and that ten of his works were recorded in the sale of the collection of the Duc de Choiseul, Minister to Louis XVI, Paris, April 6, 1772.

6 The two French print editions are Moyreau 1737 (1759). Duparc 1993, pp. 257-58, includes this information in his account of Wouwerman's popularity in European aristocratic collections.

7 Weyerman 1729-69, vol. 3 p. 157.

63 Simon Vouet

(Paris 1590 - Paris 1649)

Portrait of a Gentleman

c. 1625-27
oil on canvas
76.4 x 60.4 cm.

PROVENANCE:
Sale, Dorotheum, Vienna, October 25, 1955, no. 75; Galerie Sanct Lucas, Vienna; Private collection.

EXHIBITIONS:
Providence 1964, no. 28 (ill.); New York 1966, no. 45; College Park 1971, no. 14; New York 1972; Cleveland 1972, no. 74 (ill.); New Orleans 1997, no. 67 (ill.).

LITERATURE:
Manning 1959, p. 294, fig. 3; Crelly 1962, p. 189, no. 89; Weldon 1966, pp. 23-24, fig. 12; Antiques (Feb. 1971) p. 184 (ill.); Paris 1990-91, p. 194.

This rare early portrait by Simon Vouet presents a direct and penetrating characterization of the sitter rendered in a correspondingly bold manner – aspects which probably situate it within the painter's Italian period. The subject, seen in three-quarter profile, bust format, and set in a painted oval, inclines his head and regards his audience somewhat quizzically. He is brown-eyed with thinning, dark hair framing a full, mature, mustachioed face. A brilliant white ruff, described in dashing brush strokes, breaks the darkness of costume and background and sets off the particulars of the sitter's features.

It is likely that Vouet painted this portrait at the end of his Italian sojourn on the eve of his triumphant return to his native Paris as *Peintre du Roi* under Louis XIII in 1627.[1] As early as 1624 the tremendous official success that would take Vouet to the court in Paris was indicated in Rome by his election as Principe to the guild of Saint Luke; he was the first foreigner to be appointed. By the time Vouet painted the Weldon portrait, probably around 1625-27, he had become established in Italy in part by the patronage of the renowned collector Cassiano dal Pozzo (1588-1657) who owned approximately fifteen of his works, some of which were portraits.[2] Vouet had portrayed a number of Italian aristocrats, as well as Pope Urban VIII, and he had received important religious commissions. Only a handful of the securely attributed Italian portraits are extant, making the present painting a valuable document of the artist's early work in the genre.[3] Furthermore, in its bold tenebrist style the painting records a manner that Vouet as *Peintre du Roi* would virtually abandon as the restaurateur du bon goût,[4] the restorer of the smooth, academic aesthetic favored at the court in Paris.

The portraits ascribed to Vouet's Italian period exhibit many of the characteristics visible in the Weldon painting. They present the sitter in a bust or head format with little artifice and a broad, assured technique. Two of the portraits from this period are interpreted as self-portraits; the earliest, more tentatively identified as a likeness of the artist, is dated c. 1618-19, Musée Réattu, Arles, and the second, generally accepted to be the painter, is dated c. 1626-27, Musée des Beaux-Arts, Lyon.[5] A third work which relates to the Weldon painting is the Portrait of Giancarlo Doria, 1621, Musée du Louvre, Paris, which shows the sitter in an oval inset, but presented frontally and in a somewhat more polished style and larger format, probably as a result of the importance of the commission.[6] Finally, there is the Bravo, Herzog Anton Ulrich-Museum, Braunschweig, a portrait/genre hybrid of a sword-toting, feather-capped rake posed in three-quarter profile with head inclined like the Weldon sitter.[7]

The definitive identification of the sitter remains a mystery although two illustrious individuals have been plausibly suggested. In June Weldon's study of Vouet's male portraits, she proposed the painting as another self-portrait, dating it to the early years after the artist's return to Paris.[8] The man who stares out from the Lyon *Self-Portrait*, c. 1626-27, does indeed bear a general resemblance to the Weldon sitter; however, he appears to be considerably younger with a lower hairline and a thinner face. This interpretation is corroborated by a drawn portrait of the artist by Ottavio Leoni (1578-1630), dated 1625, which offers a much more youthful countenance than is seen in the Weldon painting.[9] Given that the Weldon and Lyon paintings share aspects of style and technique and seem to be roughly contempo-

rary, the artist could not be depicted in both. Further, in virtually all of the known likenesses of the artist, many of which are prints with identifying inscriptions, he is shown with a fashionable beard.[10]

The second proposed sitter is Vouet's patron, Cassiano dal Pozzo, an almost exact contemporary of the artist, just two years older.[11] An avid collector, antiquarian, and scholar, dal Pozzo was secretary to Cardinal Francesco Barberini, nephew of Pope Urban VIII, before he retired to devote his life to his extensive holdings of art and curiosities which comprised a virtual museum.[12] Likenesses of dal Pozzo are rare indeed. He is known from a caricature profile drawn by Bernini (1598-1680), an unreliable comparison for a portrait, and from an engraving by the Florentine artist Pietro Annichini (1610-1645), probably based on a composition of about 1630.[13] The figure in the engraving bears a generic likeness to the Weldon sitter, not enough evidence to establish a definitive identification. However, dal Pozzo was clearly fascinated by portraiture. If the Weldon painting is not a depiction of the collector himself, it may be one of the portraits that hung in his celebrated halls. His posthumous inventories indicate that a family portrait gallery was contained in his palace and that his collection included dozens of other portraits, mostly unidentified and unattributed.[14] NTM

1 The Italian period lasted from 1613 to 27. On the artist's early career, see Demonts 1913. For a biography of the painter, which is the basis for the artist's life in this entry, see the Biographie in Paris 1990-91, pp. 87-143.

In Cleveland 1972, Spear published the Weldon painting as belonging to the Italian period and discussed it in the context of many of the portraits considered in this entry. The author dated the painting to before 1627.

2 Sparti 1992 has published the posthumous inventories of the dal Pozzo collection from 1689 and 1695, from which this count has been taken. It is possible that some of the Vouet paintings were acquired after the collector's death by his younger brother Carlo Antonio dal Pozzo. Brejon de Lavergnée 1973 is a source on the French artists featured in the dal Pozzo collection.

3 See Paris 1990-91, p. 194, where Thuillier lists the early portraits, totaling just over a dozen, including those discussed here. Some of these paintings are lost and only known through engravings. Thuillier includes the present work among the "rare portraits that may be attributed to Vouet with sufficient assurance" (present author's translation). For a discussion of the expressive nature of certain early portraits which have been likened to Bernini's work, see Sutherland Harris 1991.

4 Sandrart 1675-79 (Peltzer edition, 1925, p. 256, as cited in Paris 1990-91, p. 148).

5 Both works are illustrated and catalogued in Paris 1990-91, nos. 10 and 20 respectively. The dates proposed in those entries have been repeated above.

6 Catalogued and illustrated in ibid., no. 12, where the format of the painting is discussed, and it is proposed that the oval painted frame may be a later addition. In the Weldon painting the oval appears to be part of the original composition.

7 Catalogued and illustrated as Portrait d'un Homme, dit Le Spadassin, in Paris 1990-91, no. 7.

8 Weldon 1966, pp. 23-24.

9 Portrait of Simon Vouet in 1625, Karlsruhe, Staatliche Kunsthalle, Kupferstich-Kabinett, illustrated in Paris 1990-91, p. 94.

10 In addition to the self-portraits discussed above, the known likenesses of the artist include the following: an engraving by François Perrier, after Vouet's lost self-portrait of 1632, illustrated in ibid., p. 144; an engraving by R. van der Vorst, after Van Dyck, for the Iconography, illustrated in Crelly 1962, frontispiece; and François Tortebat's painting, Portrait de Simon Vouet âgé, Versailles, illustrated in Paris 1990-91, p. 140.

11 This identification was suggested by Thuillier, ibid., p. 194.

12 For an introduction to dal Pozzo, see Haskell 1980, pp. 98-117. On dal Pozzo's collection, see Santi 1992.

13 The Bernini drawing is illustrated in Haskell 1980, plate 17a, and the engraving by Annichini, which was used as the frontispiece to Carlo Dati's biography of dal Pozzo, the Synopsis, published in 1664, has been proposed as a likeness based on a lost model dating to c. 1630, when the collector was about forty-two years old (as discussed in Brejon de Lavergnée, p. 94, note 5, where the engraving is reproduced on p. 79). Haskell 1980, p. 100, note 2, mentions another portrait of the collector, location unknown, probably by Ottavio Leoni, known from an inventory.

14 Sparti 1992 provides transcriptions of the inventories of 1689 and 1695 in the appendices which are indexed. Of those portraits that are given to specific artists, a handful are attributed to Vouet. While none of the portraits attributed to the artist may be identified with the present painting, it is possible that it is among the many unidentified, unattributed portraits.

Bibliography

CATALOGUES

Allentown 1965
Allentown, Pennsylvania, Allentown Art Museum. *Seventeenth Century Painters of Haarlem.* 1965.

Amsterdam 1924
Amsterdam, D. Komter. Exhibition. 1924.

Amsterdam 1929
Amsterdam, Rijksmuseum. *Tentoonstelling van Oude Kunst door de Vereeniging van Handelaren in Oude Kunst in Nederland.* 1929.

Amsterdam 1932
Amsterdam, Kunsthandel J. Goudstikker. *Hollandsche winterlandschappen uit de 17de eeuw.* 1932.

Amsterdam 1934
Amsterdam, Kunsthandel P. de Boer. *De Helsche en de Fluweelen Brueghel.* 1934.

Amsterdam 1936
Amsterdam, Kunsthandel J. Goudstikker. *Salomon van Ruysdael.* Introduction by J. Goudstikker. 1936.

Amsterdam 1963
Amsterdam, Kunsthandel P. de Boer. *Catalogue of Old Pictures Exhibited at the Gallery of P. de Boer.* 1963.

Amsterdam 1963A
Amsterdam, Kunstveiling S.J. Mak van Waay/H.S. Nienhuis. *Schilderijen, aquarellen en etsen, Verzameling B. de Geus van den Heuvel.* 1963.

Amsterdam 1966-67
Amsterdam, Kunsthandel P. de Boer. *Collection d'hiver 1966/67.*

Amsterdam 1970
Amsterdams Historisch Museum. *17e-eeuwse schilderijen uit de verzameling Willem Russell.* 1970.

Amsterdam 1976
Amsterdam, Rijksmuseum. *Tot Lering en Vermaak, betekenissen van Hollandse genrevoorstellingen uit de zeventiende eeuw.* Catalogue by E. de Jongh et al. 1976.

Amsterdam 1983
Amsterdam, Gallery P. de Boer. *A Fruitful Past.* Catalogue by S. Segal. 1983.

Amsterdam 1984
Amsterdam, Kunsthandel K. & V. Waterman. *Masters of Middelburg: Exhibition in the Honour of Laurens J. Bol.* Catalogue by N. Bakker et al. 1984.

Amsterdam 1993-94
Amsterdam, Rijksmuseum. *Dawn of the Golden Age. Northern Netherlandish Art 1580-1620.* 1993-94.

Amsterdam/Boston/Philadelphia 1987-88
Amsterdam, Rijksmuseum. *Masters of 17th-Century Dutch Landscape Painting.* Catalogue by P.C. Sutton et al. Also shown at Boston, Museum of Fine Arts, and Philadelphia Museum of Art. 1987/88.

Amsterdam/Jerusalem 1991
Amsterdam, Joods Historisch Museum. *Het Oude Testament in de Schilderkunst van de Gouden Eeuw.* Catalogue by C. Tümpel et al. Also shown at Jerusalem, Israel Museum. 1991.

Amsterdam/Toronto 1977
Amsterdams Historisch Museum. *The Dutch Cityscape in the 17th Century and Its Sources.* Also shown at Toronto, Art Gallery of Ontario. 1977.

Antwerp 1991
Antwerp, Museum voor Schone Kunsten. *David Teniers de Jonge. Schilderijen - Tekeningen.* Catalogue by Margaret Klinge. 1991.

Arnhem 1958
Arnhem, Gemeentemuseum. *Collectie J. C. H. Heldring.* 1958.

Arnhem 1960-61
Arnhem, Gemeentemuseum. *Collectie B. Geus van den Heuvel.* 1960-61.

Auckland 1982
Auckland City Art Gallery. *Still Life in the Age of Rembrandt.* Catalogue by E. de Jongh. 1982.

Basel 1987
Basel, Kunstmuseum. *Im Lichte Hollands. Holländische Malerei des 17. Jahrhunderts aus den Sammlungen des Fürsten von Liechtenstein und aus Schweitzer Besitz.* Catalogue by P. ten Doesschate-Chu. 1987.

Basel/Tübingen 1990
Basel, Kunsthalle. *Frans Post 1612-1680.* Also shown at Tübingen, Kunsthalle.

Berkeley 1966
Berkeley, M.H. de Young Museum. *European Works of Art in the M.H. de Young Museum.* 1966.

Berlin 1932
Berlin, Galerie Schaffer. *Hundert seltene Holländer.* 1932.

Berlin 1988
Berlin, Charlottenburg Palace. *International Arts and Antiques.* 1988.

Berlin/Amsterdam/London 1991-92
Berlin, Gemäldegalerie. *Rembrandt: The Master and his Workshop. Paintings.* Catalogue by C. Brown, J. Kelch and P. van Thiel. Also shown at Amsterdam, Rijksmuseum, and London, National Gallery. 1991-92.

Berlin/Amsterdam/London 1991-92a
Berlin, Gemäldegalerie. *Rembrandt: The Master and his Workshop. Drawings and Etchings.* Catalogue by H. Bevers, P. Schatborn and B. Welzel. Also shown at Amsterdam, Rijksmuseum, and London, National Gallery. 1991-92.

Birmingham 1995
Birmingham, Birmingham Museum of Art. *The Golden Age of Dutch Painting.* Curator, J. Wetenhall, 1995.

Birmingham 1995A
Birmingham Museum of Art Newsletter. May/June 1995.

Boston 1992
Boston, Museum of Fine Arts. *Prized Possessions: European Paintings from Private Collections of Friends of the Museum of Fine Arts, Boston.* 1992. Catalogue by P.C. Sutton. 1992.

Boston/Toledo 1993-94
Boston, Museum of Fine Arts. *The Age of Rubens.* Catalogue by P. C. Sutton et al. Also shown at Toledo Museum of Art, 1993-94.

Braunschweig 1979
Braunschweig, Herzog Anton Ulrich-Museum. *Jan Lievens ein Maler im Schatten Rembrandts.* 1979.

Brussels 1980
Brussels, Palais des Beaux-Arts. *Brueghel: Une Dynastie des Peintres.* 1980.

Chicago 1984
Chicago, Richard L. Feigen & Co. *A Gregorian Salon.* Chicago 1984.

Cleveland 1972
Cleveland Museum of Art. *Caravaggio and His Followers.* Catalogue by R. E. Spear. 1972.

College Park 1971
College Park, University of Maryland Art Gallery. *Simon Vouet 1590-1649.* 1971.

Cologne 1876
Kunsthistorische Ausstellung zu Köln. Berlin, 1876.

Cologne/Utrecht 1985-86
Wallraf-Richartz-Museum, Cologne. *Roelant Saverij in seiner Zeit.* Also shown at Utrecht, Centraal Museum. 1985-86.

Cologne/Utrecht 1991-92
Cologne, Wallraf-Richartz-Museum. *I Bamboccianti. Niederländische Malerrebellen in Rom des Barock.* Catalogue by D. Levine et al. Also shown at Utrecht, Centraal Museum. 1991-92.

Delft 1952-53
Delft, Stedelijk Museum het Prinsenhof. *Kerst tentoonstelling: Nederlandse meesters uit particulier bezit.* 1952-53.

Delft 1963
Delft, Stedelijk Museum het Prinsenhof. *XVe Oude Kunst-en Antiekbeurs der Vereniging van Handelaren in Oude Kunst in Nederland.* 1963.

Dordrecht 1955
Dordrechts Museum. *Boom, bloem en plant.* 1955.

Dordrecht 1958
Dordrechts Museum. *Adriaen Coorte Stillevenschilder.* 1958.

Dordrecht 1978
Dordrechts Museum. *Aelbert Cuyp en zijn familie, schilders te Dordrecht.* 1978.

Dordrecht 1992-93
Dordrechts Museum. *De Zichtbare Werelt. Schilderkunst uit de Gouden Eeuw in Hollands oudste stad.* 1992-93.

Dordrecht/Leeuwarden 1988-89
Dordrechts Museum. *Meesterlijk vee, Nederlandse veeschilders 1600-1900.* Also shown at Leeuwarden, Fries Museum. 1988-89.

Dortmund 1954
Museum für Kunst und Kulturgeschichte Dortmund. *Ausstellung Meisterwerke alter Malerei.* 1954.

Essen 1988
Essen, Villa-Hügel. *Prag um 1600. Kunst und Kultur am Hofe Rudolfs II.* 1988.

Essen 1997-98
Kulturstiftung Ruhr Essen. *Pieter Breughel der Jüngere - Jan Brueghel der Ältere. Flämische Malerei um 1600. Tradition und Fortschritt.* Catalogue edited by K. Ertz and C. Nitze-Ertz. Also shown at Vienna, Kunsthistorisches Museum, and Antwerp, Koninklijk Museum voor Schone Kunsten. 1997-98.

Frankfurt 1993
Frankfurt, Schirn Kunsthalle. *Leselust. Niederländische Malerei vom Rembrandt bis Vermeer.* 1993.

Frankfurt 1993-94
Frankfurt, Historisches Museum. *Georg Flegel 1566-1638. Stilleben.* 1993-94.

Genoa 1997
Genoa, Palazzo Ducale. *Van Dyck a Genoa. Grande pittura e collezionismo.* Catalogue by S.J. Barnes. 1997.

Ghent 1954
Musée des Beaux-arts de Gand. *Roelandt Savery 1576-1639.* Catalogue by P. Eeckhout. 1954.

Haarlem 1936
Haarlem, Frans Halsmuseum. *Nederlandsch Kunstverbond. Tentoonstelling van oude kunst in het Frans Halsmuseum.* 1936.

Haarlem 1986
Haarlem, Frans Halsmuseum. *Portretten van echt en trouw - Huwelijk en gezin in de Nederlandse kunst van de zeventiende eeuw.* Catalogue by E. de Jongh. 1986.

Haarlem/Worcester 1993
Haarlem, Frans Halsmuseum. *Judith Leyster: A Dutch Master and Her World.* Also shown at Worcester Art Museum. 1993.

The Hague 1994-95
The Hague, Mauritshuis. *Paulus Potter: Paintings, Drawings and Etchings.* Catalogue by A. Walsh, E. Buijsen and B. Broos. 1994-95.

The Hague/Antwerp 1991
The Hague. Hoogsteder & Hoogsteder. *The Hoogsteder Exhibition of Dutch Landscapes.* Also shown at Antwerp, Heesenhuis Museum. 1991.

The Hague/Antwerp 1994
The Hague. Hoogsteder & Hoogsteder. *The Hoogsteder Exhibition of Music and Painting in the Golden Age.* Catalogue by E. Buijsen and L.P. Grijp. Also shown at Antwerp, Heesenhuis Museum. 1994.

The Hague/Cambridge 1981-82
The Hague, Mauritshuis. *Jacob van Ruisdael 1628/29-1682.* Catalogue by S. Slive. Also shown at Cambridge, Fogg Art Museum. 1981-82.

The Hague/San Francisco 1990-91
The Hague, Mauritshuis. *Great Dutch Paintings from America.* Catalogue by B. Broos. Also shown at the Fine Arts Museum of San Francisco. 1990-91.

Hannover 1954
Hannover, Niedersächsischen Landesgalerie. *Katalog der Gemälde alter Meister in der niedersächsischen Landesgalerie.* Catalogue by G. von der Osten. 1954.

Hanover/Raleigh/Houston/Atlanta 1991-93
Hanover, Dartmouth College, Hood Museum of Art. *The Age of the Marvelous.* J. Kenseth (editor). Also shown at Raleigh, North Carolina Museum of Art, Houston, Museum of Fine Arts, and Atlanta, High Museum of Art. 1991-93.

Indianapolis/San Diego 1958-59
Indianapolis, John Herron Art Museum. *The Young Rembrandt and His Times.* Also shown at San Diego, Fine Arts Museum. 1958-59.

Laren 1958
Laren, Singer Museum. *Kunstbezit rondom Laren.* 1958.

Laren 1963
Laren, Singer Museum. *Modernen van toen.* 1963.

Leiden 1991
Leiden, Stedelijk Museum de Lakenhal. *Rembrandt en Lievens in Leiden "een jong en edel schildersduo."* Catalogue by C. Vogelaar et al. 1991.

Leiden/Arnhem 1960
Leiden, Stedelijk Museum de Lakenhal. *Jan van Goyen.* Also shown at Arnhem, Gemeentemuseum. 1960.

London 1888
London, Royal Academy of Arts. *Royal Academy Exhibition.* 1888.

London 1955
London, Alfred Brod Gallery. *Autumn Exhibition of Dutch and Flemish Masters.* 1955.

London 1957
London, Alfred Brod Gallery. *Summer Exhibition.* 1957.

London 1958
London, Alfred Brod Gallery. *Annual Spring Exhibition of Old Masters.* 1958.

London 1958A
London, Alfred Brod Gallery. *Annual Autumn Exhibition of Old Masters.* 1958.

London 1959
London, Alfred Brod Gallery. *Annual Autumn Exhibition of Old Masters.* 1959.

London 1960
London, H. Terry-Engell Gallery. *Silent World.* 1960.

London 1961
London, Alfred Brod Gallery. *Annual Spring Exhibition of Paintings of Old Dutch and Flemish Masters.* 1961.

London 1961A
London, Alfred Brod Gallery. *Annual Autumn Exhibition of Paintings of Old Dutch and Flemish Masters.* 1961.

London 1963
London, Alfred Brod Gallery. *Annual Autumn Exhibition of Paintings of Old Dutch and Flemish Masters.* 1963.

London 1964
London, Alfred Brod Gallery. *Annual Spring Exhibition of Old Master Paintings.* 1964.

London 1970
London, Leonard Koetser Ltd. *Spring Exhibition of Flemish, Dutch and Italian Old Masters.* 1970.

London 1972
London, Leonard Koetser Ltd. *Autumn Exhibition of Fine Dutch, Flemish and Italian Old Master Paintings.* 1972.

London 1975-76
London, Alan Jacobs Gallery. *Fine XVIIth-Century Dutch and Flemish Old Masters.* Winter 1975-76.

London 1976
London, John Mitchell & Sons Ltd. *The Inspiration of Nature.* 1976.

London 1984
London, Thomas Agnew & Sons Ltd. *Thirty-five Paintings from the Collection of the British Rail Pension Fund.* 1984.

London 1986
London, National Gallery. *Dutch Landscape: The Early Years, Haarlem and Amsterdam.* Catalogue by C. Brown. 1986.

London 1991
London, Richard L. Feigen & Company. *Bartholomeus Breenbergh.* Catalogue by M. Roethlisberger. 1991.

London 1992
London, Guildhall Art Gallery. *Dutch and Flemish Seventeenth-Century Paintings: The Harold Samuel Collection.* Catalogue by P.C. Sutton. 1992.

London 1993
London, John Mitchell & Son Ltd. *Pick of the Bunch from the Fitzwilliam Museum.* 1993.

London 1996
London, Tate Gallery. *Dynasties, Painting in Tudor and Jacobean England 1530-1630.* 1996.

London/Paris/Bern/Brussels 1972
London, Victoria and Albert Museum. *Flemish Drawings of the Seventeenth Century from the Collection of Frits Lugt, Institut Néerlandais, Paris.* Also shown at Paris, Institut Néerlandais, Bern, Kunstmuseum, and Brussels, Royal Library of Belgium. 1972.

Los Angeles/Boston/New York 1981-82
Los Angeles County Museum of Art. *A Mirror of Nature. Dutch Paintings from the Collection of Mr. and Mrs. Edward William Carter.* Catalogue by J. Walsh Jr. and C. Schneider. Also shown at Boston, Museum of Fine Arts, and New York, Metropolitan Museum of Art. 1981-82.

Madrid 1994
Madrid, Museo Thyssen-Bornemisza. *The Golden Age of Dutch Landscape Painting*. Catalogue by P.C. Sutton. 1994.

Minneapolis/Toledo/Los Angeles 1990-91
The Minneapolis Institute of Art. *Mirror of Empire: Dutch Marine Art of Seventeenth Century*. Catalogue by G. Keyes. Also shown at The Toledo Museum of Art, and Los Angeles County Museum of Art. 1991-92.

Montreal 1990
Montreal Museum of Fine Arts. *Italian Recollections: Dutch Painters of the Golden Age*. Catalogue by F.J. Duparc and L.L. Graif. 1990.

Münster/Baden-Baden 1979-80
Münster, Westfälisches Landesmuseum für Kunst und Kulturgeschichte. *Stilleben in Europa*. Also shown at Baden-Baden, Staatliche Kunsthalle. 1979-80.

New Brunswick 1983
New Brunswick, N.J., *The Jane Voorhees Zimmerli Art Museum*. *Haarlem: The Seventeenth Century*. Catalogue by F. Fox Hofrichter et al. 1983.

New Orleans 1997
New Orleans Museum of Art. *In the Eye of the Beholder. Northern Baroque Paintings from the Collection of Henry H. Weldon*. Catalogue by N.T. Minty. 1997.

New York 1965
New York, Finch College Museum of Art. *A Loan Exhibition, Still Life Painters. Pieter Aertsen to Georges Braque*. 1965.

New York 1966
New York, Finch College Museum of Art. *The Collection of Mr. and Mrs. Henry H. Weldon*. 1966.

New York 1968
New York, H. Schickman Gallery. *Exhibition of Dutch and Flemish Paintings*. 1968.

New York 1972
New York, Metropolitan Museum of Art. *Portrait of the Artist*. 1972.

New York 1985-86
New York, Metropolitan Museum of Art. *Liechtenstein, The Princely Collections*. 1985-86.

New York 1992-93
New York, Metropolitan Museum of Art. *Masterworks from the Musée des Beaux-Arts, Lille*. 1992-93.

New York 1995
New York, Otto Naumann. Ltd. *Inaugural Exhibition of Old Master Paintings*. Winter 1995.

New York/Coral Gables 1986
New York, National Academy of Design. *Natura Viva. Animal Paintings in the Medici Collections*. Catalogue by M. Mosco and M.M. Simari. Also shown at Coral Gables, Lowe Museum of Art. 1986.

New York/Fort Worth 1991
New York, Pierpont Morgan Library. *Van Dyck Drawings*. Catalogue by C. Brown. Also shown at Fort Worth, Kimbell Art Museum. 1991.

Northwick Park 1864
A Catalogue of Pictures, Works of Art, etc. at Northwick Park. 1864.

Norwich 1964
Norwich, Castle Museum. *Fine Paintings from East Anglia*. 1964.

Osaka/Tokyo/Sydney 1990
Osaka, Nabio Museum of Art. *Flowers and Nature: Netherlandish Flower Paintings of Four Centuries*. Catalogue by S. Segal. Also shown at Tokyo Station Gallery, and Sydney, Art Gallery of New South Wales. 1990.

Ottawa 1968-69
Ottawa, National Gallery of Canada. *Jacob Jordaens 1593-1678*. Catalogue by M. Jaffé. 1968-1969.

Ottawa 1980
Ottawa, National Gallery of Canada. *The Young van Dyck*. Catalogue by A. McNairn. 1980.

Paris 1894
Paris, Sedelmeyer Gallery. *Catalogue of 100 Paintings*. 1894.

Paris 1898
Paris, Sedelmeyer Gallery. *300 Paintings by Old Masters*. 1898.

Paris 1907
Paris, Sedelmeyer Gallery. *The Rodolphe Kann Collection*. Catalogue by W. Bode. 1907.

Paris 1911
Paris, Musée du Jeu de Paume. *Exposition rétrospective des Grands et Petits maîtres hollandaises*. Catalogue by A. Dayot. 1911.

Paris 1978
Paris, Galerie J. Kraus. *Tableaux et dessins des maîtres anciens hollandais et flamands*. 1978.

Paris 1981
Paris, Institut Néerlandais. *Antoon van Dyck et son Iconographie. Eaux-fortes, gravures et dessins de la Fondation Custodia*. 1981.

Paris 1983
Paris, Institut Néerlandais. *Reflets du Siècle d'Or. Tableaux Hollandais du dix-septième siècle, Collection Frits Lugt*. Catalogue by S. Nihom-Nijstad. 1983.

Paris 1990-91
Paris, Grand Palais. *Vouet*. Catalogue by J. Thuillier et al. 1990-91.

Philadelphia/Berlin/London 1984
Philadelphia Museum of Art. *Masters of Seventeenth-Century Dutch Genre Painting*. Also shown at Berlin, Gemäldegalerie, and London, Royal Academy of Arts. 1984.

Prague 1835
Prague, Privatgesellschaft patriotischer Kunstfreunde. *Verzeichnis der Kunstwerke welche sich in der Gemälde-Galerie der Privatgesellschaft patriotischer Kunstfreunde befinden*. 1835.

Prague 1889
Prague, Rudolphinum. *Katalog der Gemälde-Galerie im Künstlerhause Rudolphinum zu Prag*. 1889.

Prague 1997
Prague, Royal Castle. *Rudolf II and Prague*. Catalogue by E. Fucíková et al. 1997.

Princeton 1979
Princeton University, The Art Museum. *Van Dyck as a Religious Artist*. Catalogue by J. Rupert Martin and G. Feigenbaum. 1979.

Princeton 1980
Princeton University, The Art Musuem. *Italian Baroque Paintings from New York* Private Collections. Catalogue by J.T. Spike. 1980.

Providence 1964
Providence, Rhode Island School of Design. *Northern Baroque Paintings and Drawings from the Collection of Mr. and Mrs. Henry H. Weldon*. Catalogue by D.G. Carter, 1964.

Red Bank 1965
Red Bank, N.J., Monmouth Museum. *The Spell of the Sea*. 1965.

Rotterdam 1991
Rotterdam, Museum Boymans-van Beuningen. *Perspectives. Saenredam and the Architectural Painters of the 17th Century*. Catalogue by J. Giltaij and G. Jansen. 1991.

Rotterdam 1994-95
Rotterdam, Historisch Museum Het Schielandthuis. *Rotterdamse Meesters uit de Gouden Eeuw*. Catalogue by N. Schadee. 1994-95.

Rotterdam/Berlin 1997
Museum Boijmans Van Beuningen Rotterdam. *Praise of Ships and the Sea. The Dutch Marine Painters of the 17th Century*. Catalogue by J. Giltaij and J. Kelch. Also shown at Staatliche Museen zu Berlin, Gemäldegalerie im Bodemuseum. 1997.

San Francisco/Baltimore/London 1997-98
Fine Arts Museums of San Francisco. *Masters of Light. Dutch Painters in Utrecht during the Golden Age*. Catalogue by J.A. Spicer with L.F. Orr. Also shown at Baltimore, The Walters Art Gallery, and London, The National Gallery. 1997-98.

Schwerin 1982
Schwerin, Staatliches Museum. *Holländische und Flämische Malerei des 17. Jahrhunderts*. 1982.

Utrecht 1965
Utrecht, Centraal Museum. *Nederlandse 17e eeuwse Italianiserende landschapschilders*. Catalogue by A. Blankert, 1965 (rev. ed., Soest, 1978).

Utrecht 1993
Utrecht, Centraal Museum. *Het Gedroomde Land. Pastorale schilderkunst in de Gouden Eeuw*. 1993.

Vienna 1873
Vienna, Österreichischen Galerie. *Gemälde alter Meister aus Wiener Privatbesitz*. 1873.

Vienna 1979-80
Vienna, Galerie Sanct Lucas. *Gemälde alter Meister*. 1979-80.

Vienna 1982
Vienna, Akademie der bildenden Künste. *Niederländer und Italien. Italianisante Landschafts- und Genremalerei von Niederländern des 17. Jahrhunderts*. Catalogue by R. Trnek. 1982.

Vienna 1991
Vienna, Kunsthistorisches Museum. *Die Gemäldegalerie des Kunsthistorischen Museums in Wien*. Vienna, 1991.

Warsaw 1969
Warsaw, National Museum. *Catalogue of Paintings of Foreign Schools*. 1969.

Washington 1990-91
Washington, National Gallery of Art. *Anthony van Dyck*. Catalogue by A.K. Wheelock Jr., S.J. Barnes, J.S. Held et al. 1990-91.

Washington 1999
Washington, National Gallery of Art. *From Botany to Bouquets: Flowers in Northern Art*. Catalogue by A.K. Wheelock Jr. 1999.

Washington/Amsterdam 1996-97
Washington, National Gallery of Art. *Jan Steen: Painter and Storyteller*. Catalogue by H. Perry Chapman, W.T. Kloek and A.K. Wheelock Jr. Also shown at Amsterdam, Rijksmuseum. 1996-97.

Washington/Boston 1989
Washington, National Gallery of Art. *Still Lifes of the Golden Age: Northern European Paintings from the Heinz Family Collection*. Catalogue by I. Bergström, ed. by A.K. Wheelock Jr. Also shown at Museum of Fine Arts, Boston. 1989.

Washington/Detroit/Amsterdam 1980-81
Washington, National Gallery of Art. *Gods, Saints and Heroes: Dutch Paintings in the Age of Rembrandt*. Catalogue by A. Blankert et al. Also shown at Detroit, Institute of Arts, and Amsterdam, Rijksmuseum. 1980-81.

Washington/Fort Worth 1996-97
Washington, National Gallery of Art. *Georges de La Tour and his World*. Catalogue by P. Conisbee. Also shown at Fort Worth, Kimbell Art Museum. 1996-97.

Washington/The Hague 1995-96
Washington, National Gallery of Art. *Johannes Vermeer*. A.K. Wheelock Jr. (editor). Also shown at The Hague, Mauritshuis. 1995-96.

Washington/London/Haarlem 1989-90
Washington, National Gallery of Art. *Frans Hals*. Catalogue by S. Slive et al. Also shown at London, Royal Academy of Arts, and Haarlem, Frans Halsmuseum. 1989-90.

Williamstown/Sarasota 1994-95
Williamstown, Sterling and Francine Clark Art Institute. *A Golden Harvest. Paintings by Adam Pynacker*. Catalogue by L.B. Harwood. Also shown at Sarasota, John and Mable Ringling Museum of Art. 1994-95.

Yokohama 1990
Yokohama, Sogo Museum of Art. *Anthony van Dyck*. Catalogue by C. Brown et al. 1990.

Zurich 1956
Zurich, Kunsthaus. *Unbekannte Schönheit*. 1956.

Zurich 1989
Zurich, David Koetser Gallery. *Winter Exhibition 1989-90*.

Zurich 1990
Zurich, David Koetser Gallery. *Fine Old Master Paintings Principally of the Dutch and Flemish Schools*. 1990.

Zurich 1991-92
Zurich, David Koetser Gallery. *Fine Old Master Paintings*. 1991-92.

Zurich 1993
Zurich, David Koetser Gallery. *Recent Acquisitions*. 1993.

BOOKS AND ARTICLES

Alpers 1971
S. Alpers. *The Decoration of the Torre de la Parada (Corpus Rubenianum Ludwig Burchard, Part IX)*. Brussels, 1971.

Arndt 1972
K. Arndt. "Pieter Bruegel der Ältere und die Geschichte der 'Waldlandschaft'," *Jahrbuch der Berliner Museen* 14 (1972) pp. 69-121.

Bachmann 1982
F. Bachmann. *Aert van der Neer, 1603/4-1677*. Bremen, 1982.

Balis 1994
A. Balis. "Boston and Toledo, Ohio, The Age of Rubens," *Burlington Magazine* 136 (January 1994) pp. 51-53.

Balis/Díaz Padrón/van de Velde/Vlieghe 1989
A. Balis et al. *La Peinture Flamande au Prado*. Antwerp, 1989.

Barnes 1989
S.J. Barnes. " 'The Uomini Illustri...' Cultural Differentiation and Cultural Identity in the Visual Arts," *Studies in the History of Art* 27. Washington, 1989, pp. 81-92.

Bartsch 1978-
A. von Bartsch. *The Illustrated Bartsch*. W.L. Strauss (editor). New York, 1978- .

Beck 1960
H.-U. Beck. "Jan van Goyen: The Sketchy Monochrome Studies of 1651," *Apollo* 71 (June 1960) pp. 176-78.

Beck 1973
H.-U. Beck. *Jan van Goyen 1596-1656, ein Oeuvreverzeichnis*. Amsterdam, 1973.

Bellori 1672
P. Bellori. *Le vite de pittori, scultori et architetti moderni*. Genoa, 1672.

Berardi 1998
M. Barardi. "Science into Art: Rachel Ruysch's Early Development as a Still-Life Painter." Ph.D. Dissertation, University of Pittsburgh, 1998.

Bergström 1956
I. Bergström. *Dutch Still-Life Painting in the Seventeenth Century*. London 1956.

Bergström 1974
I. Bergström. "Marseus - peintre de fleurs, papillons et serpents," *L'Oeil* (Dec. 1974), pp. 24-29.

Bergström 1983
I. Bergström. "Baskets with flowers by Ambrosius Bosschaert the Elder and their repercussions on the art of Balthasar van der Ast," *Tableau* 6 (1983) pp. 66-75.

Bernt 1962
W. Bernt. *Die Niederländischen Maler des 17. Jahrhunderts*. Munich, 1962 (subsequent eds. 1969, 1970 and 1979-80).

de Bie 1661
C. de Bie. *Het Gulden Cabinet van de edele vry schilder-const*. Antwerp, 1661.

Bock 1986
H. Bock et al. *Gemäldegalerie Berlin. Gesamtverzeichnis der Gemälde*. London, 1986.

Bock/Rosenberg 1931
E. Bock and J. Rosenberg. *Die Zeichnungen alter Meister in Kupferstichkabinett. Die niederländischen Meister*. Frankfurt am Main, 1931.

Bode 1906
W. Bode. *Rembrandt und seine Zeitgenossen*. Leipzig, 1906.

Bode 1909
W. Bode. *Great Masters of Dutch and Flemish Painting*. London, 1909.

Bode 1913
W. Bode. *The Collection of Pictures of the Late Herr A. de Ridder in his Villa at Schönberg*. Berlin 1913 (English trans. of first ed., Berlin, 1910).

Bode 1914
W. Bode. *Catalogue of the Collection of Baron Albert von Oppenheim*. Berlin, 1914.

Bode 1919
W. Bode. *Die Meister der holländischen und vlämischen Malerschulen*. Leipzig, 1919.

Bol 1952-53
L.J. Bol. "Adriaen S. Coorte, stilleven-schilder," *Nederlands Kunsthistorisch Jaarboek* 4 (1952-53) pp. 193-232.

Bol 1960
L.J. Bol. *The Bosschaert Dynasty. Painters of Flowers and Fruit*. Leigh-on-Sea, 1960.

Bol 1973
L.J. Bol, *Die holländische Marinemalerei des 17. Jahrhunderts*. Braunschweig, 1973.

Bol 1977
L. J. Bol. *Adriaen Coorte*. Amsterdam, 1977.

Bol 1982
L. J. Bol. *Goede onbekenden. Hedendaagse herkenning en waardering van verscholen, voorbijgezien en onderschat talent*. Utrecht, 1982.

Bol 1989
L. J. Bol. *Adriaen Pietersz. van de Venne, Painter and Draughtsman*. Doornspijk, 1989.

van den Boogaart 1979
E. van den Boogaart (editor). *Johan Maurits van Nassau-Siegen 1604-1679. A Humanist Prince in Europe and Brazil*. The Hague, 1979.

Borenius 1921
T. Borenius. *Catalogue of the Collection of Pictures at Northwick Park*. London, 1921.

Bott 1966
G. Bott. "Stilleben des 17. Jahrhunderts - Jacob Marrell," *Kunst in Hessen und am Mittelrhein* 4 (1966) pp. 85-117.

Bredius 1915-22
A. Bredius. *Künstler-Inventare: Urkunden zur Geschichte der holländischen Kunst des XVI., XVII., und XVIII. Jahrhunderts*. The Hague, 1915-22.

Bredius 1917
A. Bredius. "The Still-Life Painter Abraham Calraet," *Burlington Magazine* 30 (1917) pp. 172-79.

Brejon de Lavergnée 1973
A. Brejon de Lavergnée. "Tableaux de Poussin et d'autres artistes français dans la collection dal Pozzo: deux inventaires inédits," *Revue de l'Art* 19 (1973) pp. 79-84.

Brenninkmeijer-de Rooij 1990
B. Brenninkmeijer-de Rooij. "Zeldzame bloemen, Fatta tutti del naturel' door Jan Breghel I," *Oud Holland* 104 (1990) pp. 218-48.

Brenninkmeijer-de Rooij 1996
B. Brenninkmeijer-de Rooij. *Roots of Seventeeth-century Flower Painting: Miniatures, Plant Books, Paintings.* Leiden, 1996.

Briels 1987
J. Briels. *Vlaamse schilders in de Noordelijke Nederlanden in het begin van de Gouden Eeuw 1585-1630.* Haarlem, 1987.

Brongers 1964
G.A. Brongers. *Nicotiana Tabacum: The History of Tobacco and Tobacco Smoking in the Netherlands.* Groningen, 1964.

Broos 1987
B. Broos. *Meesterwerken in Het Mauritshuis.* The Hague, 1987.

Broos 1996
B.P.J. Broos. "Aelst, Willem van," in *The Dictionary of Art.* vol. 1, London, 1996, pp. 165-66.

Broulhiet 1938
G. Broulhiet. *Meindert Hobbema (1638-1709).* Paris 1938.

Brown/MacLaren 1992
N. MacLaren. *National Gallery Catalogues: The Dutch School, 1600-1900* (revised by C. Brown). London, 1992.

Buijsen 1993
E. Buijsen, *The Sketchbook of Jan van Goyen from the Bredius-Kronigcollection.* The Hague, 1993.

Bullard/Stearns 1995
E.J. Bullard and S.E. Stearns. *Handbook of the Collection, New Orleans Museum of Art.* New Orleans, 1995.

Burchard 1978
L. Burchard. "Christ Blessing the Children by Anthony van Dyck," *Burlington Magazine* 72 (1978) pp. 25-30.

Burke 1976
J.D. Burke. *Jan Both: Paintings, Drawings and Prints.* New York, 1976 (Ph.D. Dissertation, Harvard University, 1972).

Campori 1870
G. Campori. *Raccoltà di Catalogi ed Inventarii inediti di Quadri....* Modena, 1870.

Chapman 1990
H. Perry Chapman. *Rembrandt's Self-Portraits: A Study in Seventeenth-Century Identity.* Princeton, 1990.

Chevalier 1984
A. Chevalier. "La Collection de tableaux de Jacques-Joseph de Bousairolles 1741-1814." MA thesis. Université de la Sorbonne, 1984.

Chong 1987
A. Chong. "The Drawings of Cornelis van Poelenburch," *Master Drawings* 25 (1987), pp. 3-62.

Chong 1992
A. Chong. *Aelbert Cuyp and the Meanings of Landscape.* Ph.D. Dissertation, New York University, 1992.

Compin 1978
I. Compin. "La donation Hélène et Victor Lyon," *La Revue du Louvre* 23, 5/6 (1978) pp. 380-95.

Crelly 1962
W.R. Crelly. *The Painting of Simon Vouet.* New Haven/London, 1962.

Cust 1900
L. Cust. *Anthony van Dyck: An Historical Study of his Life and Works.* London, 1900.

van Damme 1990
J. van Damme. "De Antwerpse tafereelmakers en hun merken. Identificatie en betekenis," *Jaarboek van het Koninklijk Museum voor Schone Kunsten* (1990), pp. 193-236.

Davies 1978
A. Davies. *Allart van Everdingen.* New York, 1978.

Demonts 1913
L. Demonts. "Essai sur la formation de Simon Vouet en Italie," *Bulletin de la Sociéte de l'Histoire de l'Art Français* (1913) pp. 309-48.

Denucé 1932
J. Denucé. *Inventare von Kunstsammlungen zu Antwerpen um 16. und 17. Jahrhundert.* Antwerp, 1932.

Denucé 1934
J. Denucé. *Lettres et Documents concernant Jan Bruegel I et II,* in *Sources pour l'histoire d'art flamand,* vol. 3. Antwerp/The Hague, 1934.

Dirkse 1978
P. Dirkse. "Pieter de Grebber: Haarlems schilder tussen begijnen, kloppen en pastoors," *Jaarboek Haarlem* (1978) pp. 109-27.

Dobrzycka 1966
A. Dobrzycka. *Jan van Goyen, 1596-1656.* Poznan, 1966.

van der Does 1668
J. van der Does. *'s Graven-hage, met de voornaemste plaetsen en vermaecklijkheden.* The Hague, 1668.

Dumas 1991
C. Dumas. *Haagse Stadsgezichten 1550-1800. Topografische Schilderijen van het Haags Historisch Museum.* Zwolle, 1991.

Dunbar 1990
P.N. Dunbar. *The New Orleans Museum of Art. The First Seventy-Five Years.* Baton Rouge/London, 1990.

Duparc 1993
F. Duparc. "Philips Wouwerman, 1619-1668," *Oud Holland* 107 (1993) pp. 257-86.

Durantini 1972
M.F. Durantini. *Pieter van Laer and the Bamboccianti.* Berkeley, 1972.

van der Dussen 1640
A. van der Dussen. "Rapport van den Staet de Geconquesteerde Landen in Brasijl, gedaen door d'Heer A. v. der Dussen aen de Vergaderinghe der XIX ter Camer Amsterdam, den 4 April, 1640" Rijks-Archief, West Ind. Comp.

Ekkart/Schneider 1973
R.E.O. Ekkart and H. Schneider. *Jan Lievens. Sein Leben und seine Werke.* Amsterdam, 1973.

Erasmus 1908
K.K.W. Erasmus. *Roelant Savery, sein Leben und seine Werke.* Halle, 1908.

Ertz 1979
K. Ertz. *Jan Brueghel der Ältere (1568-1625): Die Gemälde.* Cologne, 1979.

Ertz 1984
K. Ertz. *Jan Brueghel der Jüngere.* Freren, 1984.

Ewald 1965
G. Ewald. "Studien zur Florentiner Barockmalerei," *Pantheon* (Sept./Oct. 1965) pp. 302-13.

Faré 1974
M. Faré. *Le Grand Siècle de la Nature Morte en France: Le XVIIe Siècle.* Fribourg/Paris, 1974.

Franchini Guelfi 1977
F. Franchini Guelfi. "Otto Marseus van Schriek a Firenze," *Antichità Viva* 16 (1977) pp. 15-26.

Franken 1878
D. Franken. *Adriaen van de Venne.* Amsterdam, 1878.

Friedländer 1905
M.J. Friedländer. "Das Inventar der Sammlung Wyttenhorst," *Oud Holland* 23 (1905) pp. 63-68.

Gaskell 1989
I. Gaskell. *The Thyssen-Bornemisza Collection, Seventeenth-Century Dutch and Flemish Painting.* London, 1989.

van Gelder 1950
J.G. van Gelder. *Catalogue of the Collection of Dutch and Flemish Still-life Pictures Bequeathed by Daisy Linda Ward.* Ashmolean Museum, Oxford, 1950.

Gifford 1983
E. Melanie Gifford. "A Technical Investigation of Some Dutch Tonal Landscapes," published by the American Institute for the Conservation of Historic and Artistic Works, in *Preprints,* 11th Annual Meeting, Baltimore, 1983.

Glück 1931
G. Glück. *Van Dyck, des Meisters Gemälde.* New York, 1931.

Godefroy 1990
L. Godefroy. *The Complete Etchings of Adriaen van Ostade.* (Trans. from French ed., Paris, 1930). San Francisco, 1990.

Goedde 1989
L. Goedde. *Tempest and Shipwreck in Dutch and Flemish Art.* University Park, 1989.

Grant 1956
M.H. Grant. *Rachel Ruysch.* Leigh-on-Sea, 1956.

Guimarães 1957
A. Guimarães. "Na Holanda, com Frans Post," *Revista do Instituto Historico e Geografico Brasileiro* 235 (1957) pp. 85-295.

Haak 1984
B. Haak. *The Golden Age. Dutch Painters of the Seventeenth Century.* New York, 1984.

Hannema 1955
D. Hannema. *Catalogue Raisonné of the Pictures of the Collection of J.C.H. Heldring.* Rotterdam, 1955.

Harwood 1988
L. B. Harwood. *Adam Pynnacker (c. 1620-1673).* Doornspijk, 1988 (Ph.D. Dissertation, Courtauld Institute, 1985).

Haskell 1980
F. Haskell. *Patrons and Painters. Art and Society in Baroque Italy.* New Haven/London, 1980 (rev. ed. of first ed. 1963).

Haverkamp-Begemann 1976
E. Haverkamp-Begemann. "The youthful work of Andries Both: his landscape drawings," *Print Review* 5 (1976), pp. 88-95.

Haverkamp-Begemann 1997
E. Haverkamp-Begemann. "Introduction," to New Orleans 1997, pp. viii-ix.

Hazeleger 1979
R. Hazeleger. "Pieter Fransz. de Grebber, schilder tot Haerlem." Ph.D. Dissertation, Utrecht, 1979.

Held 1976
J. Held. "Zwei Rubens Probleme," *Zeitschrift für Kunstgeschichte* 39 (1976) pp. 34-53.

Held 1980
J. Held. *The Oil Sketches of Peter Paul Rubens.* Princeton, 1980.

Hind 1915
A.M. Hind. "Van Dyck: His Original Etchings and His Iconography," *Print Collectors Quarterly* 5 (1915) pp. 3-36, 221-252.

Hind 1926
A.M. Hind. *Catalogue of the Drawings by Dutch and Flemish Artists Preserved in the Department of Prints and Drawings in the British Museum.* London, 1926.

Hofstede de Groot 1907-1928
C. Hofstede de Groot. *Beschreibendes und kritisches Verzeichnis der Werke der hervorragendsten holländischen Maler des XVII. Jahrhunderts*, 10 vols., Esslingen am N. and Paris, 1907-28; English translation of vols. 1-8, London, 1908-27.

Hollstein 1949-
F.W.H. Hollstein. *Dutch and Flemish Etchings, Engravings and Woodcuts.* Amsterdam, 1949- .

Honour 1962
H. Honour. *Chinoiserie the Vision of Cathay.* New York, 1962.

De Hoop Scheffer 1980
D. de Hoop Scheffer. *A. Sadeler to R. Sadeler II*, in Hollstein 1949- , vol. 21, 1980.

Horn 1989
H.J. Horn. *Jan Cornelisz Vermeyen, Painter of Charles V and His Conquest of Tunis.* Doornspijk, 1989.

Houbraken 1718-21
A. Houbraken. *De Groote Schouburgh der neder-lantsche konstschilders en schilderessen.* Amsterdam, 1718-21.

Impey 1977
O. Impey. *Chinoiserie: The Impact of Oriental Styles on Western Art and Decoration.* London, 1977.

Jaffé 1967
M. Jaffé. "Rubens and Raphael," in *Studies in Renaissance and Baroque Art presented to Anthony Blunt on his 60th Birthday.* London/New York, 1967.

Jaffé 1977
M. Jaffé. *Rubens and Italy.* Oxford, 1977.

Jaffé 1989
M. Jaffé. *Rubens, Catalogo Completo.* Milan, 1989.

James 1994
R. James. Van 'boerenbuysen' en 'stilstaende dingen," in Rotterdam 1994-95, pp. 133-142.

Janeck 1968
A. Janeck. *Untersuchung über den holländischen Maler Pieter van Laer, genannt Bamboccio.* Würzburg, 1968.

Jantzen 1910
Hans Jantzen. *Das niederländischen Architekturbild.* Leipzig, 1910.

Jones Hellerstedt 1981
K. Jones Hellerstedt. "A Traditional Motif in Rembrandt's Etchings: The Hurdy-Gurdy Player," *Oud Holland* 95 (1981) pp. 16-30.

de Jonge 1932
C.H. de Jonge. "Utrechtsche schilders der XVIIde eeuw in de verzameling van Willem Vincent, Baron van Wyttenhorst," *Oudheidkundig Jaarboek* 1 (1932) pp. 120-34.

Joppien 1979
R. Joppien. "The Dutch Vision of Brazil. Johan Maurits and His Artists," in *Johan Maurits van Nassau-Siegen 1604-1679. A Humanist Prince in Europe and Brazil.* Editor, E. van den Boogaart. The Hague, 1979, pp. 297-376.

Kauffmann 1973
C.M. Kauffmann. *Victoria and Albert Museum. Catalogue of Foreign Paintings, Before 1800.* London, 1973.

Kaufmann 1988
T. D. Kaufmann. *The School of Prague: Painting at the Court of Rudolf II.* Chicago, 1988 (rev./trans. of *L'École de Prague. La Peinture à la cour de Rudolphe II.* Paris, 1985).

Kelch 1971
J. Kelch. "Studien zu Simon de Vlieger als Marinemalerei." Ph.D. Dissertation, Freie Universität, Berlin, 1971.

Kersten and Lokin 1996
M.C.C. Kersten and D.H.A.C. Lokin. *Delftse meesters, tijdgenoten van Vermeer.* Zwolle 1996.

Kelly 1920
F.M. Kelly. "Mytens and his Portraits of Charles I," *Burlington Magazine* 37 (1920), pp. 84-89.

Keyes 1984
G. Keyes. *Esaias van den Velde (1587-1630).* Doornspijk, 1984.

Knuttel 1917
G. Knuttel. *Das Gemälde des Seelenfischfangs von Adriaen van de Venne.* The Hague, 1917.

Knuttel 1935
G. Knuttel. *Gemeentemuseum 's-Gravenhage: Catalogus van schilderijen, aquarellen en teekeningen.* The Hague, 1935.

Kronig 1914
J.O. Kronig. *A Catalogue of the Paintings at Doughty House Richmond and Elsewhere in the Collection of Sir Frederick Cook...*, vol. 2, Dutch and Flemish Schools. London, 1914.

de Kruyff 1892
A.D. de Kruyff, "Iets over den schilder Jacob Marrell," *Oud Holland*, 10 (1892), pp. 57-60, 189.

Larsen 1962
E. Larsen. *Frans Post. Interprète du Brésil.* Amsterdam/Rio de Janeiro, 1962.

Larsen 1980
E. Larsen. *L'Opera completa di van Dyck 1613-1626.* Milan, 1980.

Larsen 1988
E. Larsen. *The Paintings of Anthony van Dyck.* Freren, 1988.

Laskin/Pantazzi 1987
M. Laskin and M. Pantazzi (editors). *Catalogue of the National Gallery of Canada, Ottawa: European and American Painting, Sculpture, and Decorative Arts. Volume I, 1300-1800.* Ottawa, 1987.

Lawrence 1991
C. Lawrence. *Gerrit Adriaensz. Berckheyde.* Doornspijk, 1991.

Liedtke 1984
W. Liedtke. *Flemish Paintings in the Metropolitan Museum of Art.* New York, 1984.

Liedtke 1988
W. Liedtke. "Towards a History of Dutch Genre Painting II: The South Holland Tradition," in *The Age of Rembrandt: Studies in Seventeenth-Century Dutch Painting. Papers in Art History for the Pennsylvania State University.* vol. 3. R.E. Fleischer and S. Scott Munshower (editors). University Park, 1988.

Liedtke 1991
Walter Liedtke. "The Court Style: Architectural Painting in The Hague and London," in Rotterdam 1991, pp. 30-42.

Limouze 1990
D. Limouze. "Aegidius Sadeler (c. 1570-1629): Drawings, Prints and Art Theory." Ph.D. Dissertation, Princeton University, 1990.

MacGregor 1989
A. MacGregor, ed. *The Late King's Goods. Collections, Possessions and Patronage of Charles I in the Light of the Commonwealth Sale Inventories.* London and Oxford, 1989.

McNeil Kettering 1983
A. McNeil Kettering. *The Dutch Arcadia, Pastoral Art and its Audience in the Golden Age.* Montclair, 1983.

de Maere/Wabbes 1994
J. de Maere and M. Wabbes. *Illustrated Dictionary of 17th-Century Flemish Painters.* Brussels, 1994.

Maier-Preusker/Müller Hofstede, forthcoming
W. Maier-Preusker and J. Müller Hofstede. *Philips Wouwerman, 1619-1668, The Paintings.* Doornspijk.

van Mander 1604
C. van Mander. *Het Schilder-Boeck.* Haarlem, 1604.

Manning 1959
R. L. Manning. "Some Important Paintings by Simon Vouet in America," in *Studies in the History of Art Dedicated to William E. Suida on his Eightieth Birthday,* London, 1959, pp. 294-303.

Marlier 1969
G. Marlier. *Pierre Bruegel le Jeune.* Brussels, 1969.

Maucquoy-Hendrickx 1991
M. Maucquoy-Hendrickx. *L'Iconographie d'Antoine van Dyck. Catalogue raisonné.* Brussels, 1991 (rev. ed. of first ed., Brussels, 1954).

Miedema 1973
H. Miedema. *Karel van Mander. Den grondt der edel vry schlderconst.* Utrecht, 1973.

Miedema 1994
H. Miedema. *Karel van Mander. The Lives of the Illustrious Netherlandish and German Painters.* Doornspijk, 1994.

Millar 1960
Sir O. Millar. "Abraham van der Doort's Catalogue of the Collections of Charles I," *Walpole Society* 37 (1960).

Mireur 1909-12
H. Mireur. *Dictionnaire des ventes d'art.* Paris, 1910-12.

Mitchell 1973
Peter Mitchell. *European Flower Paintings.* London, 1973.

Monconys 1666
Mons. de Monconys. *Journal des Voyages de Monsieur de Monconys.* Lyon, 1666.

Montias 1987
J.M. Montias. "Cost and Value in Seventeenth-Century Dutch Art," *Art History* 10 (December 1987) pp. 455-466.

Montias 1991
J.M. Montias. "Works of Art in Seventeenth-Century Amsterdam," in *Art in History/History in Art.* D. Freedberg and J. de Vries (editors). Santa Monica, 1991.

Moyreau 1737 (1759)
J. Moyreau. *Oeuvres de Phpe Wouwermans Hollandois Gravées d'après ses Meilleurs Tableaux qui sont dans les plus beaux cabinets de Paris et ailleurs.* Paris, 1737 (second enlarged ed., Paris, 1759).

Müllenmeister 1988
K.J. Müllenmeister. *Roelant Savery. Kortrijk 1576-1639 Utrecht. Hofmaler Kaiser Rudolf II in Prag. Die Gemälde mit kritischem Oeuvrekatalog.* Freren, 1988.

Müller 1927
C. Müller. "Abraham Bloemaert als Landschaftsmaler," *Oud Holland* 44 (1927) pp. 193-208.

Müller Hofstede 1968
J. Müller Hofstede. "Rubens und Jan Brueghel: Diana und Ihre Nymphen," *Jahrbuch der Berliner Museen* 10/11 (1968) pp. 200-32.

Muñoz/Pollack 1912
A. Muñoz and L. Pollack. *Pièces de choix de la collection du comte Grégoire Stroganoff à Rome.* Rome, 1912.

Niemeyer 1959
J. Niemeyer. "Het topografisch element in enkele riviergezichten van Salomon van Ruysdael nader beschouwd," *Oud Holland* 74 (1959) pp. 51-56.

Pigler 1956
A. Pigler. *Barockthemen. Eine Auswahl von Verzeichnissen zur Ikonographie des 17. und 18. Jahrhunderts,* 2 vols., Budapest, 1956.

de Piles 1708
R. de Piles. *Cours de Peinture par Principes.* Paris, 1708.

Playter 1972
C. Bigler Playter. "Willem Duyster and Pieter Codde. The Duystere Werelt of Dutch Genre Painting." Ph.D. Dissertation, Harvard University, 1972.

Plokker 1984
A. Plokker. *Adriaen Pietersz. van de Venne (1589-1662). De grisailles met spreukbanden.* Leuven, 1984.

Puyvelde 1934
L. van Puyvelde. "Unknown works by Jan Brueghel," *Burlington Magazine* 64 (July 1934) pp. 16-21.

Puyvelde 1959
L. van Puyvelde. *Van Dyck.* Paris, 1959.

Raupp 1984
H.-J. Raupp. *Untersuchungen zu Künstlerbildnis und Künstlerdarstellung in den Niederlanden im 17. Jahrhundert.* Hildesheim/New York, 1984.

Réau 1950
L. Réau. *Les maîtres anciens de la collection Baszanger.* Geneva, 1950.

Reinold 1981
L. K. Reinold. "The Representation of the Beggar as Rogue in Dutch Seventeenth-Century Art." Ph.D. Dissertation, University of California, Berkeley, 1981.

Reiss 1975
S. Reiss. *Aelbert Cuyp.* London, 1975.

Rijksdienst Beeldende Kunst 1992
Rijksdienst Beeldende Kunst. *Old Master Paintings,* Zwolle/The Hague, 1992.

Ripa 1644
C. Ripa. *Iconologia of Uytbeeldingen des verstands...* (first Dutch ed., trans. by D. P. Pers, Amsterdam, 1644).

Robinson 1992
W.W. Robinson. "Nicolaes Maes: Some Observations on his Early Portraits," in *Rembrandt and His Pupils: Papers given at a Symposium in Nationalmuseum Stockholm.* G. Cavalli-Björkman (editor). Stockholm, 1992.

Robinson 1997
W.W. Robinson. *The Early Works of Nicolaes Maes, 1653-1661.* Ann Arbor, 1997 (Ph.D. Dissertation, Harvard University, 1996).

Roethlisberger 1981
M. Roethlisberger. *Bartholomeus Breenbergh. The Paintings.* Berlin/New York, 1981.

Roethlisberger 1991
M. Roethlisberger. *Bartholomeus Breenbergh.* London, 1991.

Roethlisberger/Bok 1993
M. Roethlisberger and M.J. Bok. *Abraham Bloemaert and his Sons. Paintings and Prints.* Doornspijk, 1993.

Rosenberg 1900
A. Rosenberg. *Adriaen und Isack van Ostade.* Bielefeld, 1900.

Rosenberg 1928
J. Rosenberg. *Jacob van Ruisdael.* Berlin, 1928.

Royalton-Kisch 1988
M. Royalton-Kisch. *Adriaen van de Venne's Album in the Department of Prints and Drawings in the British Museum.* London, 1988.

Saint-Yves 1748
C.L. de Saint-Yves. *Observations sur les Arts, et sur quelques Morceaux de Peinture et de Sculpture, exposés au Louvre en 1748...* Leiden, 1748.

Salerno 1977
L. Salerno. *Landscape Painters of the Seventeenth Century in Rome.* Rome, 1977.

von Sandrart 1675-79
J. von Sandrart. *Teutsche Academie....* Nuremberg, 1675-9.

von Sandrart 1675/1925
J. von Sandrart. *Academie der Bau-, Bild-, und Mahlerey-Künste von 1675.* (A.R. Peltzer) Munich, 1925.

Schaeffer 1909
E. Schaeffer. *Van Dyck: Des Meisters Gemälde.* Stuttgart/Leipzig 1909 (translated as *The Work of Anthony van Dyck,* New York, 1913).

Salerno 1977
L. Salerno. *Pittori di Paessaggio del Seicento a Roma,* 3 vols., Rome, 1977-80.

Schnackenburg 1970
B. Schnackenburg. "Die Anfänge des Bauerinteriurs bei Adriaen van Ostade," *Oud Holland* 85 (1970) pp. 158-69.

Schnackenburg 1981
B. Schnackenburg. *Adriaen van Ostade, Isack van Ostade: Zeichnungen und Aquarelle.* Hamburg, 1981.

Schneider 1990
C. Schneider. *Rembrandt's Landscapes.* New Haven, 1990.

Schulz 1978
W. Schulz. *Cornelis Saftleven 1607-1681, Leben und Werke.* Berlin/NewYork, 1978.

Seelig 1997
G. Seelig. *Abraham Bloemaert (1566-1651): Studien zur Utrechter Malerei um 1620.* Berlin 1997.

Síp 1961
J. Síp. *Dutch Paintings* [in the National Gallery, Prague]. London, 1961.

Síp 1968
J. Síp. "Notities bij het stilleven van R. Ruysch," *Nederlands Kunsthistorisch Jaarboek* 19 (1968) pp. 157-70.

Slive 1959
S. Slive. "A Family Portrait by Nicolaes Maes," *Annual Report of the Fogg Art Museum 1957-1959* (1959).

Sluijter 1986
E.J. Sluijter. *De 'Heydensche Fabulen' in de Noordnederlandse schilderkunst, circa 1590-1670.* The Hague, 1986.

Sluijter-Seijfert 1984
N. Sluijter-Seifert. "Cornelis van Poelenburgh, ca 1593-1667. Ph.D. Dissertation, Leiden, 1984.

Sluijter-Seijfert 1984
N. Sluijter-Seifert. "Breenbergh, Bartholomeus," in *The Dictionary of Art.* vol. 4, London, 1996, pp. 733-35.

Smith 1829-42
J. Smith. *A Catalogue Raisonné of the Works of the Most Eminent Dutch, Flemish and French Painters,* 9 vols., London, 1829-42.

Smith 1938
R.C. Smith. "The Brazilian Landscapes of Frans Post," *Art Quarterly* 1 (1938) pp. 239-267.

Smith 1982
D.R. Smith. *Masks of Wedlock. Seventeenth-Century Dutch Marriage Portraiture.* Ann Arbor, 1982.

de Sousa-Leão 1973
J. de Sousa-Leao. *Frans Post 1612-1680.* Amsterdam, 1973.

Sparti 1992
D. Sparti. *Le collezioni dal Pozzo. Storia di una famiglia e del suo museo nella Roma seicentesca.* Modena, 1992.

Spicer 1983
J. Spicer. *The Drawings of Roelandt Savery (1576-1639).* Ann Arbor, 1983 (Ph.D. Dissertation, Yale University, 1979).

Spicer 1994
J. Spicer. "Anthony van Dyck's Iconography: An Overview of its Preparation," in *Van Dyck 350, Studies in the History of Art,* 46. Washington 1994, pp. 327-64.

Spicer 1997
Spicer, J. "Roelandt Saverij and the 'Discovery' of the Alpine Waterfall," in Prague 1997, pp. 146-156.

Stechow 1955
W. Stechow. "Jan Both and the Re-Evaluation of Dutch Italianate Landscape Painting," in *Actes du XVIIè Congrès International d'Histoire de l'Art.* The Hague, 1955, pp. 425-32.

Stechow 1966
W. Stechow. *Dutch Landscape Painting of the Seventeenth Century.* London, 1966.

Stechow 1975
W. Stechow. *Salomon van Ruysdael. Eine Einführung in seine Kunst, mit kritischem Katalog der Gemälde.* Berlin 1975 (rev. ed. of first ed., Berlin, 1938).

Sudek 1931
E. Sudek. "Bettlerdarstellungen vom Ende des XV. Jahrhunderts bis zu Rembrandt." Ph.D. Dissertation, Strasbourg, 1931.

Sumowski 1983
W. Sumowski. *Gemälde der Rembrandt Schuler.* London/Pfalz, 1983.

Sutherland Harris 1991
A. Sutherland Harris. "Vouet, le Bernin, et la «ressemblance parlante»," in *Simon Vouet, Actes du colloque international, Galeries nationales du Grand Palais, 5-6-7 février 1991,* pp. 193-208.

Sutton 1990
P.C. Sutton. *Northern European Paintings in the Philadelphia Museum of Art.* Philadelphia, 1990.

Swillens 1957
P.T.A. Swillens. *Schilderslexicon.* Utrecht, 1957.

Taylor 1995
P. Taylor. *Dutch Flower Painting 1600-1720.* London/New Haven, 1995.

van Thiel 1986
P.J.J. van Thiel. Review of Plokker 1984. *Oud Holland* 100 (1986) pp. 66-71.

Thieme/Becker 1907-50
U. Thieme and F. Becker (editors). *Allgemeines Lexikon der bildenden Künstler von der Antike bis zur Gegenwart,* 37 vols., Leipzig, 1907-50.

Torresan 1975
Di Paolo Torresan. "Per una rivaluazione di Pieter Codde," *Antichità Viva* 14 (1975) pp. 12-23.

Valentiner 1919
W.R. Valentiner. *Zeiten der Kunst und der Religion.* Berlin, 1919.

Valentiner 1924
W.R. Valentiner. *Nicolaes Maes.* Stuttgart/Berlin/Leipzig, 1924.

Valentiner/Wescher 1950
W.R. Valentiner and P. Wescher. *Louis and Mildred Kaplan Collection.* New York, 1950.

Vey 1962
H. Vey. *Die Zeichnungen Anton van Dycks.* Brussels, 1962.

Vroom 1980
N.R.A. Vroom. *A Modest Message as Intimated by the Painters of the 'Monochrome Banketje'.* Schiedam, 1980.

Waagen 1854
G. Waagen. *Treasures of Art in Great Britain.* London, 1854.

van de Waal 1931
H. van de Waal. *Jan van Goyen.* Amsterdam, 1931.

Waddingham 1964
M.R. Waddingham. "Andries and Jan Both in France and Italy," *Paragone* n.s. 171 (1964) pp. 13-43.

Walford 1981
E. Walford. "Jacob van Ruisdael and the Perception of Landscape," Ph.D. Dissertation, Cambridge University, 1981.

Walford 1991
E. Walford. *Jacob van Ruisdael and the Perception of Landscape.* New Haven/ London, 1991.

Walsh 1971
J. Walsh. "Jan and Julius Porcellis, Dutch Marine Painters." Ph.D. Dissertation, Columbia University, 1971.

Walsh 1974
"The Dutch marine painters Jan and Julius Porcellis; 1 - Jan's early career; 2- Jan's maturity and 'de jonge Porcellis'," *Burlington Magazine* (1974) 116 , pp. 653-62, 734-45.

Warner 1975
Ralph Warner. *Dutch and Flemish Flower and Fruit Painters of the XVIIth and XVIIIth Centuries.* Amsterdam, 1975.

Waterhouse 1978
E. Waterhouse. "Anthony van Dyck, Suffer Little Children To Come Unto Me," *Masterpieces in the National Gallery of Canada,* no. 11. Ottawa, 1978.

Welcker 1979
C. Welcker. *Hendrick Averkamp (1585-1634) bijge-naamd "de Stomme van Campen" en Barent Averkamp (1612-1679), "Schilders tot Campen."* (rev. ed. of first ed., Zwolle, 1933). Doornspijk, 1979.

Weldon 1966
J. deH. Weldon. "The Male Portraits of Simon Vouet." MA thesis, Columbia University, 1966.

Weyerman 1729-69
J.C. Weyerman. *De levens-beschryvingen der Nederlandsche Konstschilders.* The Hague, 1729-69.

Wheelock 1995
A.K. Wheelock Jr. *Dutch Paintings of the Seventeenth Century. The Collections of the National Gallery of Art Systematic Catalogue.* Washington, 1995.

Wheelock 1995A
A.K. Wheelock Jr. *Vermeer and the Art of Painting.* New Haven/London, 1995.

White 1982
C. White. *The Dutch Pictures in the Collection of Her Majesty the Queen.* Cambridge, 1982.

Wiegand 1971
W. Wiegand. "Ruisdael-Studien: Ein Versuch zur Ikonologie der Landschaftmalerei." Ph.D. Dissertation, Hamburg, 1971.

van den Wijngaert 1943
F. van den Wijngaert. *Antoon van Dyck.* Antwerp, 1943.

van der Willigen 1970
A. van der Willigen. *Les Artistes de Harlem. Notices historiques avec un précis sur la gilde de St. Luc.* Nieuwkoop, 1970 (trans. of Dutch ed., 1866).

Winternitz 1943
E. Winternitz. "Bagpipes and Hurdy-Gurdies in their Social Setting," *Bulletin of the Metropolitan Museum of Art* 2 (1943).